Date Due

OCT 26			
DEC 16			
JAN 4			
JAN 24			
JUN 10			
JUL 5			
NOV 28			
DEC 20			
MAR-2			
APR-4			
APR 10			
Date Due			
Date Due 5/31/1993			
SEP 2 8			
DEC 1 8 2000			

M

DISC   TURE

Discussions of Moby-Dick

DISCUSSIONS OF LITERATURE

General Editor JOSEPH H. SUMMERS, Washington University

D I S C U S S I O N S

O F

MOBY-DICK

Edited with an Introduction by

Milton R. Stern

THE UNIVERSITY OF CONNECTICUT

D. C. Heath and Company

BOSTON

CONTENTS

INTRODUCTION

THE DATES with which we indicate the birth and death of Herman Melville are 1819–1891. How neat those numbers are. They allow us to make a clean temporal category of mysteries and contradictions and developments and relationships that have been meat and drink for critics and biographers and that have only indicated once more that though we may know the art we may not know the man. Behind the public facade, beyond the private life, transcending the impervious and mocking dates, broods the artist. We have long since buried the man and not so long since redeemed the artist. The history of this resurrection in fame demands different numbers, not nearly so pat and easy as those on the certificates in city hall.

We might date the death of Melville's fame at 1851 and place the rebirth seventy years later. By the time *Pierre* was written, in 1851, Melville was considered mad, or a good popular writer gone wrong, or he was not considered at all. *Pierre*, coming hard on the heels of a whaling book that had bewildered his public, lost Melville an extensive audience, which he had first gained with *Typee* in 1846, and which he was not to recapture until thirty years after his death. In fact, in the eighteen seventies and eighties Melville was so obscure that he could not be found by travelers who wished to visit him; a New York paper considered that he was generally supposed dead; and when he *did* die, an obituary even offered notice of the demise of one Henry Melville. The definition of his ghost among those who knew him is one measure of the stature of his contemporary fame. Stedman, in his obituary notices of Melville (New York *Daily Tribune*, October, 1891; New York *World*, October 11, 1891; and *Review of Reviews*, November, 1891), recalled him as one of our most astute ethnologists of the South Seas. The titles of two of the notices, "Marquesan Melville" and "Melville of Marquesas," are symptomatic of the place in literary history to which the author of *Moby-Dick*, "Benito Cereno," *Billy Budd*, and "The Encantadas" had been relegated by his age. If he was anything, he was "the man who had lived among cannibals."

As Hugh Hetherington points out, however, the story of Melville's fame is not really that simple. And Stanley Hyman, in an excellent article ("Melville the Scrivener," *New Mexico Quarterly*, XXIII [1953], 381–415) too long for inclusion in this collection, insists that we recognize the continuity of Melville's fame and of Melville criticism. For instance, William Clark Russell kept Melville's name alive in England during the eighteen eighties by dedications, reviews, and correspondence. In 1892 Russell appeared in an American magazine, the influential *North American Review*, in order to chastise Americans (the article was called "A Claim for American Literature") for overlooking their own best authors, notably writers of the sea. Another Englishman, Robert Buchanan, wrote "Socrates in Camden" for the August 15, 1885, issue of the *Academy*, in which he insisted that Melville and Whitman were the gigantic imaginative geniuses of American letters. In Canada Professor Archibald MacMechan came under the sway of Melville's prose and tried to insure the strength of Melville's name by numerous communications, most notably "The Best Sea-Story Ever Written" in the October 1899 issue of the respected *Queen's Quarterly*. And, of course, Melville was remarked by contemporaries like Robert Louis Stevenson and biographers of a slightly later age like H. S. Salt (1851–1939).

For all practical purposes, however, Melville was lost to public knowledge until the nineteen twenties, when a new era began for him. Hyman gives credit to the 1919 *Review*, with its two-part article by Frank Jewett Mather, Jr., for the revival of Melville studies. But the claim really belongs to Raymond Weaver, who published *Herman Melville, Mariner and Mystic* in 1921; who edited the Constable edition of Melville's works; and who, with the permission of Melville's granddaughter, Mrs. Eleanor Melville Metcalf, took the manuscript of *Billy Budd* from the family papers and first published it in 1924. By the end of the nineteen twenties, Melville had been noted by bibliophiles, academics, and literary historians like Russell Blankenship, Percy H. Boynton, Vernon L. Parrington, Fred L. Pattee, Michael Sadleir, and W. P. Trent; by literary figures like Arnold Bennett, Van Wyck Brooks, Viola Meynell, Henry S. Canby, John Erskine, Matthew Josephson, D. H. Lawrence, Carl Van Doren, Carl Van Vechten, T. E. Lawrence, and W. H. Hudson; three books had been devoted exclusively to him: John Freeman's *Herman Melville* (1926), Lewis Mumford's *Herman Melville* (1929), and Meade Minnigerode's *Some Personal Letters of Herman Melville* (1922); and Fame with a capital F was consolidated when Warner Brothers filmed *The Sea Beast* in 1925.

The Melville materials that have appeared since 1921, if laid page to page, would reach from Melville's New York birthplace to the Pacific graveyard of the *Pequod*. The variety of the materials is determined by every conceivable range of interpretative and biographical opinion. Stemming from the warped and warping readings of Weaver, through the distortions of Mumford, on up to the present day, we have criticisms that see Melville's fiction as documentation for psychobiographical statements about homosexuality, Oedipal fixations, sex-fear, sex-lust, infantilism, castration complex, an unhappy marriage, envy of the father, poverty, social pretension, or any kind of pretension, extension, or intention you wish. Even sophisticated contemporary critics like Arvin (who has written one of the best of all the Melville studies) and Chase have utilized Freudian assumptions, Jungian readings, religious archetypalism, and the symbology of systematic political thought to arrive at statements that sometimes seem to be illuminations of the critic's mind rather than of the prose at issue.

On the other hand, there are critics who contend that a book like *Moby-Dick* is not really "about" anything. In 1947 Montgomery Belgion could still say, "In fact . . . readers need to shun . . . every allegation that the book holds a concealed meaning. . . . Unquestionably this theory . . . that in reality *Moby-Dick* has a cosmic theme cannot hold. It is a hindrance, not a help, to the fullest enjoyment and appreciation of the book. And so must be any other theory of a concealed meaning. . . ." ("Heterodoxy on *Moby-Dick*?" *Sewanee Review*, LV [1947], 108–125.) As recently as 1951, E. E. Stoll, entertaining different motives for hostility to the discovery of "meanings," asserted that the whole to-do over *Moby-Dick* is simply a mistaken attempt to fabricate a great American literature: "Now that we are the greatest of peoples, we must have a literature to match." ("Symbolism in *Moby-Dick*," *Journal of the History of Ideas*, XII [1951], 440–446.) Wryly dissociating himself from "trends," Mr. Stoll suggested that continuing investigation of the book is a product of "the prevalent taste for symbolism itself." The book is ambiguous, he says, like all good stories, but not really symbolical. As for adventure, *Moby-Dick* is a suspense yarn, "but," we are warned, "not one of really ecumenical or perennial importance." Simply, it is "the story of a man's lifelong revenge upon a whale for thwarting him in his money-making designs upon its blubber."

In opposition to Messrs. Belgion and Stoll, most readers will agree with William Gleim's statement ("A Theory of *Moby-Dick*," *New England Quarterly*, II [1929], 402–419) that if "the reader will approach Melville's point of view with the understanding that the book is composed partly of parable and allegory [how one would like some definition of those terms!], if he will read with a separate intention, he will find a treasure of hidden meanings, the existence of which the casual reader would never suspect." Yet when the reader watches Mr. Gleim proceed to make a Swedenborg-like equation of meaning for almost every blessed item, and to salvage some "treasures" which might better have remained unsuspected, he is inclined to wish a plague on the houses of both the literalist and the symbolist. Having said this, I should make it clear that I have no objection to criticism that proceeds from the assumptions of symbolism, Freudianism, Jungianism, religion, myth, psychology, sociology, politics. Every ism is one more potential instrument for the intelligent critic. I simply insist that criticism illuminate the work of art rather than the assumptions that are brought to it. The work is the inevitable and obdurate fact. If the critic has the right to say, "If the facts and my theory don't agree, so much the worse for the facts," then the editor has an equal right to reverse the order of priorities. I believe that the essays in this collection tend to place the facts first.

Very few readers today will insist that there are not whelming meanings, structures, or techniques to be discovered in *Moby-Dick*. The writers of these essays are all agreed that there are. Yet it will be noticed that these writers, most of them, are not literary revolutionaries, but are safe and respected academics; at least most of

the journals and magazines from which their pieces are reprinted are "scholarly" rather than "literary." Because of the coincidence (or is it?) of the movement of our vital critics to the universities and of the Melville revival, there really are very few good Melville pieces that do not come from one academic source or other, primarily American. Indeed, the very best pieces come from precisely such sources.

Academic or not, many excellent essays have been excluded from this volume because of limitations of space. Book-length studies of Melville, in which some of the best pieces of criticism are to be found, are also unrepresented here. The interested reader should consult directly the following books about Melville:

Arvin, Newton: *Herman Melville* (New York, 1950)

Baird, James: *Ishmael* (Baltimore, 1956)

Chase, Richard: *Herman Melville* (New York, 1949)

Hillway, Tyrus, and Mansfield, Luther S., eds.: *Moby-Dick Centennial Essays* (Dallas, 1953)

Howard, Leon: *Herman Melville* (Berkeley, 1951)

Leyda, Jay: *The Melville Log* (2 vols.; New York, 1951)

Metcalf, Eleanor Melville: *Herman Melville, Cycle and Epicycle* (Cambridge, Mass., 1953)

Olson, Charles: *Call Me Ishmael* (Chicago, 1947)

Percival, M. O.: *A Reading of Moby-Dick* (Chicago, 1950)

Rosenberry, E.: *Melville and the Comic Spirit* (Cambridge, Mass., 1955)

Sedgwick, W. E.: *Herman Melville: The Tragedy of Mind* (Cambridge, Mass., 1944)

Stern, Milton R.: *The Fine Hammered Steel of Herman Melville* (Urbana, 1957)

Thompson, Lawrance: *Melville's Quarrel with God* (Princeton, 1952)

Thorp, Willard, ed.: *Herman Melville* (New York, 1938)

Vincent, Howard P.: *The Trying Out of Moby-Dick* (Boston, 1949)

Wright, Nathalia: *Melville's Use of the Bible* (Durham, N.C., 1949)

Important criticism of Melville is to be found also in the following books:

Auden, W. H.: *The Enchafèd Flood* (New York, 1950)

Feidelson, Charles, Jr.: *Symbolism and American Literature* (Chicago, 1953)

Levin, Harry: *The Power of Blackness* (New York, 1958)

Matthiessen, F. O.: *American Renaissance* (New York, 1941)

Bibliographies and checklists of articles and other books are to be found in Stern and Thorp, listed above; in Floyd Stovall, ed., *Eight American Authors* (New York, 1956); Tyrus Hillway, ed., *Doctoral Dissertations on Herman Melville* (Greeley, Colorado, 1953); J. H. Birss, G. Roper, and S. C. Sherman, eds., *Annual Melville Bibliography* (Providence Public Library, 1951); Volume III of R. Spiller et al., eds., *Literary History of the United States* (New York, 1948); and the cumulative bibliographies of *American Literature* and *PMLA*.

MILTON R. STERN

Moby-Dick

Hugh W. Hetherington

Early Reviews of *Moby-Dick*

I. INTRODUCTION

SINCE so much ink has been expended on the inability of his own century to comprehend or appreciate Melville, there is need for a conscientious examination of what was actually written about *Moby-Dick* when it appeared. It is commonly agreed that among the very large number of reviewers of *Typee*, few were not delighted, and that among the much smaller number of reviewers of *Pierre*, practically all were repelled. But what about the book today regarded as Melville's masterpiece?

For over thirty years the general impression has been that in its own day *Moby-Dick* was virtually condemned and then forgotten. Lewis Mumford envisaged a highly dramatic rejection of the book. Among the many who have accepted this doctrine of the rejection are scholars of such distinction as John Freeman, F. O. Matthiessen, Alexander Cowie, Howard P. Vincent, and (somewhat more cautiously) Newton Arvin. For example, Matthiessen says that the favorable reviews in Harper's and the Literary World "were out of keeping with the general run of comments." Vincent is explicit:

At the time when *Moby Dick* was launched in 1851, few Americans attended the ceremony; and

they were not lavish in their praise nor very intelligent in their criticism. Generally those who saw *Moby Dick* sail into the sea of books contented themselves with disapproving comments as to her unseaworthiness. Not long after, they forgot her.

On the other hand, Thorp has protested against the "rejection legend," saying that there was as much said in praise as in blame.

Two articles dealing exclusively with the reception of *Moby-Dick* have appeared. The earlier and less well known is the more judicious. David Potter discovered a few previously overlooked reviews, and in "Reviews of *Moby-Dick*," published in the *Journal of Rutgers University Library* for June, 1940, he concluded that most of the early reviews of *Moby-Dick* were favorable, though few grasped its greatness and many condemned the style. John D. McCloskey's more recent and frequently quoted article in the *Philological Quarterly* for January, 1946, is unsound. He discovered no reviews which were not previously known, and did not even take the trouble to examine several listed by Potter and other investigators. His assumption that the American reception, at least, was favorable was based merely on a reinterpretation of certain reviews which had been known to scholars for years and

Reprinted by permission from *Moby-Dick Centennial Essays*, ed. Tyrus Hillway and Luther S. Mansfield (Dallas, Texas: Southern Methodist University Press, 1953).

had seemed to most of them very hostile, but from which he sifted some compliments. His conclusion is entirely untenable: "Although British opinion was about evenly divided, American critical opinion was predominantly favorable, there being no original American reviews discovered in this study, which can be classed as, on the whole, unfavorable." The latter part of this statement could have been made only by one who had not read the hostile article in the *Albion,* the completely unfavorable comments in the *Democratic Review* and the Boston *Post,* the severe strictures in *Today,* and the violent condemnation in the *Southern Quarterly Review,* none of which McCloskey mentions. McCloskey's article, moreover, lacks perspective, because he paid little attention to what happened after February, 1852, a vital part of the story.

The present study is based on a far more extensive examination of magazines and particularly newspapers than has been made by Potter, McCloskey, or other scholars. *Moby-Dick* was much more widely recognized by reviewers than has been realized. At least thirty-three American magazines and newspapers gave it some sort of attention before March, 1852, by way of excerpts, notices, or actual reviews. Nine British periodicals commented on it during the same period. It has not been possible to examine as many British as American newspapers, but the few available had nothing about the book. After February the reviews apparently ceased, but a handful of articles during the next few years considered Melville's works as a whole.

Certain differences between British and American reviewing customs should be kept in mind. The habit of inserting extremely short notes on new books seems to have been less common in England, where the more modern custom of either not mentioning a book at all or giving it a quite thorough scrutiny tended to prevail. In spite of the much longer list of American items, there was actually an almost equal number of careful studies of the book in American and British periodicals. Some of the brief American notices obviously or even admittedly *preceded* a complete reading of the book. Two of the most thorough and most laudatory reviews, however, have hitherto lain hidden in American newspapers, and in important newspapers at that.

The first reviews of *Moby-Dick* seem to have appeared on October 25, 1851. They were naturally English, as the book was published in London on or about October 16 under the title of *The Whale,* while *Moby-Dick, or The Whale* was not published in New York until November 14. The latest known reviews came out in the February, 1852, issues of magazines. These reviews devoted to the one book may be called the "immediate reaction." During the next six years (1852–58) there were four articles which sought to evaluate all that Melville had so far written. These, together with such other scanty items as can be collected for these years, may be called the "delayed reaction." It will be demonstrated that the "immediate reaction" was quite different from the "delayed reaction."

II. BRITISH REVIEWS IN 1851

It must not be forgotten that in those days there was widespread humility in America in the presence of British critical pronouncements, which were frequently reprinted on this side of the Atlantic. E. P. Whipple, a busy critic much heeded in mid-nineteenth-century America, wrote: "If the Quarterly Review or Blackwood's Magazine speaks well of an American production, we think we can praise it ourselves." Poe expressed most vehemently his "disgust" at American subserviency to British criticism:

It is not too much to say that, with us, the opinion of Washington Irving—of Prescott—of Bryant —is a mere nullity in comparison with that of any anonymous sub-sub editor of the Spectator, the Athenaeum, or the "London Punch." It is not saying too much to say this. . . . Every publisher in this country will admit it to be a fact.

Five reviewers had their say in England before the first American published an opinion. Important in getting a true perspective regarding the effect of the printed criticism on the public and on Melville is the fact that the first two known reviews came out on the same day, in two of the very magazines Poe thought so oppressively influential, and were bitterly and elaborately adverse.

The *Athenaeum* became so stirred up as to lose some of the calm which usually accompanied its condescensions toward American writers. "An ill-compounded mixture of romance and matter of fact," it exclaimed. "The rant and electrical verb might have been permitted if not interrupted by 'the facts of Scoresby and the figures of Crocker.'" Its final word was: "Mr. Melville has to thank himself only if his horrors and heroics are flung aside by the general reader as so much trash belonging to the worst school of Bedlam literature,—since he seems not so much unable to learn as disdainful of learning the craft of an artist."

Although the *Spectator* found the purely nautical parts interesting, and the minor but not the major characters good, and granted that at some places the author evinced a "vigorous and fertile fancy," the total effect of its article was severe and crushing in the highest degree. "The rhapsody belongs to wordmongering where ideas are the staple; where it takes the shape of narrative or dramatic fiction it is phantasmal—an attempted description of what is impossible in nature and without probability in art," said the *Spectator*, and went on to say that "a little knowledge is made the excuse for a vast many words," and that "the 'marvelous' injures the book by disjointing the narrative, as well as by its inherent lack of interest. . . ."

The real basis for its attack, however, was that the book did not conform to the canons of the novel, as can be seen from this:

Such a groundwork is hardly natural enough for a regular built novel, though it might form a tale, if properly managed. But Mr. Melville's mysteries provoke wonder at the author rather than terror at the creation; the soliloquies and dialogues of Ahab, in which the author attempts delineating the wild imaginings of monomania, and exhibiting some profoundly speculative views of things in general, induce weariness or skipping; while the whole scheme mars, as we have said, the nautical continuity of the whole. . . . It is a canon with some critics that nothing should be introduced into a novel which it is physically impossible for the author to have known.

The *Spectator* then reprimanded the author for shifting the mental point of view. As for the catastrophe, it overrode "all rule," because all, narrator included, sank. (The English edition, of course, did not contain the Epilogue, in which Ishmael's rescue is described.) "Such is the go-ahead method."

From these two terrific blows, Melville, always so sensitive to censure, may never have completely recovered. He should have felt, however, somewhat consoled by a very complimentary review which followed shortly, even if it was in an English magazine of less prestige. On October 27, *John Bull* contained an almost entirely favorable and indeed laudatory comment of some length. Although *John Bull* could not "but deeply regret" "some heathenish and worse than heathenish talk" heard on board the *Pequod*, and felt it was a "pity that he should have defaced his pages by occasional thrusts against revealed religion," the bulk of the article was devoted to generous praise.

John Bull particularly congratulated the author for making so poetic and interesting such an unpromising subject:

Of all the extraordinary books from the pen of Herman Melville this is out and out the most extraordinary. Who would have looked for philosophy in whales, or for poetry in blubber? Yet few books which professedly deal in metaphysics, or claim the parentage of the muses, contain as much true philosophy and as much genuine poetry as the tale of the *Pequod's* whaling expedition.

The reader would find the world of whales, *John Bull* assured him, "as brimful of matters of deepest interest as any other sublunary world." The book had charm even though it might not "fall within the ordinary canons of beauty." This particular bit of defense might almost have been written by Lewis Mumford. *John Bull*, like the *Spectator*, perceived that *The Whale* was not exactly a novel, but regarded the divergence as a mark of superiority, and approved the philosophy:

The ashes of truth, too, which sparkle on the surface of the foaming sea of thought through which the author pulls his readers in the wake of the whale ship—the profound reflections uttered by the author in the wild, watery chase in their own quaint forms of thought and speech,—and the graphic representations of human nature in the startling disguises under which it appears on the deck of the *Pequod*—all these things combine to raise *The Whale* far beyond the level of an ordinary work of fiction. It is not a mere tale of adventure, but a whole philosophy of life that it unfolds.

The extensive review in the *Atlas* is difficult to categorize as favorable or unfavorable, as it mingled disparagement with adulation. It came out in two instalments, the first on November 1 and the second on November 8, each consisting of some six very long closely printed columns. The first "Notice" was somewhat more hostile than the second, and it may be hazarded that as the reviewer approached the last pages of the book he came gradually, somewhat against his will, to submit to Melville's necromancy. He had read the work carefully, perhaps more than once, and offered by far the most complete summary and analysis to be found in the nineteenth century. The tone of the detailed plot summary was quite satirical in the first paragraphs, but became less so near the end.

In both "Notices" the *Atlas* oscillated between exasperation at Melville and acknowledgment of his power. To illustrate the former mood:

Extravagance is the bane of the book, and the stumbling block of the author. He allows his fancy not only to run riot, but absolutely to run amuk, in which poor defenseless Common Sense is hustled and belabored in a manner melancholy to contemplate. Mr. Melville is endowed with a fatal facility for the writing of rhapsodies. Once embarked on a flourishing topic he knows not when or how to stop. He flies over the page as Mynheer Van Clam flew over Holland. . . .

On the other hand, it offered such tributes as these:

. . . the whole written in a tone of exaltation and poetic sentiment which has a strange effect upon the reader's mind in refining and elevating the subject of discourse, and at last making him look upon the whale as a sort of awful and insoluble mystery. . . . In none of his previous works are finer or more highly soaring imaginative powers put forth. In none of them are so many profound, and fertile, and thoroughly original veins of philosophic speculation, or perhaps rather philosophic fancy struck. In none of them, too, is there a greater affluence of curious, quaint, and out of the way learning brought to bear upon the subject in hand. In none of them are the descriptions of seafaring and whaling matters so wonderfully graphic, and in none of them is there to be found a more thorough command over the strength and beauties of the language.

The conclusion is as fair a sample perhaps as can be found:

. . . as we close it we feel as if waking from what was partly a gorgeous vision, partly a nightmare dream, but both vision and dream intense, over-mastering in their power, the spell of a magician who works wildly, recklessly, but with a skill and a potency which few, we should think, will be disposed to deny or resist.

It was the book's magic which on November 8 enthralled the *Leader*, also. In a much shorter review than that in the *Atlas*, but one quite without adverse remarks, the *Leader* stressed that the Americans greatly excelled in handling the supersensual. "No European pen still has the power to portray the Unseen so vividly as to hush the incredulous"—but "to do this American literature is without a rival. What *romance* writer can be named with Hawthorne? Who knows the terrors of the sea like Herman Melville?" *The Whale* is ". . . a strange, wild, weird book, full of poetry and full of interest. . . . One tires terribly of ballrooms, dinners, and the incidents of town life! One never tires of Nature, though the daring imagery often grows riotously extravagant."

Then the ghostly terrors which Herman Melville so skillfully invokes have a strange fascination. In vain reason rebels. Imagination is absolute; ordinary superstitions related by vulgar pens have lost their power over all but the credulous; but Imagination has a credulity of its own respondent to power. So it is with Melville's superstitions; we believe them imaginatively.

The *Leader* relished

. . . the thrilling pages of Melville's *Whale* . . . a strange, wild work with the tangled overgrowth and luxuriant vegetation of American forests, not the trim orderliness of an English park. Criticism may pick holes in this work; but no criticism will thwart its fascination . . . the "Whiteness of the Whale" . . . should be read at midnight alone, with nothing heard but the sounds of the wind moaning without, and the embers falling into the grate within.

The *Examiner*, on the same day (November 8), however, regarded the book with exasperated hostility. After a very sarcastic summary of the plot, the *Examiner* exclaimed:

We cannot say that we recognize in this writer any advance on the admirable qualities displayed in his earlier books—we do not see that he even cares to put forth the strength of which he has shown himself undoubtedly possessed. If there is not carelessness in the book now under notice, there is at least so much wilfulness, that our enjoyment is small even of what we must admit to be undeniably clever in it.

Again recurred the complaint that *Moby-Dick* failed to conform to the canons of the novel: "But all the regular rules of narra-

tive or story are spurned and set at defiance. . . . Certainly since Tom Thumb, there has been no such tragedy." The *Examiner* consigned the book to those curious about whales, a subject not to its liking, and concluded: "Mr. Melville is a man of too real an imagination, and a writer with too singular a mastery over language and its resources, to have satisfied our expectations with such an extravaganza as this."

The *Literary Gazette,* nearly a month later, on December 6, was likewise greatly disturbed over Melville's failure to heed the conventional requirements of the novel: "This is an odd book, professing to be a novel; wantonly eccentric; outrageously bombastic; in places charmingly and vividly descriptive." The *Gazette* disliked his using materials from encyclopedias "as stuffing." "Bad stuffing it makes, serving only to try the patience of his readers, and to tempt them to wish both him and his whales at the bottom of an unfathomable sea. . . . The story of this novel scarcely deserves the name . . . a preposterous yarn. . . ."

Admitting that "There are sketches of scenes at sea, of whaling adventures, storms, and shiplife, equal to any we have ever met with," and quoting a description of an attack on a whale, the *Gazette* concluded:

Mr. Melville has earned a deservedly high reputation for his performances in descriptive fiction. He has gathered his own materials, and travelled along fresh and untrodden literary paths, exhibiting powers of no common order, and great originality. The more careful, therefore, should he be to maintain the fame he so rapidly acquired, and not waste his strength on such purposeless and unequal doings as these rambling volumes about spermaceti whales.

Such commentary about a book of which Arvin has recently said, "Not many imaginative works have so strong and strict a unity," is exceedingly harsh.

Like other British periodicals, the *Gazette* reprimanded Melville for drowning his narrator. Without the Epilogue, not contained in the English edition, which explains that Ishmael alone was "left to tell the tale," it is only the most careful reader who has realized that the author had in the last chapters accounted for Ishmael's being alive. The Epilogue is undoubtedly a great asset, and its absence would justifiably aggravate the British puzzlement at Melville's disregard of the "rules of fiction." The earliest British reviews could hardly have reached New York before November 8. As Melville was then in Pittsfield, and the American edition appeared on November 14, it is unlikely that there was time for the writing and adding of the Epilogue. Probably Bentley, the British publisher, had received the Epilogue along with the rest of the manuscript, but had carelessly or deliberately omitted it.

III. AMERICAN REVIEWS IN 1851

Moby-Dick was published in New York on November 14, 1851. Two brief advance notices, by persons who had only sampled the book, appeared in the *Daily Evening Transcript* in Boston and the *Evening Journal* in Albany on November 12. The Boston paper had a mere note of welcome to a work which would "be eagerly sought" by those who remembered the writer's "first two nautical works"; and the Albany paper, recalling *Typee* and *Omoo* with rich enjoyment, thought the new work opened "promisingly."

An American review by J. Watson Webb appeared in the *Courier and New York Enquirer* on November 14, the very day of *Moby-Dick's* publication. It was, if short, highly favorable, and was notable in declaring definitely that Melville's latest work was his best, and that its author was a genius:

His purity and freshness of style and exquisite tact in imparting vividness and lifelikeness to his sketches long since gained him hosts of admirers on both sides of the water. The book has all the attractiveness of any of its predecessors; in truth it possesses more of a witching interest, since the author's fancy has taken in it a wilder play than

ever before. It is ostensibly taken up with whales and whaler, but a vast variety of characters and subjects figure in it, all set off with an artistic effect that irresistibly captivates the attention. The author writes with the gusto of true genius, and it must be a torpid spirit indeed that is not enlivened with the raciness of his humor and the redolence of his imagination.

Four American periodicals showed cognizance of *Moby-Dick* on November 15. In Hartford the distinguished *Courant* was moderately friendly, finding the book pleasant but not very important. It echoed the British accusation that Melville disregarded the rules of the novel. His works hovered between truth and fiction: "There is the same want of unity of subject—of a regular beginning and end—of the form and shape and outline of a well built novel which we find in real life. But there is too much romance and adventure of 'imminent perils' and hair-breadth escapes, to be anything but fiction." Significant, however, was the *Courant's* decision that the author was improving and that *Moby-Dick* was his best: "The present story is the most interesting and best told of any of the group," though all showed "abandonment to all the easy slipshod luxuries of storytelling."

The same day the New Haven *Register* printed the last part of chapter lxi, vouched for the book's superiority to the many other accounts of whaling which the reviewer had read, and predicted for the work "a great run."

The Boston *Daily Evening Traveller*, also on November 15, seemed to enjoy the book, though puzzled by its form, worried as to its proportions of truth and fiction, and shocked at its blasphemy:

We have a new book, from one of the most sprightly and entertaining writers of our day. It appears to be a sort of hermaphrodite craft—half fact and half fiction. . . . There is so much of caricature and exaggeration mixed with what may be fact that it is not easy to discriminate. Many of Mr. Melville's descriptions are extremely graphic, lifelike and entertaining. He certainly holds the pen of a ready writer; but he indulges frequently in profaneness, and occasionally in indelicacies, which materially detract from the merits of the book, which exhibits much tact, talent and genius.

Also on the same day the *Literary World* showed that it considered Melville important by devoting to *Moby-Dick* the leading article of the week; but it reserved the important criticism it had to offer for the following week.

Another shocked enjoyer was the New Haven *Daily Palladium*, which on November 17 predicted that the "lively, roving story of Moby-Dick" would be "as popular as any other work" of the author. It commended the "thrilling sketches of sea life, whale captures, shark massacres," but deplored the "irreverence and profane jesting" in the colloquies of the "weather-beaten jacks," even though true to life, and granted that the book possessed "all the interest of the most exciting fiction," while at the same time it contained much valuable information.

The provinces again proved shockable when the next day in Albany the *Argus* found the book "the production of a man of genius," abounding in "bright, witty, and attractive things"; worried that the "line between the credible and the apocryphal" was not "always very distinct"; and denounced the "irreverence" which would "greatly impair its interest with many who will nevertheless admire its bold and graphic sketches."

On November 19 the Boston *Daily Bee* headed its back page "Moby-Dick" in large type, and remarked that it was "said to be the best written and most entertaining book put forth by that popular and clever author."

Another and completely favorable review on November 19 was in the New Bedford *Mercury*, which was naturally interested in the whaling aspects. It said it had read many volumes about whaling voyages, but never before one containing so much natural history, nor in "so attractive a

guise." The *Mercury* was not irritated that Ishmael had shipped from Nantucket rather than New Bedford, and averred that "although the whole book is made to serve as a 'tub for the whale,' the characters and subjects which figure in it are set off with artistic effect, and with irresistible attraction for the reader." Promised extracts appeared the next day. This praise from the chief of the whaling ports is of especial interest in view of the fact that a careful search through the leading papers in three other whaling ports—Sag Harbor, New London, and Nantucket—revealed no mention of *Moby-Dick*.

The New York Evangelist, which reviewed *Moby-Dick* on November 20, might have been expected to be disturbed over Melville's impieties, but no. It thought the book odd but exciting and artistic. It began, however, censoriously, lamenting that "Mr. Melville" had "grown wilder and more untameable with every adventure," had tended to wander from "verisimilitude," and "now in this last venture" had "reached the very limbo of eccentricity"; yet it ended with these flattering words:

The extraordinary descriptive powers which Typee disclosed are here in full strength. More graphic and terrible portraitures of hair-breadth 'scapes we never read. The delineation of character, too, is exquisitely humorous, sharp, individual, and never-to-be-forgotten. The description of Father Mapple's sermon is a powerful piece of sailor oratory: and passages of great eloquence, and artistic beauty and force are to be found everywhere. It will add to Mr. Melville's reputation as a writer, undoubtedly, and furnish, incidentally, a most striking picture of sea adventure.

So far, in the six days since the American edition had appeared, there had not been a single completely adverse commentary. Not a single American periodical had failed to acknowledge the book as fascinating, if not a downright work of genius, although there had been some censure. Now came from Boston the first real blow, from the *Post*, which had been so hard on *White Jacket*. Of *Moby-Dick* it said:

We have read nearly one half; and are satisfied that the *Athenaeum* is right in calling it "an ill-compounded mixture of romance and matter of fact." It is a crazy sort of affair, stuffed with conceits and oddities of all kinds, put in *artificially, deliberately,* and affectedly, by the side of strong, terse and brilliant passages of incident and description.

The *Post* then quoted the most hostile portions of the hostile *Athenaeum* review.

The four early American reviews of *Moby-Dick* which were outstanding for their thoroughness were all essentially favorable, varying from the qualifiedly commendatory to the rhapsodically enthusiastic. They were in the *Literary World, Harper's Monthly,* and the *Tribune,* all in New York, and in the *National Intelligencer,* in Washington. The first two are now well known, but the latter two, although in themselves very striking and although published in important newspapers, have hitherto escaped attention. Those in the *Literary World* and the *Tribune* came out on November 22, the other two not until December.

The oft-quoted review in the *Literary World* was probably by Melville's quite intimate friend Evert A. Duyckinck, who, however, mingled with his praise enough censure and even ridicule to make his article the least favorable of the big American four; yet he seems to have had real insight into Melville's underlying intentions.

In his rather lengthy critique, Duyckinck gave expression to the current astonishment at the unusual aesthetic form of the book by calling it "an intellectual chowder." He condemned "this piratical running down of creeds and opinions, the conceited indifferentism of Emerson, or the run-a-muck style of Carlyle" as "out of place and uncomfortable." What a nineteenth-century note is struck in that word "uncomfortable"! He was shocked at Melville's having spoken disrespectfully of the angel Gabriel. On the other hand, he enjoyed the "vivid narration"; he found the account of the Sperm Whale "wholly delightful"; he was one of the three reviewers who applied the term "allegorical"; he considered the great monster an effective embodiment "in strongly drawn lines of mental association of the vaster moral evil of the world." Surely the following statement of Duyckinck's was perceptive: "The pursuit of the White Whale thus interweaves with the literal perils of the fishery a problem of fate and destiny." His last sentence placed the book high: "It is still a great honor, among the crowd of successful mediocrities which throng our publishers' counters and know nothing of divine impulses, to be in the company of these nobler spirits on any terms."

Second to none in significance among the early reviews was the one which appeared in the New York *Daily Tribune,* also on November 22. It may well have been written by the editor himself, Horace Greeley, who is known to have reviewed *Omoo* enthusiastically. Quite extensive and consisting entirely of praise was this commentary on *Moby-Dick*—indeed, all that the most exacting Melvillian could desire. The *Tribune* began by referring to the tradition concerning an invincible whale, and saying that the present volume was "a 'Whaliad,' or the Epic of that veritable old leviathan," who laughed at his pursuers. After a good summary of the plot the *Tribune* continued ardently:

The narrative is constructed in Herman Melville's best manner. It combines the various features which form the chief attractions of his style, and is commendably free from the faults which we have before had occasion to specify in this powerful writer. The intensity of the plot is happily relieved by minute descriptions of the most homely processes of the whale fishery. We have occasional touches of subtle mysticism, which is not carried to such an inconvenient excess in Mardi, but it is here mixed up with so many tangible and odorous realities, that we always safely alight from the excursion through mid-air upon the solid deck of the whaler. We are recalled to this world by the fumes of "oil and blubber," and are made to think more of the contents of barrels than of allegories. . . . The work is also full of episodes, descriptive of strange and original phases of character. One of these is the meeting of the writer and Queequeg. . . .

Recent critics, especially Lewis Mumford, have offered this type of defense of the book, contending that the whaling material gives needed "ballast" or solidity to the speculation and the imaginative flights.

Much less cordial was the *Albion*, which presented on the same November 22 an article in the "great merits, great faults" category. Granting that *Moby-Dick* was "not lacking much of being a great work" and defending the possibility of locating a particular whale, it continued:

Not only is there an immense amount of reliable information . . . the *dramatis personae*, mates, harpooners, carpenters, and cooks, are all vivid sketches done in the author's best style. What they do and how they look is brought to one's perception with wondrous elaboration of detail; and yet this minuteness does not spoil the broad outlines of each.

But the illusion passed away when Mr. Melville tried to write dialogue; the *Albion* condemned "the stuff and nonsense spouted forth by the crazy captain" and maintained that "the rarely imagined character has been grievously spoiled, nay altogether ruined by a vile over daubing with a coat of book-learning and mysticism; there is not method in his madness; and we must pronounce the chief feature of the work a perfect failure, and the work inartistic." It admitted, however, that there was "choice reading" for one who could skip "judiciously."

A brief notice in the New York *Commercial Advertiser* on November 28 was almost entirely hostile. Most readers, it believed, would be at first repulsed by the "eccentricity," for "such a salmagundi of fact, fiction, and philosophy, composed in a style which combined the peculiarities of Carlyle, Marryat and Lamb, was never seen before." It found the cetology "pleasant," but regretted that Mr. Melville was "guilty

of sneering at the truth of revealed religion."

On November 29 and December 6, the Cincinnati *Daily Gazette* printed in two instalments without comment "The Town-Ho's Story."

Melville's close friend N. P. Willis may have been the writer of the entirely approving though certainly not profound note in the *Home Journal* for November 29:

If we mistake not, the author of "Typee" and "White Jacket," conscious of the vivid expectation excited in the reading public by his previous books, resolved to combine in the present all his popular characteristics, and so fully justify his fame . . . the result is a very racy, spirited, curious and entertaining book, which affords quite an amount of information, excites the sympathies, and often charms the fancy.

As has been seen, *Moby-Dick* really received a great deal of attention in America during November; there was some falling off in the number of notices in December. On December 1, however, the New Bedford *Daily Evening Standard* and on December 2 the New York *Evening Post* reprinted the favorite chapter xli. Both papers praised the vivid writing about whaling. The New York paper said that Melville in describing "a marvelous chase by a whaling monomaniac after the 'Moby Dick,' the fabulous leviathan of sailors . . . probably let us into the realities of actual whaling as minutely and faithfully as any sea-author has ever done." In *Holden's Magazine* for December, 1851, the editor, Evert A. Duyckinck, reprinted the review he had previously inserted in the *Literary World*.

Now famous is the remarkable review of *Moby-Dick* in the December, 1851, number of *Harper's Magazine*. Although only a column and a half long, it was given the place of honor as the first and longest of the "Literary Notices" for that month. The author, as was demonstrated with reasonable certitude in the present writer's doctoral dissertation, was George Ripley. Ripley, eschewing a single touch of disapproval, expressed his conviction that the book was the summit of Melville's achievement. Among the early reviewers he was the most explicit in declaring that although Melville had cast his materials in a highly original mold, his success had justified his choice. Ripley pointed out the strange contrasts between the passages of statistical exactitude about whaling and the "weird phantom-like character of the plot." "These sudden and violent transitions," said Ripley, "form a striking feature of the volume. Difficult of management in the highest degree, they are wrought with consummate skill. To a less gifted author, they would inevitably have proved fatal. He has not only deftly avoided their dangers, but made them an element of power." Ripley relished the "fine vein of humor" in the earlier chapters, found the character of Captain Ahab "wonderful," and extolled the "unique portrait gallery, which every artist must despair of rivalling."

Like Duyckinck and the *Tribune* he suggested the presence of allegory, saying that "beneath the whole story the subtle, imaginative reader may perhaps find a pregnant allegory intended to illustrate the mystery of human life," and that "the genius of the author for moral analysis is scarcely surpassed by his wizard power of description."

It must be remembered, of course, that Harper and Brothers had published *Moby-Dick;* on the other hand, Ripley, a Transcendentalist, could have been expected to evince sympathetic insight into the philosophical aspects of the book.

In the Washington *National Intelligencer* for December 16 appeared an extremely imposing and hitherto overlooked review covering almost a whole fine-printed newspaper page. The writer may have been William Allen Butler, a member of the Duyckinck group. He was evidently much excited about the book. In a very long introduction in which he talked about literary canonization and the blindness of critics to contemporary greatness, he implied that he had before him something of immense sig-

nificance. Even he, however, felt he must complain about Melville's "irreverent wit" and condemn the "ribald orgies" of the forecastle scene. Yet after some paragraphs of ecstatic praise of *Typee*, he swung into even more fervent laudation of the present volume, which

presents a most striking and truthful portraiture of the whale and his perilous capture . . . a prose Epic of Whaling . . . no one can deny it to be the production of a man of genius. . . . The descriptive powers of Mr. Melville are unrivalled, whether the scenes he paints reveal "old ocean into tempest tossed," or are laid among the bright hillsides of some Pacific island, so warm and undulating that the printed page on which they are so graphically depicted seems almost to palpitate beneath the sun.

The next passage contained the most ardent eulogy given to *Moby-Dick* during the century:

Language in the hands of this master becomes like a magician's wand, evoking at will "thick coming fancies" and peopling the "chambers of imagery" with hideous shapes of terror or winning forms of beauty and loveliness. Mr. Melville has a strange power to reach the sinuosities of thought, if we may so express ourselves; he touches with his lead and line depths of pathos that few can fathom, and by a single work can set a whole chime of sweet or wild emotions into a pealing concert. His delineation of character is actually Shakespearean—a quality which is even more prominently evinced in "Moby-Dick" than in any of his antecedent efforts.

The humor pleased this reviewer:

The humor of Mr. Melville is of that subdued yet unquenchable nature which spreads such a charm over the pages of Sterne . . . (as shown in the) . . . irresistible comic passages scattered at irregular intervals through "Moby-Dick," and occasionally we find in this singular production the traces of that "wild imagining" which throws such a weird-like charm about the Ancient Mariner of Coleridge.

His very complete summary showed deep imaginative sympathy and stressed the themes—Ishmael's reasons for going to sea, and Ahab's vision of the white whale as the incarnation of all wickedness. He concluded that "this ingenious romance . . . for variety of incident and vigor of style" could "scarcely be exceeded."

IV. REVIEWS IN JANUARY AND FEBRUARY, 1852

In the reviews in the *Intelligencer* and *Harper's, Moby-Dick* reached the peak of its American fame during its author's lifetime. During January, 1852, the curve of its reputation was already definitely a falling one. Although eight American magazines noticed the book during this month, of these only one, *Peterson's,* wrote favorably at any length. *Godey's Lady's Book* and *Knickerbocker* were complimentary, and *Hunt's* less so, but all three were very brief. *Littell's Living Age* reprinted highly adulatory material from the *Courier and New York Enquirer,* but three magazines denounced the book—two, *Today* and the *Democratic Review,* and one, the *Southern Quarterly Review,* with fanatical violence.

According more praise than disparagement, *Peterson's Magazine* preferred the narrative to the philosophical elements, and thought that if the work had been "compressed one half and all the transcendental chapters omitted, it would have been decidedly the best sea novel in the language"; but by attempting to combine narrative and philosophy "Mr. Melville has spoilt his book." Still, *Peterson's* went on, the "demerit of 'Moby Dick' is only comparative. It is not an indifferent work but a very superior one after all." The whaling scenes were powerful, and "the concluding chapters" were "really beyond rivalry." Here was another example of the special American interest in the whaling materials. Warm as was *Peterson's* enthusiasm for the nautical parts, its review showed much less approbation of the work as a totality than had some of the November and December reviews.

Godey's brief note was amiable, but that was all. It thought the work was "itself a perfect literary whale, and worthy of the pen of Herman Melville, whose reputation as an original writer has been established the world over." *Knickerbocker* had even less to say, although nothing unapproving: "Under the title *Moby Dick,* Mr. Melville has taken up this whale and made him the subject of one of his characteristic and striking romances. His ocean pictures are exceedingly graphic." *Hunt's Merchants' Magazine* printed some four qualifiedly friendly lines, indicating that those who expected to "find an agreeable and entertaining volume in this will not be disappointed," that in places "it may be rather diffuse, but as a whole it will be read with gratification," and that the whaling scenes were spirited.

Today: A Boston Literary Journal could find a few passages to approve, but was in the main very antagonistic. It advanced what was before long to be the prevailing judgment: *Typee* was fine, but "the merit of Mr. Melville's books has decreased almost in the order of their production." *Today* made four adverse points: (1) The valuable material about whaling was obscured by "dreamy philosophy and indistinct speculation." (2) The excellent adventures of Ishmael and Queequeg were ruined by the impiety:

Some of . . . their adventures are narrated inimitably and are almost sufficient to excuse any faults in other parts of the book. Yet the humor of those parts where sacred things are made light of, as for instance, the scene in which the hero joins his pagan friend in worshipping an idol and defends his course by half a page of wretched sophistry is revolting to good taste, and may . . . be dangerous to many of those persons who will be likely to read the book. . . .

(3) The accounts of whaling would be of much value if not introduced in such a way as to cast doubt on their accuracy. (4) The book should have been pared down. As if to make some amends, *Today* finally admitted that the book had its "beauties" and enough fine and valuable passages in it "to amply repay its perusal."

In the *Democratic Review* appeared the most extended American condemnation of

Moby-Dick. The *Review* was stirred by displeasure at Melville's latest work to denounce the earlier ones. *Typee* and *Omoo* were popular, but why were they found on tables from which Byron was prohibited? the *Democratic Review* wondered, and went on:

But these were Mr. Melville's triumphs, *Redburn* was a stupid failure, *Mardi* was hopelessly dull, *White Jacket* was worse than either; and in fact, it was such a very bad book, that, until the appearance of *Moby Dick* we had set it down as the very ultimatum of weakness to which the author could attain. It seems, however, that we were mistaken. In bombast, in caricature, in rhetorical artifice—generally as clumsy as it is ineffectual—and in low attempts at humor, each of his volumes has been an advance upon its predecessors.

Like *Today*, the *Democratic Review* viewed Melville's efforts as resulting only in a descending achievement curve.

The *Democratic Review*, becoming more personal, accused Melville of an "immeasurable vanity": "From this morbid self-esteem, coupled with a most unbounded love of notoriety, spring all his rhetorical contortions, all his declamatory abuse of society, all his inflated sentiment, and all his insinuating licentiousness." The conclusion involved a further fling at the style: "But if there are any of our readers who wish to find examples of bad rhetoric, involved syntax, stilted sentiment and incoherent English, we will take the liberty of recommending to them this precious volume of Mr. Melville's."

The *Southern Quarterly Review*, after granting the book had some merits, ended with an even more violent final stab than that of the *Democratic Review*. Characteristically American was the *Southern Quarterly's* admitting that the parts relating to whaling were "interesting and informative" and that "in all the scenes where the whale is the performer or sufferer, the delineation and action are highly vivid and entertaining." "In all other respects," it announced, "the book is sad stuff and dreary or ridiculous. . . . The Quakers are dolts, the mad

Captain a bore." The last, crushing sentence declared that "the captain's ravings and those of Mr. Melville are such as would justify a writ *de lunatico* against all parties." William Gilmore Simms, the editor, may have written these words.

The widely circulated *Graham's Magazine* in its February number brought to an end the "immediate American reception" in a piece of hearty applause. It was a rather general but almost entirely adulatory critique, centering on the merits of the style:

This volume sparkles with the raciest qualities of the author's voluble and brilliant mind, and whatever may be its reception among old salts, it will be sure of success with the reading public generally. It has passages of description and narration equal to the best that Melville has written, and its rhetoric revels and riots in scenes of nautical adventure with more than usual glee and gusto. The style is dashing, headlong, strewn with queer and quaint ingenuities moistened with humor, and is a capital specimen of deliberate and felicitous recklessness, in which seeming helter-skelter movement is guided by real judgment.

Melville's teeming fancy sometimes leads him to excessive use of analogies, but

The joyous elasticity and vigor of his style . . . compensates for all faults, and even his tasteless passages bear the impress of conscious and unwearied power. His late books are not only original in the usual sense, but evince originality of nature, and convey the impression of a new individuality, somewhat composite, it is true, but still giving to the jaded reader of everyday publications, that pleasant shock of surprise which comes from a mental contact with a character at once novel and vigorous.

It is to be noted that this review, though enthusiastic, made no commitment as to the author's "genius" or "importance."

From England during January had come one more good word for the book. *Bentley's Miscellany* was generous in appreciation, and was one of the few who were sure that *Moby-Dick* was Melville at his best. Impressed with the force of the characterization of Ahab, *Bentley's* exclaimed:

Through what scenes of beauty and grandeur that monomania impels him. . . . There are descriptions in this book of unrivalled force, colored and warmed as they are by the light and heat of a most poetical imagination, and many passages might be cited of vigorous thought, of earnest and tender sentiment, of glowing fancy which . . . show . . . that Herman Melville is a man of the truest and most original genius.

It seems ungracious, but it is necessary, to remind oneself that Richard Bentley had published the book in England.

The *Dublin University Magazine* in February considered the book both good and bad. It was not without relish for the adventure passages, for the "graphic" scenes of the early chapters. Yet it condemned, as had others, the technique: "All the rules which have been hitherto understood to regulate the composition of works of fiction are despised or set at naught." It seemed uninterested in seeking any deeper significance in the book.

Moby-Dick was, so far as is known, ignored by all its author's more distinguished literary contemporaries, except Longfellow and Hawthorne. In his journal on November 15, Longfellow had written: "Read all evening in Melville's new book, 'Moby Dick or the Whale.' Very wild, strange, and interesting." This is not the place for a discussion of the subtle problem of Hawthorne's attitude toward Melville, which has been treated fully in recent studies. A famous letter of Melville's in reply to a now lost letter of Hawthorne's makes clear that the latter admired *Moby-Dick*, said or implied that it was an allegory, and in Melville's opinion understood it. There is some evidence that he might have written a review of it if Melville had encouraged him.

Lest the reader gain an exaggerated idea of the widespread interest in the book, he should be reminded that there were many notable silences on the part of magazines and newspapers and that the total number of reviews, as well as the total number of favorable reviews, was much smaller than

in the case of *Typee*. British magazines which overlooked *Moby-Dick* included the *British Quarterly Review, Frazer's Magazine*, the *Gentleman's Magazine, Notes and Queries*, the *North British Review*, and the *Quarterly Review*, none of which had ever mentioned Melville; and *Blackwood's*, the weekly *Critic*, and the *London Illustrated News*, which had written about some of his earlier books. American magazines which said nothing about *Moby-Dick* included the *North American Review* and the *Ladies' Repository*, which had never referred to Melville; and the *American Review*, the *New Englander*, the *Southern Literary Messenger*, and *Saroni's Musical Times*, which had reviewed some of his previous works. Neither the *Times* of London nor that of New York noted the book, and it was ignored by a long list of American newspapers.

V. THE DELAYED REACTION

Several critics, among them some of moderate importance, in England and America, in the half-dozen years following 1851, sought to assess the value of Melville's work as a whole. In a "Retrospective Survey of American Literature" appearing in 1852 in the *Westminster Review*, Melville got a single but favorable sentence. He was therein called "a man of unquestionable genius who struck out for himself a new path in 'Typee,' 'Omoo,' and his latest book, 'The Whale.' " Hawthorne got no more space, although called the "first and greatest" of American novelists, but much more attention was given both Irving and Cooper. Duyckinck, in his *Cyclopaedia* (1855), simply repeated what he had said in the *Literary World*.

In 1853 "Sir Nathaniel," whose real name may have been William Harrison Ainsworth, devoted one of a long series of articles on "American Authorship" in the *London New Monthly Magazine* to Melville. With amazing violence he objected to the stylistic extravagance and transcendentalism of *Moby-Dick*. His words were harsh indeed: "The style is maniacal —mad as a March hare—mowing, gibbering, screaming, like an incurable Bedlamite, reckless of keeper or straight waistcoat." He found the author "maundering, drivelling, subject to paroxisms, cramps and total eclipse." He considered the book "a huge dose of hyperbolical slang, maudlin sentimentalism, and tragic-comic bubble and squeak" and said that the hero raved "by the hour in a lingo derived from Rabelais, Carlyle, Emerson, newspapers transcendental and transatlantic." The fact that "Sir Nathaniel" was especially warm and sympathetic toward Irving and Longfellow would lend weight to the contention that Melville's work, in its more difficult aspects, was ill suited to appeal to the nineteenth-century mind. Transatlantic readers were given little chance to escape "Sir Nathaniel," as his article was twice reprinted in American magazines.

The author of "A Trio of American Sailor Authors" in the *Dublin University Magazine* in 1856, himself a writer about whaling, he said, was only less completely damnatory than "Sir Nathaniel." Melville can hardly have found much satisfaction in being told that his best work was merely an earnest that he had the ability, even the "genius" to do something worth while, if he could get away from "half-insane conceits." He said that Melville would rank high if he did not "pervert his lofty gifts," as he had done in *Moby-Dick*, a book which was "eccentric and monstrously extravagant" but valuable for its whaling information. "The merits are obscured and almost neutralized by the astounding quantity of wild, mad passages and entire chapters . . . reckless inconceivable extravagances. . . ." Somewhat inconsistently he said that the work was throughout "splendidly written in a literary sense," and that the early chapters were "superlatively excellent." What these self-contradictory remarks added up to was made plain by his saying that *White Jacket* was Melville's

finest production, and that he found "awe-striking sublimity and mystery" and "Shakespearean" characterizations not in Melville but in Cooper, a writer he thought had no faults. This article also was reprinted in America.

The American critic and fictionist Fitz-James O'Brien wrote two essays about Melville. To judge from his first essay, in 1853, *Moby-Dick* made practically no impression on him, for he mentioned it only once in this long critique, thus: "Typee . . . was healthy; Omoo nearly so; after them came Mardi with its excusable wildness; then came Moby Dick, and Pierre, with its inexcusable insanity." The last sentence is ambiguous, but apparently he did not think *Moby-Dick* even worth the attention involved in a fling at its sanity.

Four years later, in his second essay on Melville, O'Brien gave the book some attention, but only in scorn. Now he confessed that he could not understand *Moby-Dick*. He exclaimed:

What did Mr. Melville mean when he wrote "Moby Dick"? We have a right to know, for he carried us floundering on with him after his great white whale . . . now perfectly exhausted with fatigue and deafened with many words whereof we understood no syllable, and then suddenly refreshed with a brisk sea breeze and a touch of nature kindling as the dawn.

At least O'Brien was not one of those who "partook in the general comprehension of Melville's meaning" which one writer on Melville's fame "discovered" some years ago. O'Brien did use the word "genius" with reference to Melville, but lamented loudly that he was a man who distorted "the flowers of his fancy; a man born to create who resolves to anatomize; a man born to see who insists on speculating." O'Brien made it perfectly clear that for him the author's "flowers of fancy" were most fragrant in *Typee*. However complimentary he may have been to Melville's power in general, he rejected what today is considered the chief manifestation of that power. Curiously enough, he preferred *The Confidence-Man* to *Moby-Dick;* yet he did not think highly of that work either. It was simply better than Melville at his worst—his worst being *Moby-Dick.*

The record of the sales of the book in America provided further proof that while the "immediate reaction" was a partial acceptance, the "delayed reaction" was a virtual rejection. By November 25, 1851, according to Melville's accounts with Harper and Brothers, the sole American publishers of the book during his lifetime, 1,535 copies had been sold; and by February 7, 1852, 471 more. These are respectable figures for that time, but during the whole next decade only 1,236 copies, or an average of only 123 per year, were sold; and between 1863 and 1887, the year of the twenty-seventh and last account with Harper's, only 555, or an average of 23 a year. The total number of copies of *Moby-Dick* printed and sold in America up to and including 1887 was thus 3,797. During less than three years Wiley and Putnam had sold, up to January, 1849, 6,392 copies of *Typee,* and a considerable number of copies had been sold also by Harper's, who had brought out an edition of Melville's first book.

During the single year 1887 were sold 200,000 copies of *Ben-Hur* (1880), and during 1888, 290,000 copies. The sales of *Moby-Dick* were, of course, as nothing to those of Susan Warner's *The Wide Wide World* (1850) or Mrs. E. D. E. N. Southworth's *The Curse of Clifton* (1852). Mott points out that *Moby-Dick* "was a very poor seller indeed when it first appeared," and won its right to be included in his list of "Over-All Best Sellers" only by the distribution of "more than a million copies" in the United States between 1921 and 1947.

The record of the lack of new editions or even reprintings over many decades provides further negative evidence. In America there was only one reprinting between 1851 and 1892, and that was by Harper's in 1863. In England there was only one reprinting between 1851 and 1902, and that was by Bentley in 1853. For forty-nine years, then, *Moby-Dick* was not reprinted in England, where some have asserted it was continuously admired.

After O'Brien's 1857 article the rest was, for many years, silence. Perhaps not complete silence about Melville, but silence about *Moby-Dick.* As has often been said, the violent condemnation of *Pierre* in 1852 by substantially all reviewers tended to destroy interest in its author and to cause many to read back into *Moby-Dick* the despised qualities of the next book. The fact that there was far more interest than has been generally realized in *Israel Potter* (1855), the *Piazza Tales* (1856), and *The Confidence Man* (1857) merely serves to make more deafening the silence about *Moby-Dick.* As early as 1852, the Boston *Daily Transcript* could begin a brief note on *Pierre* thus: "The author of 'Typee' here wholly forsakes the sea and . . . ," with no reference to *Moby-Dick.* In reviewing the *Piazza Tales* the New Bedford *Mercury* began: "The author of Typee and Omoo, is so well known . . . ," again with no mention of *Moby-Dick.* Melville's publishers themselves did not consider it worth mentioning that he had written a book called *Moby-Dick. Pierre* was advertised by Harper and Brothers in the New York *Evening Post* of August 27, 1852, as "By Herman Melville, author of 'Typee,' 'Omoo,' 'Redburn,' etc." This advertisement was repeated without alteration on August 28 and on September 3 and 6. In the same newspaper, G. P. Putnam's advertised *Israel Potter* as "By Herman Melville, Author of 'Typee,' 'Omoo,' etc. etc." These advertisements are eloquent in their omissions. The attitude of his friends was similar. George Duyckinck in a letter in 1858 could refer to "your friend Typee Melville." It was the same away from Pittsfield. Merrell R. Davis, in his study of the reviews of Melville's 1859 lectures, says: "Melville's literary reputation in the Midwest apparently rested on *Typee* and *Omoo;* he is called 'the author of "Typee,"' or 'the author of "Typee" and "Omoo," etc.'; at no time are any other books of his mentioned by name or even casually referred to." Thirty years later, in most of his obituaries, Melville was recalled, if as a writer at all, as "the author of *Typee*." The New York *Tribune* could subsume his literary career in this sentence: "*Typee* was his best work, although he has since written a number of other stories which were published more for private than public circulation."

VI. CONCLUSIONS

The key to a true conception of the early fame of *Moby-Dick* is the distinction between the "immediate reaction" and the "delayed reaction."

The main features of the "immediate reaction" may be summarized as follows:

1. Although many periodicals ignored the book, it was much more widely examined than has hitherto been realized.

2. There was considerable and often severe censure of Melville's choice of aesthetic form and repeated insistence that he had failed to conform to the accepted canons of the novel. Five British periodicals (*Athenaeum, Spectator, Examiner, Literary Gazette,* and *Dublin University Magazine*) and four American ones (Boston *Traveller,* New Haven *Palladium,* Albany *Argus,* and New York *Commercial*) reprimanded Melville on this score. There were, however, four actual defenses of the unique form, two British (*John Bull, Leader*) and two American (*Tribune* and *Harper's*). Duyckinck was puzzled by the form rather than actually adverse.

3. By one English periodical (*John Bull*) and by six American (*Traveller, Palladium, Argus, Commercial Advertiser, National Intelligencer, Today,* and Duyckinck's *Literary World*) Melville was severely condemned for impiety. Of those

especially *John Bull* and the *Intelligencer,* and to some degree Duyckinck, were otherwise extremely complimentary to the philosophy.

4. The book was disposed of as mad by the *Athenaeum,* the Boston *Post,* and the *Southern Quarterly Review.* Such accusations may have been motivated by timid Victorian fear of the contemptuous revaluation of their way of life which they perceived in Melville.

5. Two, however, discovered significant and profound "allegory" (Duyckinck, *Harper's*), and the *Tribune* found allegory effectively extrinsified in the very real whale story, while the *Atlas* admired the "original philosophical fancy," the *Intelligencer* delighted in the "power to reach the sinuosities of thought," and *John Bull* saw in it "a whole philosophy of life." Thus not all recoiled against the book's deeper soundings.

6. Most liked the characterizations, though a few found the dialogue unrealistic or incoherent or worse. Few failed to pay tribute to the "graphic" sea scenes.

7. Melville's power to cast "a potent magic spell" was ardently attested by three (*Atlas, Leader,* and *Intelligencer*).

8. Only six reviews were completely adverse, three British (*Athenaeum, Examiner, Literary Gazette*) and three American (*Commercial Advertiser,* Boston *Post, Democratic Review*); but the hostile criticism in general was often peculiarly insulting.

9. One English (*Leader*) and twelve American periodicals printed notices which contained no censorious qualifications whatever. Of these twelve, however, six were notes giving no real evidence the book had been read, and only four (*Courier, Tribune, Graham's,* and *Harper's*) can be considered truly thoughtful.

10. There was a marked tendency for reviewers to indulge in extremes of praise or censure, sometimes both in the same article. The word "dull" was almost never used.

11. The clear line of demarcation between British and American judgments of merit, which McCloskey claims he saw, simply did not exist. There were, however, two differences between the readers on the two sides of the Atlantic. Most of the Americans had an interest in whaling as such, while few British had such an interest, and one or two of the latter were irritated that they had to read any book about whales. The greater economic importance of whaling in America counted for the book here. It is difficult to imagine an American complimenting Melville for making an unattractive subject fascinating, as did *John Bull*. Again while there was silence in England about the humor, four Americans (*Courier, Graham's,* and especially the *Intelligencer* and *Harper's*) keenly relished it. True, some Americans were shocked by the elements of irreverence or impiety in the wit.

Surely, even for the modern Melvillian, at least two British (*John Bull, Leader*) and three American (*Tribune, Intelligencer, Harper's*) articles embody adequate apperceptions of Melville's unique genius.

The main aspects of the "delayed reaction" may be thus described:

1. Although the "immediate reactions" were so varied that it is possible, by biased selection of quotations, to build up a case for either a welcome or a rejection, as has been done, the "delayed reaction" was *clearly adverse.*

2. The unfriendly "delayed reaction" had already begun to set in as early as January, 1852, during which month two Americans asserted dogmatically that Melville's writings had been getting progressively worse. The peak of the early fame of *Moby-Dick* had come in the first part of December, 1851.

3. One British and one American evaluator of Melville's whole canon rejected the book utterly.

4. There were some indications even before the violent assault on *Pierre*, and many afterward, that the book about the white whale was being rapidly forgotten, and that if its author was considered important at all, it was not as the author of *Moby-Dick*.

And finally, it seems to the present writer, as it seems to Arvin, that even in the "immediate reaction," ambivalent as it was, there were elements which might well, for Melville, have poisoned the honey which was undeniably present. It is implicit in *Pierre* that Melville believed *Moby-Dick* had failed, though no record exists that he said so directly. The first two reviews were acrimonious; the most influential British magazines were silent or essentially hostile; two of the most favorable reviews were issued by house organs of his publishers; Duyckinck and some other encouragers were personal friends; and the censure was peculiarly corrosive.

The existence in the "immediate reaction" of reviews that were adulatory, even ecstatic, even reverently perceptive of the main themes, makes the complete contemptuousness or thorough obliviousness of the "delayed reaction" not less, but *more* dramatic, and perhaps inexplicable except on the basis of such denunciations of nineteenth-century timidity and blindness as flared out in the "Melville Revival" of the twenties. True, a few watchers joyously announced in 1851 the new planet which so many were to believe was not discovered until seventy years later. But in the nineteenth century it was not the praise ("language in the hands of this master becomes like a magician's wand," "a unique portrait gallery which every writer must despair of rivalling," "the gusto of true genius," "the subtle imaginative reader may perhaps find a pregnant allegory," "it must be a torpid spirit indeed that is not enlivened with the raciness of his humor and the redolence of his imagination,") that lingered in the mind. It was always the snide phrases ("trash belonging to the worst school of bedlam literature," "rhetorical artifice clumsy as it is ineffectual," "mor-

bid self-esteem," "insinuating licentiousness," "stuff and nonsense spouted forth by
the crazy captain," "such as would justify
a writ *de lunatico*,") and the conclusion
of that "review" in the Boston *Post* ("not
worth the money asked for it, either as a
literary work or as a mass of printed
paper") that stung the memory and soon
induced amnesia.

Reginald L. Cook

Big Medicine in *Moby Dick*

"THERE is magic in it." So Ishmael, solitary survivor of the Pequod's disastrous voyage in pursuit of the White Whale, discovers in the meditation of water. So Melville discloses in *Moby Dick*, his mythopoeic tale of the golden days of the whale fishery. For some readers the magic is in the symbolism and philosophy; for a few it is in the strange wonders of cetological information; for many others it is in the spirited yarn, narrated in a sonorous, eloquent rhetoric, compounded of fun and fury.

Above all else, *Moby Dick* is a briny book. As soon as the land's behind, there is the feel of the ground-swell beneath stretched timbers, the curl of foam at the bows, the gurgle at the stern, ropeyards tingling, tall masts buckling, bowsprit plunging, and, for companions, nimble seamen who trim the yards, veteran harpooners who skilfully dart the barbed iron, and mates who have many times thrust the lance in the wide and endless waters from one side of the world to the other—tough, weather-ruddied, brawny hunters of whales with a windward look in their eyes. There is sea magic in the book—the yo-heave-o spirit of spreading sail on extended yards and halyards hard-strained through creaking blocks.

There is also a natural magic in the object of the chase—in the sperm whale with its immense head and comparatively small eye, its incredible power and remarkable propulsion. Who, among the whaling mariners, did not marvel at the breaching whale, rising vertically out of the water with such velocity that half its length is bared, or gaze in wonder at the whale

suspended perpendicularly in the water, head downward, in the interesting motion known as peaking flukes! "Excepting the sublime breach . . . this peaking of the whale's flukes is perhaps the grandest sight to be seen in all animated nature." Melville surely speaks for himself when he says in *Moby Dick:* "Standing at the masthead of my ship during a sunrise that crimsoned sky and sea, I once saw a large herd of whales in the east, all heading toward the sun, and for a moment vibrating in concert with peaked flukes. As it seemed to me at the time, such a grand embodiment of the gods was never beheld, even in Persia, the home of the fire-worshippers."

The whale's deep-diving—about two thousand feet—and its spouting are of the same order of natural magic. So also is its voracious appetite (to us), when we learn that the blue whale devours at one feeding the equivalent of six barrels of large shrimplike crustaceans, called "krill," while the sperm whale feeds on cuttlefish, especially the giant squid. Moreover, Melville is quite as fascinated by its breeding habits, for doubtless he saw whales mating in tropical waters during the fall and winter, and doubtless he saw them following the veins in migrations, moving poleward to spend the summer in Arctic or Antarctic waters.

There is to-day another kind of magic beyond the scope of *Moby Dick*. It is the magic of mechanical enterprise where the big whaling vessels of Great Britain, Norway, Japan and Holland hunt in the Indian Ocean or off the coast of Peru or in the Antarctic, completely equipped with me-

Reprinted by permission from *Accent*, VIII (Winter, 1948), 102–109.

chanical gadgets that an inventive age has provided. Among the super-gadgets are planes, Asdic (sonic submarine detectors), radar and guns. Planes sight the whales; gunners follow the sounding whale on its dive by Asdic sonic beam; and radar spots the surfaced whale. The whaling guns, so important in making the kill, and efficiently unromantic, fire modern harpoons equipped with bombs that explode after contact. This is a "magic" that out-magics the skill that lent such splendor to "that wild Scandinavian vocation" of whaling in the golden age.

"I love all men who dive," Melville wrote Evert Duyckinck. He is himself a "thought-diver." It is not alone the whale who dives deep, sounding a thousand fathoms, as it is said, beneath light and air. In *Moby Dick* Melville dives deep and comes up with blood-shot eyes. It is the magic in this deep-diving that now interests us.

In *The Golden Bough* religion is represented as a belief in a conscious and personal power which controls and directs the course of nature and human life, and the practice of conciliating the higher power. Magic, on the contrary, assumes an order and uniformity in nature which is determined by immutable laws whose operation is foreseeable and calculable. While religion believes that through persuasion it is possible to induce the superhuman force that controls the universe to favor mankind, magic applies coercion. The magician arrogates more power than the religious devotee. He assumes that by spells, enchantments and ceremonies he can manipulate the impersonal force which controls all things. In the magician's arrogant authority the humble religious devotee sees "an impious and blasphemous usurpation of prerogatives that belong to God alone."

To the medicine man of primitive cults there were no elements of chance, caprice or accident in the course of nature. By following the laws of nature, as he understood them, the medicine man believed that he would be rewarded by success. When he failed to conform strictly to the rules of his art, his spell would be broken. Thus his power was not arbitrary and unlimited. Neither does Ahab assume that he is on the inside. He is not Supreme Dictator of the Universe although he gives the prescription for such a dictator. *Moby Dick* would have been far less credible had Melville endowed Ahab with superhuman power.

There is magic in *Moby Dick*. It is the magic of Ahab whose intent dictates the form and spirit of his quest. The ungodly Ahab is bent upon supernatural revenge. He forswears the Christian God of his fathers and celebrates a blasphemous ritual. In an ascendancy of egotistic will he vents his contempt on "ye great gods." "I laugh and hoot at ye, ye cricket-players, ye pugilists . . . come forth from behind your cotton bags! Come, Ahab's compliments to ye; come and see if ye can swerve me." No suppliance here! No placative humility! Instead, the arrogance of the sorcerer who believes he can coerce the great gods. Yet Ahab proves to be mindful of the orthodox God when, on the eve of the final mortal encounter, he inquires: "Is it I, God, or who, that lifts this arm? But if the great sun move not of himself; but is an errand-boy in heaven; nor one single star can revolve, but by some invisible power; how then can this one small heart beat; this one small brain think thoughts; unless God does that beating, does that thinking, does that living, and not I."

There is a subtle consciousness in Ahab. He operates on two levels: sometimes on the Christian; more frequently on the primitive. Yet his ceremonial rituals are not aimed to influence either deity or devil. He hardly respects the power of either of them. He uses them only that the appropriate spells will inevitably produce the desired effect on his crew. There is no evidence that he believes in their efficacy in giving him ultimate power over Moby Dick, but they influence his men, and this is necessary to gain his bloody-minded end.

Ahab's magic does not follow the usual pattern of the primitive magician. He did not seek for supernatural power in a dream or vision, to be effected by fasting, stimulants or flagellant torture, as among the Plains Indian tribes of Western America, the African tribal groups, or the Melanesians. He does dream prophetically and fatefully of the hearses, and he prophesies that he will dismember his dismemberers, which subsequent events prove to be an erroneous prophecy. After the first fateful meeting with the White Whale at sea, he envisions his own greatness dramatically by exalting the egotistic will until his malaise is that of a megalomaniac paranoid. His behavior becomes strange and psychotic. He casts away his pipe, to be rid of serenity. He commands his men with overbearing looks and exaggerated actions. Yet there is comparatively little sadism and no masochism in his actions.

Ahab's reversion is important. It is linked with his personal misfortune. In the Christian world of rewards and punishments, salvation by faith, and the conciliation of powers superior to man, he is angered and puzzled by his personal fate. He is crazed by a loss which most mariners would accept as a vocational hazard. The aberrant Ahab is no ordinary mariner. In "The Quarter Deck" he states a personal quandary. Is the force which governs the world conscious or unconscious of human destiny? The orthodox mariner believes in a superhuman power that is conscious and personal. He considers deity susceptible to the insinuation of prayer and sacrifice. Ahab, victimized by an unreckoned force, asks: Is there an accountable God? He is aware of an invisible power, but he is unsure whether there is any intelligible meaning behind the inscrutable universe. All he knows is that the White Whale who has reaped his leg from his body is "outrageous strength, with an inscrutable malice sinewing it."

This is what he will wreak his hate upon; this is the object of his fiery hunt. Seeing no particular efficacy in Christian conciliation of a force that permits evil to prevail, Ahab rejects the Christian way and turns by reversion to the forms of magic—"big medicine."

To solemnize the chase of the white-headed whale he calls for a heavily charged flagon of liquor "hot as Satan's hoof" and passes it round, rallying his men to take short draughts and long swallows. He orders his harpooners to detach the iron part of their harpoons and use them as goblets. He fills these ingenious goblets to the brim and ranking the mates opposite the harpooners, he focusses the fiery chase on Moby Dick until the White Whale spouts black blood and rolls fin out. In this exuberant ceremonial he unites the crew in an indissoluble league. "Death to Moby Dick! God hunt us all if we do not hunt Moby Dick to his death!"

Another example of "big medicine" is shown when Ahab's talismanic lance is forged. Its shank is made of rods from nail-stubs gathered from the steel shoes of racing horses welded together "like glue from the melted bones of murderers." The barbs were forged of Ahab's razors, sharp as "the needle-sleet of the Icy Sea," and tempered in the blood of the three heathen harpooners, initiates in the harpoon cult, aboard the Pequod. In the baptismal tempering of the barbs, Ahab utters a blasphemous incantation: "Ego non baptizo te in nomine patris, sed in nomine diaboli!"

The most sensational display of big medicine occurs when the typhoon lashes the Pequod. Ahab rises to tremendous height arrogating elemental power. It is a powerful magic that he exhibits, confounding some but not all of his men. At the base of the main-mast he holds aloft the lightning link in his left hand, placing his foot on the kneeling Parsee, and defyingly invokes the "clear spirit of clear fire" before the awed crew (although later Stubb disabuses the credulous Flask as to the actual risk in Ahab's seemingly dangerous act). The panic-stricken crew race to the braces to fix sail and turn homeward in awful fright when they see flames of "pale, forked fire" shooting from the naked barb of Ahab's specially forged harpoon in the whale-boat's bow. Ahab snatches the harpoon, waves it torch-like and swears to transfix the first man who casts loose a rope's end. He revitalizes in the crew its oath to hunt the White Whale, "and with one blast of his breath he extinguished the flame," to the terror of many of the men.

It is his belief that the elements do not destroy him when he defies them because he is one with them. Their right worship is not love or reverence but defiance—"defyingly I worship them," he exclaims as he holds the lightning rods aloft at the height of the typhoon. Extraordinary he is, for so sensitized is his physical organism that he reacts preternaturally to changes in environment not perceptible to grosser seamen. It is Ahab who first smells the presence of the White Whale. He is like a hound on a watery slot.

Those who have not been cowed stand in awe of his acts. Even the prudent and unconvinced Starbuck is constrained to obey Ahab's commands, rebellingly. When the needles in the binnacle compass demagnetize in the storm, Ahab takes lancehead, top-maul and the smallest of the sailmaker's needles, and with "strange motions" he magnetizes the needle from the lance-head and slips the needle over the compass card. Scornfully and triumphantly he awes the men with this show of magic, proving at least to his satisfaction that he is "lord of the level load-stone." Ahab is possessed of irrepressible histrionic abilities. Like Twain's Connecticut Yankee what he does has to be theatrical or he doesn't take any interest in it.

The final chapters of *Moby Dick* are a thoroughly documented representation of the fanatical passion of Captain Ahab in his attempt to infuse his will (through magic) upon his men and upon the elemental forces of the universe. And in a sense his magic is just as fundamental as its practice by the rudest aborigines of Australia or Africa. There are, we see, ceremonial rituals, the divinations of the Parsee and Ahab's dream, demonological connotations, harpoon cults, the masked god of the White Whale, the fetishistic death-lance, chant-like exclamations. In seventeenth century New England Ahab would be accused of wizardry and condemned as a sorcerer.

Aided by civilized qualities of intelligence and gifted with "high perception," Ahab knows how to appeal to the covetousness of his crew. He victimizes them with bribes and plies them with spirits, and effectively immobilizes them by strange ascendancies of megalomania through "sheer inveteracy of will." Ahab shows few gestures of mollification. He does lower for the chase when the White Whale is out of range, which tends to settle his men. He has studied the files of old log books and traced courses on large wrinkled yellowish sea-charts. He knows the set of tides and currents; he has calculated the driftings of the sperm whale's food; he has noted the tendency of the whale to swim in arbitrary veins; he will, therefore, hunt Moby Dick in particular latitudes and anticipate him in the Season-on-the-line.

Ahab's eventual defeat is attributable to a personal failure, not to the exaction of a lawful deity or higher power. After the second day of the chase, injured but unbeaten, he tells his first mate Starbuck, "I am the Fates' lieutenant, I act under orders." So he acted, for he thought the whole act was immutably decreed. He was ready; he asserted his desperate will; the immutable laws were acknowledged; the battle was joined; he fought heroically. Somewhere in between there was a slip. In perfect self-containment he finally addresses the whale. There is no trace of Christian submission or renunciation in his attitude. There is only the major chord of overweening pride and arrogance, so typical of primitive medicine men. "Towards thee I roll, thou all-destroying but unconquering whale; to the last I grapple with thee; from hell's heart I stab at thee; for hate's sake I spit my last breath at thee."

His magic—the harpoon ritualistically forged, the crew shamanistically briefed, the contact vigilantly charted and planned —fails to destroy the force he opposes. Neither is the whale's attack unconditionally successful. In the mortal battle between the sentient Ahab and the inscrutable animate force incarnate in the White Whale, there is no clear-cut victory. If physical presence after mortal conflct is the only just measure of victory then inscrutability rules supreme over vulnerable sentience. If the spirit of man has not been conquered, and this Ahab believes when he refers to the "unconquering" whale, then victory is partial and limited, not unconditional and absolute for the whale. Ahab is physically destroyed but spiritually triumphant over adversity *sub specie aeternitatis*.

Ahab's equivocal defeat is, in a sense, the failure of magic as an effective force in the manipulation of natural forces. *Moby Dick* is not an apotheosis of magic. By inference, it is a confession of the inadequacy of magic as a means of control. Ahab is brave and proud, but in his reversion to magic he confesses human ignorance and in his physical defeat he betrays, not lack of skill but the limitation of all men before superior animate forces. Ahab's fallibility is a token of the inadequacy of magic. The inscrutable remains inscrutable, but its presence is more exactly defined. We know it for what it is: a terrifying power at the heart of things. Ahab possesses no enchantment, personal or derivative, that gives him the potency to penetrate the ultimate nature of things. His pent-up passion, his cunning and patient preparation, his exacting toil, his brilliant ingenuity, his frenzied bravado, all avail him little, actually.

There is also considerable big medicine in *Moby Dick* indirectly associated with Captain Ahab. The tattooed Queequeg worships a little hunchbacked glistening black ivory god called Yojo with guttural pagan psalmody. The Manx-man is popularly invested with abnormal powers of discernment. The impromptu ritual enacted when the Christian Ishmael "marries" the pagan Queequeg—together smoking the tomahawk pipe, pressing foreheads in embrace, dividing personal wealth and offering burnt biscuit to Yojo with salaams, are certainly evidences of "medicine." So, too, is the appearance of Fedallah: the tall, swart, black-jacketed, white-turbaned, protuberant-toothed Parsee who raises the Spirit Spout and prophesies Ahab's fate. Nor can we exclude the tattooed body of Queequeg, a perfect marvel of totemism, representing "a complete theory of the heavens and the earth and a mystical treatise on the art of attaining truth," as conceived by a prophet.

There are, moreover, correlative evidences of "medicine": Ahab's "brand," a cicatrice scoring him from head to toe, the result of his elemental strife at sea; his throne-like tripod of ivory bone on which he sits on the weather side of the deck; the vial of sand from Nantucket Soundings which Ahab carries with him like a fetish; and the red-billed savage sea-hawk stealing his hat. There are the ambiguous rumors: of the veiled prophecy of the squaw Tistig from Gayhead, the shrouded story of Ahab's scrimmage with a Spaniard before the altar in Santa, and the hinted desecration when Ahab spat in the silver calabash. Are the latter actual or imaginary events? Are they meaningful as the soothsaying Elijah's gibberish? At least they are just such rumors as would surround the sorcerer and lend credence to his supernatural power. Melville mentions the tendency of superstitious whalemen to indulge their fancies and their credulity. "The whaleman," he says, "is wrapped by influences all tending to make his fancy pregnant with many a mighty birth." The wonders of the deep (the wondrous cistern in the whale's huge head, the prodigy of his unhinged lower jaw, and the miracle of his symmetrical tail on the fabulous squid); and the heroics of the chase (Queequeg's "agile obstetrics" in rescuing Tashtego from the sinking Sperm Whale's head or jolly Stubb's exuberant chase of great whales), contribute perceptibly to the atmosphere of "big medicine" in *Moby Dick*.

Animism is touched circumspectly in the White Whale, and totemism is suggested in the whale as masked god. There are the forms and usages aboard ship as related to the mariner's tribal society—the harpooner clan—but there is no reference to tabu, unless Captain Boomer's attitude and the insane Gabriel's injunction are considered as such. Nor is there any eroticism, though one terrific orgy of Dionysian revelry and drunkenness takes place. Nor is there any exorcism of devils.

Melville has dealt carefully with the necromantic features of big medicine. Ex-tended as the mythopoeic scenes are, Melville does not over-reach himself. He resolves the issues in his book by having Ahab remain true to himself. The nefarious Ahab neither renounces the fiery hunt nor recants his reversion to demonology. His Christian apostasy is unimpugnable; to the end his sorcery is virtuous if ineffective. Melville's handling of "big medicine" is reservedly romantic. He does not offer a well worked-out formula that begins with the practice of obtaining supernatural power in dream or vision, to be effected by continence, discipline, torture, fasting, alcohol or drugs, nor one which applies the technique of concentration until the "right" vision comes. This was not, of course, his aim. The "big medicine" is used to heighten the drama and to infuse the magnificent plangent poetry with strange imagistic overtones. It does, however, contribute to the intellectual content. It reinforces Melville's meaning and in its connotations gives Ahab's actions powerful significance.

Henry A. Murray

In Nomine Diaboli

NEXT to the seizures and shapings of creative thought—the thing itself—no comparable experience is more thrilling than being witched, illumined, and transfigured by the magic of another's art. This is a trance from which one returns refreshed and quickened, and bubbling with unenvious praise of the exciting cause, much as Melville bubbled after his first reading of Hawthorne's *Mosses*. In describing *his* experience Melville chose a phrase so apt —"the shock of recognition"—that in the thirties Edmund Wilson took it as the irresistibly perfect title for his anthology of literary appreciations. Acknowledging a shock of recognition and paying homage to the delivering genius is singularly exhilarating, even today—or especially today—when every waxing enthusiasm must confront an outgoing tide of culture.

In our time, the capacities for wonder and reverence, for generous judgments and trustful affirmations, have largely given way, though not without cause surely, to their antitheses, the humors of a waning ethos: disillusionment, cynicism, disgust, and gnawing envy. These states have bred in us the inclination to dissect the subtlest orders of man's wit with ever sharper instruments of depreciation, to pour all values, the best confounded by the worst, into one mocking-pot, to sneer "realistically," and, as we say today, to "assassinate" character. These same humors have disposed writers to spend immortal talent in snickering exhibitions of vulgarity and spiritual emptiness, or in making delicate picture-puzzles out of the butt-ends of life.

In the face of these current trends and tempers, I, coming out of years of brim-ming gratefulness for the gift of *Moby-Dick*, would like to praise Herman Melville worthily, not to bury him in a winding sheet of scientific terminology. But the odds are not favorable to my ambition. A commitment of thirty years to analytic modes of thought and concepts lethal to emotion has built such habits in me that were I to be waked in the night by a cry of "Help!" I fear I would respond in the lingo of psychology. I am suffering from one of the commonest ailments of our age —trained disability.

The habit of a psychologist is to break down the structure of each personality he studies into elements, and so in a few strokes to bring to earth whatever merit that structure, as a structure, may possess. Furthermore, for reasons I need not mention here, the technical terms for the majority of these elements have derogatory connotations. Consequently, it is difficult to open one's professional mouth without disparaging a fellow-being. Were an analyst to be confronted by that much heralded but still missing specimen of the human race—the normal man—he would be struck dumb, for once, through lack of appropriate ideas.

If I am able to surmount to some extent any impediments of this origin, you may attribute my good fortune to a providential circumstance. In the procession of my experiences *Moby-Dick* anteceded psychology; that is, I was swept by Melville's gale and shaken by his appalling sea dragon before I had acquired the all-leveling academic oil that is poured on brewed-up waters, and before I possessed the weapons and tools of science—the conceptual lance,

Reprinted by permission from the *New England Quarterly*, XXIV (December, 1951), 435–452.

harpoons, cutting irons, and whatnots—which might have reduced the "grand hooded phantom" to mere blubber. Lacking these defenses I was whelmed. Instead of my changing this book, this book changed me.

To me, *Moby-Dick* was Beethoven's *Eroica* in words: first of all, a masterly orchestration of harmonic and melodic language, of resonating images and thoughts in varied meters. Equally compelling were the spacious sea-setting of the story; the cast of characters and their prodigious common target; the sorrow, the fury, and the terror, together with all those frequent touches, those subtle interminglings of unexampled humor, quizzical, and, in the American way, extravagant; and finally the fated closure, the crown and tragic consummation of the immense yet firmly welded whole. But still more extraordinary and portentous were the penetration and scope, the sheer audacity of the author's imagination. Here was a man who did not fly away with his surprising fantasies to some unbelievable dreamland, pale or florid, shunning the stubborn objects and gritty facts, the prosaic routines and practicalities of everyday existence. Here was a man, who, on the contrary, chose these very things as vessels for his procreative powers—the whale as a naturalist, a Hunter or a Cuvier, would perceive him, the business of killing whales, the whale-ship running as an oil factory, stowing-down—in fact, every mechanism and technique, each tool and gadget, that was integral to the money-minded industry of whaling. Here was a man who could describe the appearance, the concrete matter-of-factness, and the utility of each one of these natural objects, implements, and tools with the fidelity of a scientist, and while doing this, explore it as a conceivable repository of some aspect of the human drama; then, by an imaginative tour de force, deliver a vital essence, some humorous or profound idea, coalescing with its embodiment. But still more. Differing from

the symbolists of our time, here was a man who offered us essences and meanings which did not level or depreciate the objects of his contemplation. On the contrary, this loving man exalted all creatures—the mariners, renegades, and castaways on board the *Pequod*—by ascribing to them "high qualities, though dark" and weaving round them "tragic graces." Here, in short, was a man with the myth-making powers of a Blake, a hive of significant associations, who was capable of reuniting what science had put asunder—pure perception and relevant emotion—and doing it in an exultant way that was acceptable to skepticism.

Not at first, but later, I perceived the crucial difference between Melville's dramatic animations of nature and those of primitive religion-makers; both were spontaneous and uncalculated projections, but Melville's were in harmony, for the most part, with scientific knowledge, because they had been recognized as projections, checked, and modified. Here, then, was a man who might redeem us from the virtue of an incredible subjective belief, on the one side, and from the virtue of a deadly objective rationality, on the other.

For these and other reasons the reading of *Moby-Dick*—coming before psychology—left a stupendous imprint, too vivid to be dimmed by the long series of relentless analytical operations to which I subsequently subjected it. Today, after twenty-five years of such experiments, *The Whale* is still *the* whale, more magnificent, if anything, than before.

Before coming to grips with the "mystery" of *Moby-Dick* I should mention another providential circumstance to which all psychologists are, or should be, forever grateful—and literary critics too, since without it no complete understanding of books like *Moby-Dick* would be possible today. Ahead of us were two greatly gifted pioneers, Freud and Jung, who, with others, explored the manifold vagaries of unconscious mental processes and left for our inheritance their finely written works. The discoveries of these adventurers advantaged me in a special way: they gave, I thought, support to one of Santayana's early convictions, that in the human being imagination is more fundamental than perception. Anyhow, adopting this position, some of us psychologists have been devoting ourselves to the study of dreams, fantasies, creative productions, and projections—all of which are primarily and essentially emotional and dramatic, such stuff as myths are made of. Thus, by chance or otherwise, this branch of the tree of psychology is growing in the direction of Herman Meville.

To be explicit: psychologists have been recognizing in the dream figures and fantasy figures of today's children and adolescents more and more family likenesses of the heroes and heroines of primitive myths, legends, and fables—figures, in other words, who are engaged in comparable heroic strivings and conflicts and are experiencing comparable heroic triumphs and fatalities. Our ancestors, yielding to an inherent propensity of the mind, projected the more relevant of these figures into objects of their environment, into sun, moon, and stars, into the unknown deeps of the sea and of the earth, and into the boundless void of heaven; and they worshiped the most potent of these projected images, whether animal or human, as superbeings, gods, or goddesses. On any clear night one can see scores of the more luminous of such divinities parading up and down the firmament. For example, in fall and winter, one looks with admiration on that resplendent hero Perseus and above him the chained beauty Andromeda, whom he saved from a devouring monster, ferocious as Moby Dick. Now, what psychologists have been learning by degrees is that Perseus is in the unconscious mind of every man and Andromeda in every woman—not, let me hasten to say, as an inherited fixed image, but as a potential set of dispositions which may be constellated in the personality by the occurrence of a certain kind of

situation. Herman Melville arrived at this conclusion in his own way a hundred years ago, sooner and, I believe, with more genuine comprehension than any other writer.

An explanation of all this in scientific terms would require all the space permitted me and more. Suffice it to say here that the psychologists who are studying the elementary myth-makings of the mind are dealing with the germy sources of poetry and drama, the fecundities out of which great literature is fashioned. Furthermore, in attempting to formulate and classify these multifarious productions of the imagination, the psychologist uses modes of analysis and synthesis very similar to those that Aristotle used in setting forth the dynamics of Greek tragedy. In these and other trends I find much encouragement for the view that a rapprochement of psychology and literary criticism is in progress, and that it will prove fruitful to both callings. As an ideal meeting ground I would propose Melville's world of "wondrous depths."

To this Columbus of the mind, the great archetypal figures of myth, drama, and epic were not pieces of intellectual Dresden china, heirlooms of a classical education, ornamental bric-a-brac to be put here and there for the pleasure of genteel readers. Many of the more significant of these constellations were inwardly experienced by Melville, one after the other, as each was given vent to blossom and assert itself. Thus we are offered a spectacle of spiritual development through passionate identifications. Only by proceeding in this way could Melville have learned on his pulses what it was to be a Narcissus, Orestes, Oedipus, Ishmael, Apollo, Lucifer. "Like a frigate," he said, "I am full with a thousand souls."

This brings me to the problem of interpreting *Moby-Dick*. Some writers have said that there is nothing to interpret: it is a plain sea story marred here and there by irrelevant ruminations. But I shall not cite the abundant proof for the now generally accepted proposition that in *Moby-Dick*

Melville "meant" something—something, I should add, which he considered "terrifically true" but which, in the world's judgment, was so harmful "that it were all but madness for any good man, in his own proper character, to utter or even hint of." What seems decisive here is the passage in Melville's celebrated letter to Hawthorne: "A sense of unspeakable security is in me this moment, on account of your having understood the book." From this we can conclude that there *are* meanings to be understood in *Moby-Dick*, and also—may we say for our own encouragement?—that Melville's ghost will feel secure forever if modern critics can find them, and since Hawthorne remained silent, set them forth in print. Here it might be well to remind ourselves of a crucial statement which follows the just quoted passage from Melville's letter: "I have written a wicked book." The implication is clear: all interpretations which fail to show that *Moby-Dick* is, in some sense, wicked have missed the author's avowed intention.

A few critics have scouted all attempts to fish Melville's own meaning out of *The Whale*, on the ground that an interpretation of a work of art so vast and so complex is bound to be composed in large measure of projections from the mind of the interpreter. It must be granted that preposterous projections often do occur in the course of such an effort. But these are not inevitable. Self-knowledge and discipline may reduce projections to a minimum. Anyhow, in the case of *Moby-Dick*, the facts do not sustain the proposition that a critic can see nothing in this book but his own reflected image. The interpretations which have been published over the last thirty years exhibit an unmistakable trend toward consensus in respect to the drama as a whole as well as to many of its subordinate parts. Moreover, so far as I can judge, the critics who, with hints from their predecessors, applied their intuitions most recently to the exegesis of *The Whale* can be said to have arrived, if taken together, at Melville's essential mean-

ing. Since one or another of these authors has deftly said what I clumsily thought, my prejudices are strongly in favor of their conclusions, and I am whole-hearted in applauding them—Newton Arvin's most especially—despite their having left me with nothing fresh to say. Since this is how things stand, my version of the main theme of *Moby-Dick* can be presented in a briefer form, and limited to two hypotheses.

The first of them is this: Captain Ahab is an embodiment of that fallen angel or demigod who in Christendom was variously named Lucifer, Devil, Adversary, Satan. The Church Fathers would have called Captain Ahab "Antichrist" because he was not Satan himself, but a human creature possessed of all Satan's pride and energy, "summing up within himself," as Irenaeus said, "the apostasy of the devil."

That it was Melville's intention to beget Ahab in Satan's image can hardly be doubted. He told Hawthorne that his book had been broiled in hell-fire and secretly baptized not in the name of God but in the name of the Devil. He named his tragic hero after the Old Testament ruler who "did more to provoke the Lord God of Israel to anger than all the Kings of Israel that were before him." King Ahab's accuser, the prophet Elijah, is also resurrected to play his original role, though very briefly, in Melville's testament. We are told that Captain Ahab is an "ungodly, god-like" man who is spiritually outside Christendom. He is a well of blasphemy and defiance, of scorn and mockery for the gods—"cricket-players and pugilists" in his eyes. Rumor has it that he once spat in the holy goblet on the altar of the Catholic Church at Santa. "I never saw him kneel," says Stubb. He is associated in the text with scores of references to the Devil. He is an "anaconda of an old man." His self-assertive sadism is the linked antithesis of the masochistic submission preached by Father Mapple.

Captain Ahab-Lucifer is also related to a sun-god, like Christ, but in reverse. Instead of being light leaping out of darkness, he is "darkness leaping out of light." The *Pequod* sails on Christmas Day. *This* new year's sun will be the god of Wrath rather than the god of Love. Ahab does not emerge from his subterranean abode until his ship is "rolling through the bright Quito spring" (Eastertide, symbolically, when the all-fertilizing sun-god is resurrected). The frenzied ceremony in which Ahab's followers are sworn to the pursuit of the White Whale—"Commend the murderous chalices!"—is suggestive of the Black Mass; the lurid operations at the tryworks is a scene out of Hell.

There is some evidence that Melville was rereading *Paradise Lost* in the summer of 1850, shortly after, let us guess, he got the idea of transforming the captain of his whale-ship into the first of all cardinal sinners who fell by pride. Anyhow, Melville's Satan is the spitting image of Milton's hero, but portrayed with deeper and subtler psychological insight, and placed where he belongs, in the heart of an enraged man.

Melville may have been persuaded by Goethe's Mephistopheles, or even by some of Hawthorne's bloodless abstracts of humanity, to add Fedallah to his cast of characters. Evidently he wanted to make certain that no reader would fail to recognize that Ahab had been possessed by, or had sold his soul to the Devil. Personally, I think Fedallah's role is superfluous, and I regret that Melville made room for him and his unbelievable boat-crew on the ship *Pequod*. Still, he is not wholly without interest. He represents the cool, heartless, cunning, calculating, intellectual Devil of the medieval myth-makers, in contrast to the stricken, passionate, indignant, and often eloquent rebel angel of *Paradise Lost,* whose role is played by Ahab.

The Arabic name "Fedallah" suggests "dev(il) Allah," that is, the Mohammedans' god as he appeared in the mind's eye of a Crusader. But we are told that Fedallah is a Parsee—a Persian fire-worshiper, or Zoroastrian, who lives in India. Thus, Ahab, named after the Semitic apostate who was converted to the orgiastic cult of Baal, or Bel, originally a Babylonian fertility god, has formed a compact with a Zoroastrian whose name reminds us of still another Oriental religion. In addition, Captain Ahab's whaleboat is manned by a crew of unregenerate infidels, as defined by orthodox Christianity; and each of his three harpooners, Queequeg, Tashtego, and Daggoo, is a member of a race which believed in other gods than the one god of the Hebraic-Christian Bible.

Speaking roughly, it might be said that Captain Ahab, incarnation of the Adversary and master of the ship *Pequod* (named after the aggressive Indian tribe that was exterminated by the Puritans of New England), has summoned the various religions of the East to combat the one dominant religion of the West. Or, in other terms, that he and his followers, Starbuck excepted, represent the horde of primitive drives, values, beliefs, and practices which the Hebraic-Christian religionists rejected and excluded, and by threats, punishments, and inquisitions forced into the unconscious mind of Western man.

Stated in psychological concepts, Ahab is captain of the culturally repressed dispositions of human nature, that part of personality which psychoanalysts have termed the "Id." If this is true, his opponent, the White Whale, can be none other than the internal institution which is responsible for these repressions, namely the Freudian Superego. This, then, is my second hypothesis; Moby Dick is a veritable spouting, breaching, sounding whale, a whale who, because of his whiteness, his mighty bulk and beauty, and because of one instinctive act that happened to dismember his assailant, has received the projection of Captain Ahab's Presbyterian conscience, and so may be said to embody the Old Testament Calvinistic conception of an affrighting Deity and his strict commandments, the derivative puritan ethic of nineteenth-century America and the society that defended this ethic. Also, and most specifically, he symbolizes the zealous parents whose righteous sermonizings and corrections drove the prohibitions in so hard that a serious young man could hardly reach outside the barrier, except possibly far away among some tolerant, gracious Polynesian peoples. The emphasis should be placed on that unconscious (and hence inscrutable) wall of inhibition which imprisoned the puritan's thrusting passions. "How can the prisoner reach outside," cries Ahab, "except by thrusting through the wall? To me, the white whale is that wall, shoved near to me . . . I see in him outrageous strength, with an inscrutable malice sinewing it." As a symbol of a sounding, breaching, white-dark, unconquerable New England conscience what could be better than a sounding, breaching, white-dark, unconquerable sperm whale?

Who is the psychoanalyst who could resist the immediate inference that the imago of the mother as well as the imago of the father is contained in the Whale? In the present case there happens to be a host of biographical facts and written passages which support this proposition. Luckily, I need not review them, because Mr. Arvin and others have come to the same conclusion. I shall confine myself to one reference. It exhibits Melville's keen and sympathetic insight into the cultural determinants of his mother's prohibiting dispositions. In *Pierre*, it is the "high-up, and towering and all-forbidding . . . edifice of his mother's immense pride . . . her pride of birth . . . her pride of purity," that is the "wall shoved near," the wall that stands between the hero and the realization of his heart's resolve. But instead of expending the fury of frustration upon his mother, he directs it at Fate, or, more specifically, at his mother's God and the society that shaped her. For he sees "that not his mother has made his mother; but the Infinite Haughtiness had first fashioned her; and then the haughty world had further molded her; nor had a haughty Ritual omitted to finish her."

Given this penetrating apprehension, we are in a position to say that Melville's tar-

get in *Moby-Dick* was the upper-middle class culture of his time. It was *this* culture which was defended with righteous indignation by what he was apt to call "the world" or "the public," and Melville had very little respect for "the world" or "the public." The "public," or men operating as a social system, was something quite distinct from "the people." In *White-Jacket* he wrote: "The public and the people! . . . let us hate the one, and cleave to the other." "The public is a monster," says Lemsford. Still earlier Melville had said: "I fight against the armed and crested lies of Mardi (the world)." "Mardi is a monster whose eyes are fixed in its head, like a whale." Many other writers have used similar imagery. Sir Thomas Browne referred to the multitude as "that numerous piece of monstrosity." Keats spoke of "the dragon world." But closest of all was Hobbes: "By art is created that great Leviathan, called a commonwealth or state." It is in the laws of this Leviathan, Hobbes made clear, that the sources of right and wrong reside. To summarize: the giant mass of Melville's whale is the same as Melville's man-of-war world, the *Neversink*, in *White-Jacket*, which in turn is an epitome of Melville's Mardi. The Whale's white forehead and hump should be reserved for the world's heavenly King.

That God is incarnate in the Whale has been perceived by Geoffrey Stone, and, as far as I know, by every other Catholic critic of Melville's work, as well as by several Protestant critics. In fact, Richard Chase has marshaled so fair a portion of the large bulk of evidence on this point that any more from me would be superfluous. Of course, what Ahab projects into the Whale is not the image of a loving Father, but the God of the Old Dispensation, the God who brought Jeremiah into darkness, hedged him about, and made his path crooked; the God adopted by the fire-and-brimstone Puritans, who said: "With fury poured out I will rule over you." "The sword without and the terror within, shall destroy both the young man and the virgin." "I will also send the teeth of beasts up)n them." "I will heap mischiefs upon them." "To me belongeth vengeance and recompense."

Since the society's vision of deity, and the society's morality, and the parents and ministers who implant these conceptions, are represented in a fully socialized personality by an establishment that is called the Superego—conscience as Freud defined it—and since Ahab has been proclaimed the "Captain of the Id," the simplest psychological formula for Melville's dramatic epic is this: an insurgent Id in mortal conflict with an oppressive cultural Superego. Starbuck, the first mate, stands for the rational realistic Ego, which is overpowered by the fanatical compulsiveness of the Id and dispossessed of its normal regulating functions.

If this is approximately correct, it appears that while writing his greatest work Melville abandoned his detached position in the Ego from time to time, hailed "the realm of shades," as his hero Taji had, and, through the mediumship of Ahab, "burst his hot heart's shell" upon the sacrosanct Almighty and the sacrosanct sentiments of Christendom. Since in the world's judgment, in 1851, nothing could be more reproachable than this, it would be unjust, if not treacherous, of us to reason *Moby-Dick* into some comforting morality play for which no boldness was required. This would be depriving Melville of the ground he gained for self-respect by having dared to abide by his own subjective truth and write a "wicked book," the kind of book that Pierre's publishers, Steel, Flint, and Asbestos, would have called "a blasphemous rhapsody filched from the vile Atheists, Lucian and Voltaire."

Some may wonder how it was that Melville, a fundamentally good, affectionate, noble, idealistic, and reverential man, should have felt impelled to write a wicked book. Why did he aggress so furiously against Western orthodoxy, as furiously as Byron and Shelley, or any Satanic writer who preceded him, as furiously as Nietz-

sche or the most radical of his successors in our day?

In *Civilization and Its Discontents* Freud, out of the ripeness of his full experience, wrote that when one finds deepseated aggression—and by this he meant aggression of the sort that Melville voiced—one can safely attribute it to the frustration of Eros. In my opinion this generalization does not hold for all men of all cultures of all times, but the probability of its being valid is extremely high in the case of an earnest, moralistic, nineteenth-century American, a Presbyterian to boot, whose anger is born of suffering—especially if this man spent an impressionable year of his life in Polynesia and returned to marry the very proper little daughter of the chief justice of Massachusetts, and if, in addition, he is a profoundly creative man in whose androgynic personality masculine and feminine components are integrally blended.

If it were concerned with *Moby-Dick*, the book, rather than with its author, I would call *this* my third hypothesis: Ahab-Melville's aggression was directed against the object that once harmed Eros with apparent malice and was still thwarting it with presentiments of further retaliations. The correctness of this inference is indicated by the nature of the injury—a symbolic emasculation—that excited Ahab's ire. Initially, this threatening object was, in all likelihood, the father; later, possibly, the mother. But, as Melville plainly saw, both his parents had been fashioned by the Hebraic-Christian, American Calvinistic tradition, the tradition which conceived of a deity in whose eyes Eros was depravity. It was the first Biblical myth-makers who dismissed from heaven and from earth the Great Goddess of the Oriental and primitive religions, and so rejected the feminine principle as a spiritual force. Ahab, protagonist of those rejected religions, in addressing heaven's fire and lightning, what he calls "the personified impersonal," cries: "but thou art my fiery father; my sweet mother I know not. Oh, cruel! What hast thou done with her?" He calls this god a foundling, a "hermit immemorial," who does not know his own origin. Again, it was the Hebraic authors, sustained later by the Church Fathers, who propagated the legend that a woman was the cause of Adam's exile from Paradise, and that the original sin was concupiscence. Melville says that Ahab, spokesman of all exiled princes, "piled upon the whale's white hump the sum of all the general rage and hate felt by his whole race from Adam down." Remember also that it was the lure of Jezebel that drew King Ahab of Israel outside the orthodoxy of his religion and persuaded him to worship the Phoenician Astarte, goddess of love and fruitful increase. "Jezebel" was the worst tongue-lash a puritan could give a woman. She was sex, and sex was Sin, spelled with a capital. It was the church periodicals of Melville's day that denounced *Typee*, called the author a sensualist, and influenced the publishers to delete suggestive passages from the second edition. It was this long heritage of aversion and animosity, so accentuated in this country, which banned sex relations as a topic of discourse and condemned divorce as an unpardonable offense. All this has been changed, for better and for worse, by the moral revolutionaries of our own time who, feeling as Melville felt but finding the currents of sentiment less strongly opposite, spoke out, and with their wit, indignation, and logic, reinforced by the findings of psychoanalysis, disgraced the stern-faced idols of their forebears. One result is this: today an incompatible marriage is not a prison-house, as it was for Melville, "with wall shoved near."

In *Pierre* Melville confessed his own faith when he said that Eros is god of all, and Love "the loftiest religion on this earth." To the romantic Pierre the image of Isabel was "a silent and tyrannical call, challenging him in his deepest moral being, and summoning Truth, Love, Pity, Conscience to the stand." Here he seems to have had in mind the redeeming and inspiriting

Eros of courtly love, a heresy which the medieval church had done its utmost to stamp out. *This*, he felt convinced, was *his* "path to God," although in the way of it he saw with horror the implacable conscience and worldly valuations of his revered mother.

If this line of reasoning is as close as I think it is to the known facts, then Melville, in the person of Ahab, assailed Calvinism in the Whale because it blocked the advance of a conscience beneficent to evolutionary love. And so, weighed in the scales of its creator, *Moby-Dick* is not a wicked book but a *good* book, and after finishing it Melville had full reason to feel, as he confessed, "spotless as the lamb."

But then, seen from another point, *Moby-Dick* might be judged a wicked book, not because its hero condemns an entrenched tradition, but because he is completely committed to destruction. Although Captain Ahab manifests the basic stubborn virtues of the arch-protestant and the rugged individualist carried to their limits, *this* god-defier is no Prometheus, since all thought of benefiting humanity is foreign to him. His purpose is not to make the Pacific safe for whaling, nor, when blasting at the moral order, does he have in mind a more heartening vision for the future. The religion of Eros which might once have been the secret determinant of Ahab's undertaking is never mentioned. At one critical point in *Pierre* the hero-author, favored by a flash of light, exclaims, "I will gospelize the world anew"; but he never does. Out of light comes darkness: the temper of Pierre's book is no different from the temper of *Moby-Dick*. The truth is that Ahab is motivated by his private need to avenge a private insult. His governing philosophy is that of nihilism, the doctrine that the existing system must be shattered. Nihilism springs up when the imagination fails to provide the redeeming solution of an unbearable dilemma, when "the creative response," as Toynbee would say, is not forthcoming, and a man reacts out of a hot heart

—"to the dogs with the head"—and swings to an instinct, "the same that prompts even a worm to turn under the heel." This is what White Jacket did when arraigned at the mast, and what Pierre did when fortune deserted him, and what Billy Budd did when confronted by his accuser. "Nature has not implanted any power in man," said Melville,

that was not meant to be exercised at times, though too often our powers have been abused. The privilege, inborn, and inalienable, that every man has, of dying himself and inflicting death upon another, was not given to us without a purpose. These are the last resources of an insulted and unendurable existence.

If we grant that Ahab is a wicked man, what does this prove? It proves that *Moby-Dick* is a *good* book, a parable in epic form, because Melville makes a great spectacle of Ahab's wickedness and shows through the course of the narrative how such wickedness will drive a man on iron rails to an appointed nemesis. Melville adhered to the classic formula for tragedies. He could feel "spotless as the lamb," because he had seen to it that the huge threat to the social system immanent in Ahab's two cardinal defects— egotistic self-inflation and unleashed wrath —was, at the end, fatefully exterminated, "and the great shroud of the sea rolled on as it rolled five thousand years ago." The reader has had his catharsis, equilibrium has been restored, sanity is vindicated.

This is true, but is it the whole truth? In point of fact, while writing *Moby-Dick* did Melville maintain aesthetic distance, keeping his own feelings in abeyance? Do we not hear Ahab saying things that the later Pierre will say and that Melville says less vehemently in his own person? Does not the author show marked partiality for the "mighty pageant creature" of his invention, put in *his* mouth the finest, boldest language? Also, have not many interpreters been so influenced by the abused Ahab that they saw nothing in his opponent but the source of all malicious agencies, the very

Devil? As Lewis Mumford has said so eloquently, Ahab is at heart a noble being whose tragic wrong is that of battling against evil with "power instead of love," and so becoming "the image of the thing he hates." With this impression imbedded in our minds, how can we come out with any moral except this: evil wins. We admit that Ahab's wickedness has been canceled. But what survives? It is the much more formidable, compacted wickedness of the group that survives, the world that is "saturated and soaking with lies," and its man-of-war God, who is hardly more admirable than a primitive totem beast, some oral-aggressive, child-devouring Cronos of the sea. Is this an idea that a man of good will can rest with?

Rest with? Certainly not. Melville's clear intention was to bring not rest, but *unrest* to intrepid minds. All gentle people were warned away from his book "on risk of a lumbago or sciatica." "A polar wind blows through it," he announced. He had not written to soothe, but to kindle, to make men leap from their seats, as Whitman would say, and fight for their lives. Was it the poet's function to buttress the battlements of complacency, to give comfort to the enemy? There is little doubt about the nature of the enemy in Melville's day. It was the dominant ideology, that peculiar compound of puritanism and materialism, of rationalism and commercialism, of shallow, blatant optimism and technology, which proved so crushing to creative evolutions in religion, art, and life. In such circumstances every "true poet," as Blake said, "is of the Devil's party," whether he knows it or not. Surveying the last hundred and fifty years, how many exceptions to this statement can we find? Melville, anyhow, knew that *he* belonged to the party, and while writing *Moby-Dick* so gloried in his membership that he baptized his work *In Nomine Diaboli*. It was precisely under these auspices that he created his solitary masterpiece, a construction of the same high order as the Constitution of the United

States and the scientific treatises of Willard Gibbs, though huge and wild and unruly as the Grand Canyon. And it is for this marvel chiefly that he resides in our hearts now among the greatest in "that small but high-hushed world" of bestowing geniuses.

The drama is finished. What of its author?

Moby-Dick may be taken as a comment on the strategic crisis of Melville's allegorical life. In portraying the consequences of Ahab's last suicidal lunge, the hero's umbilical fixation to the Whale and his death by strangling, the author signalized not only his permanent attachment to the imago of the mother, but the submission he had foreseen to the binding power of the parental conscience, the Superego of middle-class America. Measured against the standards of *his* day, then, Melville must be accounted a *good* man.

But does this entitle him to a place on the side of the angels? He abdicated to the conscience he condemned, and his ship *Pequod*, in sinking, carried down with it the conscience he aspired to, represented by the sky-hawk, the bird of heaven. With his

ideal drowned, life from then on was load, and time stood still. All he had denied to love he gave, throughout a martyrdom of forty years, to death.

But "hark ye yet again—the little lower layer." Melville's capitulation in the face of overwhelming odds was limited to the sphere of action. His embattled soul refused surrender and lived on, breathing back defiance, disputing "to the last gasp" of his "earthquake life" the sovereignty of that inscrutable authority in him. As he wrote in *Pierre,* unless the enthusiast "can find the talismanic secret, to reconcile this world with his own soul, then there is no peace for him, no slightest truce for him in this life." Years later we find him holding the same ground. "Terrible is earth" was his conclusion, but despite all, "no retreat through me." By this stand he bequeathed to us the unsolved problem of the talismanic secret.

Only at the very last, instinct spent, earthquake over, did he fall back to a position close to Christian resignation. In his Being, was not this man "a wonder, a grandeur, and a woe"?

D. H. Lawrence

Moby Dick, or the White Whale

A HUNT. The last great hunt.

For what?

For Moby Dick, the huge white sperm whale: who is old, hoary, monstrous, and swims alone; who is unspeakably terrible in his wrath, having so often been attacked; and snow-white.

Of course he is a symbol.

Of what?

I doubt if even Melville knew exactly. That's the best of it.

He is warm-blooded, he is lovable. He is lonely Leviathan, not a Hobbes sort. Or is he?

But he is warm-blooded, and lovable. The South Sea Islanders, and Polynesians, and Malays, who worship shark, or crocodile, or weave endless frigate-bird distortions, why did they never worship the whale? So big!

Because the whale is not wicked. He doesn't bite. And their gods had to bite.

He's not a dragon. He is Leviathan. He never coils like the Chinese dragon of the sun. He's not a serpent of the waters. He is warm-blooded, a mammal. And hunted, hunted down.

It is a great book.

At first you are put off by the style. It reads like journalism. It seems spurious. You feel Melville is trying to put something over you. It won't do.

And Melville really is a bit sententious: aware of himself, self-conscious, putting something over even himself. But then it's not easy to get into the swing of a piece of deep mysticism when you just set out with a story.

Nobody can be more clownish, more clumsy and sententiously in bad taste, than Herman Melville, even in a great book like MOBY DICK. He preaches and holds forth because he's not sure of himself. And he holds forth, often, so amateurishly.

The artist was so MUCH greater than the man. The man is rather a tiresome New Englander of the ethical mystical-transcendentalist sort: Emerson, Longfellow, Hawthorne, etc. So unrelieved, the solemn ass even in humour. So hopelessly AU GRAND SERIEUX, you feel like saying: Good God, what does it matter? If life is a tragedy, or a farce, or a disaster, or anything else, what do I care! Let life be what it likes. Give me a drink, that's what I want just now.

For my part, life is so many things I don't care what it is. It's not my affair to sum it up. Just now it's a cup of tea. This morning it was wormwood and gall. Hand me the sugar.

One wearies of the GRAND SERIEUX. There's something false about it. And that's Melville. Oh, dear, when the solemn ass brays! brays! brays!

But he was a deep, great artist, even if he was rather a sententious man. He was a real American in that he always felt his audience in front of him. But when he ceases to be American, when he forgets all audience, and gives us his sheer apprehension of the world, then he is wonderful, his book commands a stillness in the soul, an awe.

In his "human" self, Melville is almost dead. That is, he hardly reacts to human contacts any more: or only ideally: or just for a moment. His human-emotional self is almost played out. He is abstract, self-analytical and abstracted. And he is more spell-bound by the strange slidings and collidings of Matter than by the things men do. In this he is like Dana. It is the material elements he really has to do with. His drama is with them. He was a futurist long before futurism found paint. The sheer naked slidings of the elements. And the human soul experiencing it all. So often, it is almost over the border: psychiatry. Almost spurious. Yet so great.

It is the same old thing as in all Americans. They keep their old-fashioned ideal frock-coat on, and an old-fashioned silk hat, while they do the most impossible things. There you are: you see Melville hugged in bed by a huge tattooed South Sea Islander, and solemnly offering burnt offering to this savage's little idol, and his ideal frock-coat just hides his shirt-tails and prevents us from seeing his bare posterior as he salaams, while his ethical silk hat sits correctly over his brow the while. That is so typically American: doing the most impossible things without taking off their spiritual get-up. Their ideals are like armour which has rusted in, and will never more come off. And meanwhile in Melville his bodily knowledge moves naked, a living quick among the stark elements. For with sheer physical, vibrational sensitiveness, like a marvellous wireless-station, he registers the effects of the outer world. And he records also, almost beyond pain or pleasure, the extreme transitions of the isolated, far-driven soul, the soul which is now alone, without any real human contact.

The first days in New Bedford introduce the only human being who really enters into the book, namely, Ishmael, the "I" of the book. And then the moment's hearts-brother, Queequeg, the tattooed, powerful South Sea harpooner, whom Melville loves as Dana loves "Hope." The advent of Ishmael's bedmate is amusing and unforgettable. But later the two swear "marriage," in the language of the savages.

For Queequeg has opened again the flood-gates of love and human connection in Ishmael.

"As I sat there in that now lonely room, the fire burning low, in that mild stage when, after its first intensity has warmed the air, it then only glows to be looked at; the evening shades and phantoms gathering round the casements, and peering in upon us silent, solitary twain: I began to be sensible of strange feelings. I felt a melting in me. No more my splintered hand and maddened heart was turned against the wolfish world. This soothing savage had redeemed it. There he sat, his very indifference speaking a nature in which there lurked no civilized hypocrisies and bland deceits. Wild he was; a very sight of sights to see; yet I began to feel myself mysteriously drawn towards him." —So they smoke together, and are clasped in each other's arms. The friendship is finally sealed when Ishmael offers sacrifice to Queequeg's little idol, Gogo.

"I was a good Christian, born and bred in the bosom of the infallible Presbyterian Church. How then could I unite with the idolater in worshipping his piece of wood? But what is worship?—to do the will of God—THAT is worship. And what is the will of God?—to do to my fellowman what I would have my fellowman do to me—THAT is the will of God."—Which sounds like Benjamin Franklin, and is hopelessly bad theology. But it is real American logic. "Now Queequeg is my fellowman. And what do I wish that this Queequeg would do to me. Why, unite with me in my particular Presbyterian form of worship. Consequently, I must unite with him; ergo, I must turn idolater. So I kindled the shavings, helped prop up the innocent little idol; offered him burnt biscuit with Queequeg; salaamed before him twice or thrice; kissed his nose; and that done, we undressed and went to bed, at peace with our own consciences and all the world. But we did not go to sleep without some little chat. How it is I know not; but there

is no place like bed for confidential dis-
closures between friends. Man and wife,
they say, open the very bottom of their
souls to each other; and some old couples
often lie and chat over old times till nearly
morning. Thus, then, lay I and Queequeg
—a cozy, loving pair—"

You would think this relation with
Queequeg meant something to Ishmael. But
no. Queequeg is forgotten like yesterday's
newspaper. Human things are only momentary excitements or amusements to the
American Ishmael. Ishmael, the hunted.
But much more, Ishmael the hunter. What's
a Queequeg? What's a wife? The white
whale must be hunted down. Queequeg
must be just "KNOWN," then dropped
into oblivion.

And what in the name of fortune is the
white whale?

Elsewhere Ishmael says he loved Queequeg's eyes: "large, deep eyes, fiery black
and bold." No doubt, like Poe, he wanted
to get the "clue" to them. That was all.

The two men go over from New Bedford
to Nantucket, and there sign on to the
Quaker whaling ship, the PEQUOD. It is
all strangely fantastic, phantasmagoric.
The voyage of the soul. Yet curiously a
real whaling voyage, too. We pass on into
the midst of the sea with this strange ship
and its incredible crew. The Argonauts
were mild lambs in comparison. And
Ulysses went DEFEATING the Circes and
overcoming the wicked hussies of the isles.
But the PEQUOD'S crew is a collection of
maniacs fanatically hunting down a lonely,
harmless white whale.

As a soul history, it makes one angry.
As a sea yarn, it is marvellous: there is
always something a bit over the mark, in
sea yarns. Should be. Then again the mask-
ing up of actual seaman's experience with
sonorous mysticism sometimes gets on
one's nerves. And again, as a revelation of
destiny the book is too deep even for sorrow. Profound beyond feeling.

You are some time before you are allowed to see the captain, Ahab: the mys-

terious Quaker. Oh, it is a God-fearing
Quaker ship.

Ahab, the captain. The captain of the
soul.

"I am the master of my fate.
I am the captain of my soul!"

Ahab!
"Oh, captain, my captain, our fearful
trip is done."

The gaunt Ahab, Quaker, mysterious
person, only shows himself after some
days at sea. There's a secret about him.
What?

Oh, he's a portentous person. He stumps
about on an ivory stump, made from sea-
ivory. Moby Dick, the great white whale,
tore off Ahab's leg at the knee, when Ahab
was attacking him.

Quite right, too. Should have torn off
both his legs, and a bit more besides.

But Ahab doesn't think so. Ahab is now
a monomaniac. Moby Dick is his monomania. Moby Dick must DIE, or Ahab
can't live any longer. Ahab is atheist by
this.

All right.

This PEQUOD, ship of the American
soul, has three mates.

1. Starbuck: Quaker, Nantucketer, a
good responsible man of reason, fore-
thought, intrepidity, what is called a de-
pendable man. At the bottom, AFRAID.

2. Stubb: "Fearless as fire, and as mechanical." Insists on being reckless and
jolly on every occasion. Must be afraid
too, really.

3. Flask: Stubborn, obstinate, without
imagination. To him "the wondrous whale
was but a species of magnified mouse, or
water-rat—"

There you have them: a maniac captain
and his three mates, three splendid seamen, admirable whalemen, first class men
at their job.

America!

It is rather like Mr. Wilson and his admirable, "efficient" crew, at the Peace Con-

ference. Except that none of the Pequod-ders took their wives along.

A maniac captain of the soul, and three eminently practical mates.

America!

Then such a crew. Renegades, castaways, cannibals: Ishmael, Quakers.

America!

Three giant harpooners, to spear the great white whale.

1. Queequeg, the South Sea Islander, all tattooed, big and powerful.

2. Tashtego, the Red Indian of the sea-coast, where the Indian meets the sea.

3. Daggoo, the huge black negro.

There you have them, three savage races, under the American flag, the maniac captain, with their great keen harpoons, ready to spear the WHITE whale.

And only after many days at sea does Ahab's own boat-crew appear on deck. Strange, silent, secret, black-garbed Malays, fire-worshipping Parsees. These are to man Ahab's boat, when it leaps in pursuit of that whale.

What do you think of the ship PEQUOD, the ship of the soul of an American?

Many races, many peoples, many nations, under the Stars and Stripes. Beaten with many stripes.

Seeing stars sometimes.

And in a mad ship, under a mad captain, in a mad, fanatic's hunt.

For what?

For Moby Dick, the great white whale.

But splendidly handled. Three splendid mates. The whole thing practical, eminently practical in its working. American industry!

And all this practicality in the service of a mad, mad chase.

Melville manages to keep it a real whaling ship, on a real cruise, in spite of all fantastics. A wonderful, wonderful voy-age. And a beauty that is so surpassing only because of the author's awful flounderings in mystical waters. He wanted to get metaphysically deep. And he got deeper than metaphysics. It is a surpassingly beau-tiful book. With an awful meaning. And bad jolts.

It is interesting to compare Melville with Dana, about the albatross. Melville a bit sententious.—"I remember the first albatross I ever saw. It was during a prolonged gale in waters hard upon the Antarctic seas. From my forenoon watch below I ascended to the over-crowded deck, and there, lashed upon the main hatches, I saw a regal feathered thing of unspotted whiteness, and with a hooked Roman bill sublime. At intervals it arched forth its vast, archangel wings.—Wondrous throbbings and flutterings shook it. Though bodily unharmed, it uttered cries, as some King's ghost in supernatural distress. Through its inexpressible strange eyes methought I peeped to secrets not below the heavens—the white thing was so white, its wings so wide, and in those for ever exiled waters, I had lost the miserable warping memories of traditions and of town.—I assert then, that in the wondrous bodily whiteness of the bird chiefly lurks the secret of the spell—"

Melville's albatross is a prisoner, caught by a bait on a hook.

Well, I have seen an albatross, too: Following us in waters hard upon the Antarctic, too, south of Australia. And in the Southern winter. And the ship, a P. and O. boat, nearly empty. And the lascar crew shivering.

The bird with its long, long wings following, then leaving us. No one knows till they have tried, how lost, how lonely those Southern waters are. And glimpses of the Australian coast.

It makes one feel that our day is only a day. That in the dark of the night ahead other days stir fecund, when we have lapsed from existence.

Who knows how utterly we shall lapse.

But Melville keeps up his disquisition about "whiteness." The great abstract fascinated him. The abstract where we end, and cease to be. White or black. Our white, abstract end!

Then again it is lovely to be at sea on the PEQUOD, with never a grain of earth to us.

"It was a cloudy, sultry afternoon; the seamen were lazily lounging about the decks, or vacantly gazing over into the lead-coloured waters. Queequeg and I were mildly employed weaving what is called a sword-mat, for an additional lashing to our boat. So still and subdued and yet somehow preluding was all the scene, and such an incantation of reverie lurked in the air that each silent sailor seemed resolved into his own invisible self.—"

In the midst of this preluding silence came the first cry: "There she blows! there! there! there! She blows!"—And then comes the first chase, a marvellous piece of true sea-writing, the sea, and sheer sea-beings on the chase, sea-creatures chased. There is scarcely a taint of earth, —pure sea-motion.

" 'Give way men,' whispered Starbuck, drawing still further aft the sheet of his sail; 'there is time to kill fish yet before the squall comes. There's white water again!—Close to!—Spring!' Soon after, two cries in quick succession on each side of us denoted that the other boats had got fast; but hardly were they overheard, when with a lightning-like hurtling whisper Starbuck said: 'Stand up!' and Queequeg, harpoon in hand, sprang to his feet.— Though not one of the oarsmen was then facing the life and death peril so close to them ahead, yet their eyes on the intense countenance of the mate in the stern of the boat, they knew that the imminent instant had come; they heard, too, an enormous wallowing sound, as of fifty elephants stirring in their litter. Meanwhile the boat was still booming through the mist, the waves curbing and hissing around us like the erected crests of enraged serpents.

" 'That's his hump. THERE! THERE, give it to him!' whispered Starbuck.—A short rushing sound leapt out of the boat; it was the darted iron of Queequeg. Then all in one welded motion came a push

from astern, while forward the boat seemed striking on a ledge; the sail collapsed and exploded; a gush of scalding vapour shot up near by; something rolled and tumbled like an earthquake beneath us. The whole crew were half-suffocated as they were tossed helter-skelter into the white curling cream of the squall. Squall, whale, and harpoon had all blended together; and the whale, merely grazed by the iron, escaped—"

Melville is a master of violent, chaotic physical motion, he can keep up a whole wild chase without a flaw. He is as perfect at creating stillness. The ship is cruising on the Carrol Ground, south of St. Helena. —"It was while gliding through these latter waters that one serene and moonlight night, when all the waves rolled by like scrolls of silver; and by their soft, suffusing seethings, made what seemed a silvery silence, not a solitude; on such a silent night a silvery jet was seen far in advance of the white bubbles at the bow—"

Then there is the description of Brit. "Steering northeastward from the Crozello we fell in with vast meadows of brit, the minute, yellow substance upon which the right whale largely feeds. For leagues and leagues it undulated round us, so that we seemed to be sailing through boundless fields of ripe and golden wheat. On the second day, numbers of right whales were seen, secure from the attack of a sperm whaler like the PEQUOD. With open jaws they sluggishly swam through the brit, which, adhering to the fringed fibres of that wondrous Venetian blind in their mouths, was in that manner separated from the water that escaped at the lip. As moving mowers who, side by side, slowly and seethingly advance their scythes through the long wet grass of the marshy meads; even so these monsters swam, making a strange, grassy, cutting sound; and leaving behind them endless swaths of blue on the yellow sea. But it was only the sound they made as they parted the brit which at all reminded one of mowers. Seen from the mastheads, especially when they paused and were stationary for a while, their vast black forms looked more like masses of rock than anything else—"

This beautiful passage brings us to the apparition of the squid.

"Slowly wading through the meadows of brit, the PEQUOD still held her way northeastward towards the island of Java; a gentle air impelling her keel, so that in the surrounding serenity her three tall, tapering masts mildly waved to that languid breeze, as three mild palms on a plain. And still, at wide intervals, in the silvery night, that lonely, alluring jet would be seen.

"But one transparent-blue morning, when a stillness almost preternatural spread over the sea, however unattended with any stagnant calm; when the long burnished sunglade on the waters seemed a golden finger laid across them, enjoining secrecy; when all the slippered waves whispered together as they softly ran on; in this profound hush of the visible sphere a strange spectre was seen by Daggoo from the mainmast head.

"In the distance, a great white mass lazily rose, and rising higher and higher, and disentangling itself from the azure, at last gleamed before our prow like a snow-slide, new slid from the hills. Thus glistening for a moment, as slowly it subsided, and sank. Then once more arose, and silently gleamed. It seemed not a whale; and yet, is this Moby Dick? thought Dagoo—"

The boats were lowered and pulled to the scene.

"In the same spot where it sank, once more it slowly rose. Almost forgetting for the moment all thoughts of Moby Dick, we now gazed at the most wondrous phenomenon which the secret seas have hitherto revealed to mankind. A vast pulpy mass, furlongs in length and breadth, of a glancing cream-colour, lay floating on the water, innumerable long arms radiating from its centre, and curling and twisting like a nest of anacondas, as if blindly to clutch at any hapless object within reach. No perceptible face or front did it have; no conceivable token of either sensation or instinct; but undulated there on the billows, an unearthly, formless, chance-like apparition of life. And with a low sucking it slowly disappeared again."

The following chapters, with their account of whalehunts, the killing, the stripping, the cutting up, are magnificent records of actual happening. Then comes the queer tale of the meeting of the JERE–BOAM, a whaler met at sea, all of whose men were under the domination of a religious maniac, one of the ship's hands. There are detailed descriptions of the actual taking of the sperm oil from a whale's head. Dilating on the smallness of the brain of a sperm whale, Melville significantly remarks—"for I believe that much of a man's character will be found betokened in his backbone. I would rather feel your spine than your skull, whoever you are—" And of the whale, he adds:

"For, viewed in this light, the wonderful comparative smallness of his brain proper is more than compensated by the wonderful comparative magnitude of his spinal cord."

In among the rush of terrible, awful hunts come touches of pure beauty.

"As the three boats lay there on that gently rolling sea, gazing down into its eternal blue noon; and as not so much as a ripple or a thought, came up from its depths; what landsman would have thought that beneath all that silence and placidity the utmost monster of the seas was writhing and wrenching in agony!"

Perhaps the most stupendous chapter is the one called THE GRAND ARMADA, at the beginning of Volume III. The PEQUOD was drawing through the Sunda Straits towards Java when she came upon a vast host of sperm whales. "Broad on both bows, at a distance of two or three miles, and forming a great semi-circle embracing one-half of the level horizon, a continuous chain of whale-jets were up-playing and sparkling in the noonday air." Chasing this great herd, past the Straits of Sunda, themselves chased by Javan pirates, the whalers race on. Then the boats are lowered. At last that curious state of inert irresolution came over the whales, when they were, as the seamen say, gallied. Instead of forging ahead in huge martial array they swam violently hither and thither, a surging sea of whales, no longer moving on. Starbuck's boat, made fast to a whale, is towed in amongst this howling Leviathan chaos. In mad career it cockles through the boiling surge of monsters, till it is brought into a clear lagoon in the very centre of the vast, mad, terrified herd. There a sleek, pure calm reigns. There the females swam in peace, and the young whales came snuffing tamely at the boat, like dogs. And there the astonished seamen watched the love-making of these amazing monsters, mammals, now in rut far down in the sea.—"But far beneath this wondrous world upon the surface, another and still stranger world met our eyes, as we gazed over the side. For, suspended in these watery vaults, floated the forms of the nursing mothers of the whales, and those that by their enormous girth seemed shortly to become mothers. The lake, as I have hinted, was to a considerable depth exceedingly transparent; and as human infants while sucking will calmly and fixedly gaze away from the breast, as if leading two different lives at a time; and while yet drawing moral nourishment, be still spiritually feasting upon some unearthly reminiscence, even so did the young of these whales seem looking up towards us, but not at us, as if we were but a bit of gulf-weed in their newborn sight. Floating on their sides, the mothers also seemed quietly eyeing us.—Some of the subtlest secrets of the seas seemed divulged to us in this enchanted pond. We saw young Leviathan amours in the deep. And thus, though surrounded by circle upon circle of consternation and affrights, did these inscrutable creatures at the centre freely and fearlessly indulge in all peaceful concernments; yea, serenely revelled in dalliance and delight—"

There is something really overwhelming in these whalehunts, almost super-human or inhuman, bigger than life, more terrific than human activity. The same with the chapter on ambergris: it is so curious, so real, yet so unearthly. And again in the chapter called THE CASSOCK—surely the oldest piece of phallicism in all the world's literature.

After this comes the amazing account of the Try-works, when the ship is turned into the sooty, oily factory in mid-ocean, and the oil is extracted from the blubber. In the night of the red furnace burning on deck, at sea, Melville has his startling experience of reversion. He is at the helm, but has turned to watch the fire: when suddenly he feels the ship rushing backward from him, in mystic reversion.—"Uppermost was the impression, that whatever swift, rushing thing I stood on was not so much bound to any haven ahead, as rushing from all havens astern. A stark, bewildered feeling, as of death, came over me. Convulsively my hands grasped the tiller, but with the crazy conceit that the tiller was, somehow, in some enchanted way, inverted. My God! What is the matter with me, I thought!"

This dream-experience is a real soul-experience. He ends with an injunction to all men, not to gaze at the red fire when its redness makes all things look ghastly. It seems to him that his gazing on fire has evoked this horror of reversion, undoing.

Perhaps it had. He was water-born.

After some unhealthy work on the ship, Queequeg caught a fever and was like to die.—"How he wasted and wasted in those few, long-lingering days, till there seemed but little left of him but his frame and tattooing. But as all else of him thinned, and his cheek-bones grew sharper, his eyes, nevertheless, seemed growing fuller and fuller; they took on a strangeness of lustre; and mildly but deeply looked out at you there from his sickness, a wondrous testimony to that immortal health in him which could not die, or be weakened. And like circles on the water, which, as they grow fainter, expand; so his eyes seemed rounding and rounding, like the circles of Eternity. An awe that cannot be named would steal over you as you sat by the side of this waning savage—"

But Queequeg did not die—and the PEQUOD emerges from the Eastern Straits, into the full Pacific. "To my meditative Magian rover, this serene Pacific once beheld, must ever after be the sea of his adoption. It rolls the utmost waters of the world—"

In this Pacific the fights go on.—"It was far down the afternoon; and when all the spearings of the crimson fight were done; and floating in the lovely sunset sea and sky, sun and whale both died stilly together; then such a sweetness and such a plaintiveness, such inwreathing orisons curled up in that rosy air, that it almost seemed as if far over from the deep green convent valleys of the Manila isles, the Spanish land-breeze had gone to sea, freighted with these vesper hymns.— Soothed again, but only soothed to deeper gloom, Ahab, who had sterned off from the whale, sat intently watching his final wanings from the now tranquil boat. For that strange spectacle, observable in all sperm whales dying—the turning of the head sunwards, and so expiring—that strange spectacle, beheld of such a placid evening, somehow to Ahab conveyed wondrousness unknown before. 'He turns and turns him to it; how slowly, but how steadfastly, his home-rendering and invoking brow, with his last dying motions. He too worships fire; . . .'"

So Ahab soliloquizes: and so the warm-blooded whale turns for the last time to the sun, which begot him in the waters.

But as we see in the next chaper, it is the Thunder-fire which Ahab really worships: that living sundering fire of which he bears the brand, from head to foot.—It is storm,

the electric storm of the PEQUOD, when the corposants burn in high, tapering flames of supernatural pallor upon the masthead, and when the compass is reversed. After this all is fatality. Life itself seems mystically reversed. In these hunters of Moby Dick there is nothing but madness and possession. The captain, Ahab, moves hand in hand with the poor imbecile negro boy, Pip, who has been so cruelly demented, left swimming alone in the vast sea. It is the imbecile child of the sun hand in hand with the northern monomaniac, captain and master.

The voyage surges on. They meet one ship, then another. It is all ordinary day-routine, and yet all is a tension of pure madness and horror, the approaching horror of the last fight. "Hither and thither, on high, glided the snow-white wings of small unspecked birds; these were the gentle thoughts of the feminine air; but to and fro in the deeps, far down in the bottomless blue, rushed mighty leviathans, sword-fish and sharks; and these were the strong, troubled, murderous thinkings of the masculine sea—" On this day Ahab confesses his weariness, the weariness of his burden. "But do I look very old, so very, very old, Starbuck? I feel deadly faint, and bowed, and humped, as though I were Adam staggering beneath the piled centuries since Paradise—" It is the Gethsemane of Ahab, before the last fight; the Gethsemane of the human soul seeking the last self-conquest, the last attainment of extended consciousness—infinite consciousness.

At last they sight the whale. Ahab sees him from his hoisted perch at the mast-head.—"From this height the whale was now seen some mile or so ahead, at every roll of the sea revealing his high, sparkling hump, and regularly jetting his silent spout into the air."

The boats are lowered, to draw near the white whale. "At length the breathless hunter came so nigh his seemingly unsuspectful prey that his entire dazzling hump was distinctly visible, sliding along the sea as if an isolated thing, and continually set in a revolving ring of finest, fleecy, greenish foam. He saw the vast involved wrinkles of the slightly projecting head beyond. Before it, far out on the soft, Turkish rugged waters, went the glistening white shadow from his broad, milky forehead, a musical rippling playfully accompanying the shade; and behind, the blue waters interchangeably flowed over the moving valley of his steady wake; and on either side bright bubbles arose and danced by his side. But these were broken again by the light toes of hundreds of gay fowl softly feathering the sea, alternate with their fitful flight; and like to some flagstaff rising from the pointed hull of an argosy, the tall but shattered pole of a recent lance projected from the white whale's back; and at intervals one of the clouds of soft-toed fowls hovering, and to and fro shimmering like a canopy over the fish, silently perched and rocked on this pole, the long tail-feathers streaming like pennons.

"A gentle joyousness—a mighty mildness of repose in swiftness, invested the gliding whale—"

The fight with the whale is too wonderful, and too awful, to be quoted apart from the book. It lasted three days. The fearful sight, on the third day, of the torn body of the Parsee harpooner, lost on the previous day, now seen lashed on to the flanks of the white whale by the tangle of harpoon lines, has a mystic dream-horror. The awful and infuriated whale turns upon the ship, symbol of this civilized world of ours. He smites her with a fearful shock. And a few minutes later, from the last of the fighting whale boats comes the cry: " 'The ship! Great God, where is the ship?'—Soon they, through the dim, bewildering mediums, saw her sidelong fading phantom, as in the gaseous Fata Morgana; only the uppermost masts out of the water; while fixed by infatuation, or fidelity, or fate, to their once lofty

perches, the pagan harpooners still maintained their sinking lookouts on the sea. And now concentric circles seized the lone boat itself, and all its crew, and each floating oar, and every lance-pole, and spinning, animate and inanimate, all round and round in one vortex, carried the smallest chip of the PEQUOD out of sight—"

The bird of heaven, the eagle, St. John's bird, the Red Indian bird, the American, goes down with the ship, nailed by Tashtego's hammer, the hammer of the American Indian. The eagle of the spirit. Sunk.

"Now small fowls flew screaming over the yet yawning gulf; a sullen white surf beat against its steep sides; then all collapsed; and then the great shroud of the sea rolled on as it rolled five thousand years ago."

So ends one of the strangest and most wonderful books in the world, closing up its mystery and its tortured symbolism. It is an epic of the sea such as no man has equalled; and it is a book of exoteric symbolism of profound significance, and of considerable tiresomeness.

But it is a great book, a very great book, the greatest book of the sea ever written. It moves awe in the soul.

The terrible fatality.

Fatality.

Doom.

Doom! Doom! Doom! something seems to whisper it in the very dark trees of America. Doom!

Doom of what?

Doom of our white day. We are doomed, doomed. And the doom is in America. The doom of our white day.

Ah, well, if my day is doomed, and I am doomed with my day, it is something greater than I which dooms me, so I accept my doom as a sign of the greatness which is more than I am.

Melville knew. He knew his race was doomed. His white soul, doomed. His great white epoch, doomed. Himself, doomed. The idealist, doomed. The spirit, doomed.

The reversion. "Not so much bound to

any haven ahead, as rushing from all havens astern."

That great horror of ours! It is our civilization rushing from all havens astern.

The last ghastly hunt. The White Whale.

What then is Moby Dick?—He is the deepest blood-being of the white race. He is our deepest blood-nature.

And he is hunted, hunted, hunted by the maniacal fanaticism of our white mental consciousness. We want to hunt him down. To subject him to our will. And in this maniacal conscious hunt of ourselves we get dark races and pale to help us, red, yellow, and black, east and west, Quaker and fire-worshipper, we get them all to help us in this ghastly maniacal hunt which is our doom and our suicide.

The last phallic being of the white man. Hunted into the death of upper consciousness and the ideal will. Our blood-self subjected to our will. Our blood-consciousness sapped by a parasitic mental or ideal consciousness.

Hot-blooded   sea-born   Moby   Dick. Hunted by monomaniacs of the idea.

Oh God, oh God, what next, when the PEQUOD has sunk?

She sank in the war, and we all are flotsam.

Now what next?

Who knows? Quien sabe? Quien sabe, señor?

Neither Spanish nor Saxon America has any answer.

The PEQUOD went down. And the PEQUOD was the ship of the white American soul. She sank, taking with her Negro and Indian and Polynesian, Asiatic and Quaker and good, businesslike Yankees and Ishmael: she sank all the lot of them.

Boom! as Vachel Lindsay would say.

To use the words of Jesus, IT IS FINISHED.

Consummatum est!

But *Moby Dick* was first published in 1851. If the Great White Whale sank the ship of the Great White Soul in 1851, what's been happening ever since?

Post mortem effects, presumably.

Because, in the first centuries, Jesus was Cetus, the Whale. And the Christians were the little fishes. Jesus, the Redeemer, was Cetus, Leviathan. And all the Christians all his little fishes.

Harry Slochower

Moby Dick: The Myth of Democratic Expectancy

THE myth is the answer to the question of a basic universal theme. Its legitimacy and living form spring, however, from a specific cultural economy in which the myth is rooted. The universality of *The Divine Comedy* arises out of the historic forces of the Italian and Catholic tradition, that of *Hamlet* and *Faust* out of the English and German Renaissance. Aside from the influence of a national or folk culture, the myth is also conditioned by a sense of heritage from a past which goes far back, imbedded in the deep layers of folk-memory. Myth is the incarnation of the eternal present and of a chartered future through the remembrance of things past. The living myth looks ahead by looking back. Does America have these conditions for the myth? Has not our historic span been too brief to have formed such native memories?

Despite our relatively short historic life, we do possess an indigenous lore. We have our legends of Indians, pioneers, and gold-seekers, our Kit Carsons, Paul Bunyans, and Mike Finks. To be sure, these go back only a few centuries or less. But, because of the accelerated changes in American life in the wake of rapid technical development, the era of the Indian, the adventurous pioneer, and the daring western Robin Hood seems to belong to an immemorial past.

The myth imbedded in these pictures of earliest American life is that of a land offering a surfeit of opportunities, "a golden land," as America has been known to countless immigrants. The myth of America is that of a new, open, expanding world in which "the sky is the limit," and where one can hit it rich, where *anybody*, regardless of his origins, can go "from rags to riches." [1] This success story is supplemented by the idea (as found in the early Chaplin pictures) that here the little man can maneuver amidst the big and powerful and can even manage to outwit them. In place of fixed ancestral norms, we have the open future of limitless possibilities. The classic mythical category of creation becomes the category of the quest for the newest and the latest. [2] "Expectancy" as the most definitive American mood is embodied in two of our major intellectual movements—Transcendentalism and pragmatic operationalism.

The mythic form of the quest is the journey. Our legendary figures are "outdoor" heroes, wandering like Paul Bunyan and Davy Crockett through woods and forests, like Mike Fink and Huck Finn down the rivers, like Captain Ahab and Wolf Larsen toward the Pacific, like Walt Whitman throughout the continent. They are American in their direct, empirical approach and in the practical nature of their pursuits—gold, whales, or seals. These legendary and symbolic journeys are the projection of the feverish migrations in our earlier history. The task faced by our pioneers was not to re-create a new commune by gaining control of forest,

[1] This has been particularly the European version of the American myth. In Franz Kafka's *Amerika*, for example, Karl Rossman leaves Europe to find employment in the free nature-theater of Oklahoma. Here, *everybody* is welcome and no one is even asked about his qualifications.

[2] One thinks of our New Year celebrations with their unreserved impiety toward the old and their unbounded expectancy of the new year. Twelve months later, we treat the new as hopelessly old.

Reprinted by permission from the *American Quarterly*, II (1950), 259–269.

land, and river. Theirs was the problem of Prometheus without his traditional involvements with Zeus and Hermes.

The ebb and flow of migratory living did not allow the hardening of a traditional core or the formation of a steady mythic reference. Instead, it encouraged the ego toward unlimited play of "free enterprise." It permitted an exaggerated, willful independence and adventurism, unchecked by restrictive feudal memories. In Emerson and Whitman (later in William James and John Dewey), this transcendence appears as *good* expectancy.

But there were those who saw a threat in unrestricted freedom, individualism, and futurism. And, indeed, these contained the basis of a Nietzschean, "I will, therefore I am" and its later existentialist variation "I exist, therefore I am free," leading to the ethics of the sea—and land-wolves. For the Puritans and for Jonathan Edwards, the myth of expectancy appears ambiguous, if not evil. By the time of Theodore Dreiser, William Faulkner, and Robinson Jeffers, it has lost most of its legitimacy. The success story of Dreiser's "Titan" becomes suspect and the efforts of the little man to hit it rich provide the foundation for an "American tragedy." The magic short cut to the happy ending receives even more acid treatment in Faulkner and Jeffers. Among our contemporary writers, the myth of expectancy appears frozen (O'Neill's *The Iceman Cometh*), cornered (Tennessee Williams' *A Streetcar Named Desire*), pitiful (Arthur Miller's *Death of a Salesman*), and self-destructive (Clifford Odets' *The Big Knife*).

However, the celebration of rugged, self-reliant individualism was necessarily tempered from the beginning by the enormity of the task of exploring and controlling a new world. Although the pioneer would regard himself an independent "colony," minding his own business, he had to lean on the "good neighbor policy." Moreover, his individualism was not, from its incep-

tion, exclusive, was not a racial, national, or geographic exceptionalism. America is the expression of a *common* effort. Many races, religions, and customs found themselves on one boat which led them away from the restrictive and divisive hierarchies of the Old World.

This factor shapes the nature of the American myth. The isolative individualism of its hero is checked by his international affiliation. Fatherlessness does not result in conscienceless freedom, but is replaced by the idea of brotherhood. The good neighbor, the buddy, and the friend are substituted for the European father. Fraternity, or the myth of democratic expectancy, is the American equivalent of European paternity.

But what constitutes the core of this fraternity? Who is the "American"? Is it Melville's New Englander who yearns for the South Seas? Is it Mark Twain's southerner with his chivalry and slave plantations, or his Huck and Jim who strike out for freedom? Is it the western rancher? Is it the Indian, the Negro, and the foreigner? Is it Dreiser's Quaker, Willa Cather's bishop, Mike Gold's Jew? It is all of these international elements, as yet not formed into an organic mold.

There are some who think of the ideal America in terms of the "melting pot." But this would give us a flat "common man," bordering on choral anonymity. Such rubber-stamped coordination makes for uniformity, but not for unity. It would, in any case, destroy the basis for a living myth, which depends on the preservation of differentiated folk traditions within a communal body.

Herman Melville stands at the watershed moment of this historic cycle, between individualism and coordination, between freedom and equality. America in the mid-century still harbored vast, unexplored possibilities of adventure and fortune. But Melville is among those who are beginning to question the ethic of expansionism and coordination. Ahab's Pacific journey objectifies this ambivalent attitude. It is an extension of the continental experience, a venture into the promising unknown. At the same time, the sea journey expresses disillusionment with the land. The opening paragraphs of the novel touch on this motivation: Having little or no money in his purse, and with nothing in particular to interest him on shore, Ishmael decides to see the watery part of the world. This is his "substitute for pistol and ball." He reflects that this desire for the sea may be seen on a dreamy Sabbath afternoon when the eyes of thousands are fixed in ocean reveries. They are the eyes of men who on weekdays are "pent up in lath and plaster —tied to counters, nailed to benches, clinched to desks." And Ishmael observes that "should you ever be athirst in the great American desert" of the land, then try this experiment. Thus, Melville's Pacific is at once a continuation of the American myth of expectancy and an expression of disenchantment with it. Herein, Melville meets with Goethe whose Faust likewise affirms and questions the myth of modern expansionism.

THE COLLECTIVE BURDEN

The myth would establish a universal analogy, the specific story, theme, and characters serving as a microcosmic model. The Pequod is a kind of Noah's Ark, harboring elements from all corners of the savage and civilized world. In the end, this world is engulfed by a deluge, with a smaller "ark" carrying away one who escaped to tell the story. Its hero would catch the great fish Leviathan, but unlike the Messiah, his intent is not to divide it among the faithful. He is not an aid to his commune but its destroyer. The devil's price —thou must not love—is exacted to its fullest on the social level as well. It appears in Ahab's relation to the crew.[3]

Ahab is the single ruler over his social universe. All must submit to his will and

[3] I am indebted here to suggestions made by Benjamin Appel.

do his bidding to the point of jeopardizing their collective existence. But what is the legitimacy of Ahab's rule? What is the cause in which they are sacrificed?

In the classical myth, the "cause" has a public, all-human reference—to bring peace to Thebes and Athens, to build the city of Rome, to revive the Golden Age of Chivalry, to rid the state of Denmark of its rottenness, to build a Faustian free city. To be sure, in all instances, a personal need is interwoven with the public task; but in the end, the individual need is a function of the public frame-work.

The exclusive stake in the chase of Moby Dick is the righting of a *personal wrong* suffered by Ahab. It is Ahab's leg which the White Whale bit off. It is his and only his person which was violated, his private need and private pique which are alone involved. To the crew, whaling is a practical business, a form of employment. They have no special interest in Moby Dick. It is in Ahab's interests and his interests solely that the crew is endangered and perishes. Ahab succeeds in persuading the crew that his objective is identical with their own. They are somehow hypnotized by their leader's demon and they act as if they were all a collective Ahab. The transformation is achieved by something akin to black magic.

Ahab succeeds in imposing his "sultanism" because at this stage of American development, there is as yet no cohesive commune. The crew belong in the category of "Loose-Fish," which Melville defines as "fair game for anybody who can soonest catch it."[4] Ahab's crew are somewhere between individual differentiation

[4] In "Fast-Fish and Loose-Fish," Melville carries the social analogy further: "What was America in 1492 but a Loose-Fish, in which Columbus struck the Spanish standard by way of waifing it for his royal master and mistress? What was Poland to the Czar? What Greece to the Turk? What India to England? What at last will Mexico be to the United States? All Loose-Fish. What are the Rights of Man and the Liberties of the World but Loose-Fish?"

and "the melting pot." They are unable to act jointly in their common interests and are not sufficiently ego-centered to rebel anarchically. They are the raw, eclectic (sexless) form of the American lower depths toward the middle of the nineteenth century. Artistically, Melville shows this by making them all (with the exception of Queequeg) more or less depersonalized stereotypes.

Herein lies Ahab's power over his crew. While they are as yet unformed, Ahab is a finished and closed mold. By virtue of his completely organized form, Ahab can silence their vague, rebellious murmurings, can melt their will down to the point where it merges with his purpose.

Ahab's relation to the crew is the hero pitted *against* the collective. He curses the "mortal inter-debtedness" of man and frets that he, who would be "a sovereign being in nature," must depend on the carpenter for a bone to stand on. In Schopenhauer, the goal of the willful ego is the nothingness of nirvana, that which Freud later called the death-wish. In both, the individual is at the end "socialized" in a cosmic collective. Modern existentialism —which claims Melville as one of its forerunners—contains a variant of this dialectic. Its individual would also be "as free as air." It begins with "nothing," and by a series of "leaps," reaches death or shipwreck.[5] Similarly for Ahab. His commanding voice is muffled into infantile voicelessness and his dictatorial ego is communalized in the womb of the sea.[6]

[5] See our discussion "The Function of Myth in Existentialism," Yale French Studies, spring 1948.

[6] A number of mythic parallels suggest themselves: The fate which overtakes Ahab is similar to that of the hunter Actaeon, who invades the privacy of the virgin goddess Diana; of Pentheus, who sought to view the secret ritual of his mother Agave; of Oedipus, who is blinded by recognition of his incestuous life. When, at the end, Ahab beholds Moby Dick, about to pierce the hull of the Pequod, he staggers, smites his forehead, and cries out: "I grow blind; hands! stretch out before me that I may yet grope my way. Is't night?"

REHABILITATION

The mythic process moves from creation through the quest toward re-creation. But Ahab never reaches understanding of the nature of his quest and the White Whale remains for him an ineffable, undefined, though visible object. In *Moby Dick,* the quest is kept to its egocentric or demonic phase and is not transmuted into the communal blessing. Ahab's *hybris* is closer to the idea of religious sin than to mythic error or crime. His fate contains a warning of what is in store for a man who would be God, a sermon on the theme that "mortal greatness" is "disease." As is the case with Faustus, such monomania leads to the destruction of the self. Ahab himself feels that he can do nothing to avert this. In the manner of Calvinistic predestination, he declares, "the whole act's inscrutably decreed."

Ahab lacks the communal norm which rehabilitates the hero in the literary myth. He has contempt for the common man, keeps a distance from the crew and even from his mates. While Ahab's ruthless egotism is not for material ownership and gain, his "irresistible dictatorship" foreshadows that free individual enterprise which Jack London pictures in *The Sea Wolf* and which later became the ethic of the "robber barons." [7]

[7] In F. O. Matthiessen's formulation, Ahab anticipates much of America's development: "The strong-willed individuals who seized the land and gutted the forests and built the railroads were no longer troubled with Ahab's obsessive sense of evil, since theology had receded. . . . They tended to be . . . as blind to everything but their one pursuit, as unmoved by fear or sympathy, as confident in assuming an identification of their wills with immutable plan or manifest destiny, as liable to regard other men as merely arms and legs for the fulfilment of their purposes. . . . [Melville] also provided an ominous glimpse of what was to result when the Emersonian will to virtue became in less innocent natures the will to power and conquest."

Jack London's Wolf Larsen approximates the combined features of Ahab and Moby Dick. He is both fascinating and terrifying, unites intellect with the "savage instincts" of a beast of prey. Like

The refusal or inability of this hero to accept the fact of "mortal inter-debtedness" keeps him from Greek and Christian reconciliation. This Oedipus confronts but does not solve the riddle of the Sphinx; this St. George gives battle but does not slay the Dragon. This Protestant hero maintains his self-assertiveness to the last and thereby becomes the herald of disaster, a curse to himself and the commune.

Yet, *Moby Dick* is not altogether lacking in communal reference. To be sure, the collective is here not an Athenian chorus, not the noble citizen of the Roman state, not even Hamlet's "distracted multitude," but is "chiefly made up of mongrel renegades and castaways, and cannibals." Yet, Melville writes in praise of the "democratic God" who selects champions "from the kingly commons," who gave power to "the swart convict Bunyan," to "the pampered arm of old Cervantes," and who picked up Andrew Jackson "from the pebbles." He would celebrate "that democratic dignity which, on all hands, radiates without end from God." Ahab himself is a "democratic" hero, one who does not possess the "dignity of kings and robes." But Melville's paean is first of all to Ahab's mates, to the "Knights and Squires," all "momentous men," to the harpooners, to the arm "that wields a pick or drives a spoke." They all belong to the "same ancient Catholic Church . . . the great and everlasting First Congregation." Melville translates the transcendental democracy of Emerson and the idyllic internationalism of Thoreau into a realistic ship-commune.

In a sense, it is the crew that compose the tragic in *Moby Dick*. They are placed in a situation with which they cannot cope; yet, they face it with courage and fight the battle unflinchingly. Now, the crew

accepts Ahab, sensing his "humanities." Their acceptance is an element of grace which contributes toward his redemption. Starbuck hears Ahab exposing his personal wounds in "The Symphony." All witness his human relationship to little Pip. They see suffering written on his face, as he stands there "in all the nameless regal overbearing dignity of some mighty woe." In such moments, the Satanic hero almost becomes the sacrificial scapegoat.

In this phase, Ahab has remarkable affinity to the figure of the Fisher King, connected with the legend of the Holy Grail. As developed by Jessie L. Weston's *From Ritual to Romance*, the Fisher King is incapacitated by the effects of a wound and becomes known as the Maimed King. In the Grail legend, the wound of the King is a punishment for his sinful passion toward a pagan princess, and the nature of the wound suggests injury to the reproductive energy. The Fisher King, who is either in middle life or an aged man, is healed by his successor, a youthful figure.

Ahab would be at once the middle-aged Fisher King and the young hero who saves him, both the Satanic rebel and the redeeming Messiah.[8] He fights the colossus although he knows he will be defeated, and he emerges with the dignity of the tragic, which arises from his very flaw. This flaw and the redemption are foreshadowed in "The Sermon" which states the two main motifs of the book.

The text of Father Mapple's sermon is "And God had prepared a great fish to swallow up Jonah." Jonah's sin lay "in his willful disobedience of the command of God." Jonah finally makes his confession and accepts his punishment as just, and the sermon holds him to be "a model of repentance." However, Father Mapple

---

Ahab, Larsen is only outwardly formidable. Actually, he is a very sick man, goes blind, and dies in a helpless state. In Larsen's own terminology, he moves from a living "to do" toward a deathly "to be," an existence without movement.

[8] Miss Weston notes that in Christian art and tradition, "the Lance or Spear, as an instrument of the Passion, is found in conjunction with the Cross, nails, sponge, and Crown of Thorns." We find this conjunction in Ahab's spear and his mark of crucifixion, which is "completed" as he gives up the spear and is strangled.

poses the dilemma which comes with the Judaic-Christian, specifically the Protestant, epoch. For, states Father Mapple, "if we obey God, we must disobey ourselves," and his sermon is partly in praise of being true to one's "own inexorable self." He concludes: "Delight is to God, a far, far upward and inward delight—who against the proud gods and commodores of this earth, ever stands forth his inexorable self."

To this self, Ahab has been true, and to that extent, he is a tragic and redeemable figure.[9] Like Job, he insists on maintaining his own ways before God. But he does not rise to the recognition of the communal elements in his own self, and in the end Ahab reverses Job, as well as the Greek and Christian mythic heroes.[10] Only in his relation to Pip, and when he urges Starbuck to stay on the boat to be saved, does Ahab reveal some social pathos.

Melville's *Moby Dick* is the first major American literary myth sounding the central motifs of creation and quest. Its distinctive American quality lies in its uncertain attitude toward creation. Dante and the mythmakers before him accepted creation as their natural and communal heritage and were concerned with its how, not its what or why. Their heroes end with the assured promise that their labors are to become part of a new tradition or recreation. Even Hamlet feels himself bound to origins, although his father appears in "such a questionable shape," and finally he gives his dying voice to a new king. The American mythic hero is still in search of his creative sources and in doubt as to the possibility of their transformation and succession.[11]

The American renaissance, as Matthiessen's study shows, was not a *re*-birth, but America's first maturity. Melville's *Moby Dick* shares some of the features of the other Renaissance myths, has some of the breadth, the sense of varied experience and expansiveness of Hamlet, Faust, and Siegfried. But its hero does not reach the tertiary phase of reintegration precisely because he questions or cannot find his primary sources. Indeed, the quest itself is carried on with inner reservations. *Moby Dick* comes at the point when industrialism begins its forward movement. Ahab and Ishmael leave the solid land, where men are "nailed to benches." But on the ocean, Ahab continues the way of the land, driving himself and others toward conquest. Yet, he knows that his progress is circular, that his pursuit of the White Whale is a pursuit of death. In this sense, *Moby Dick* questions a "progress" which does not rest on a basic platform. Herein, the work carries the mythic insight that if America is to know progress, it must recollect and transmute its creative beginnings.

Melville stands close enough to our European heritage to have felt the need to seek for parental sources. Mark Twain, Walt Whitman, Carl Sandburg, have sought to find a tradition in terms of America's native experience. This note is also implicit in Melville who thought that Americans are "the peculiar, chosen people —the Israel of our time; we bear the ark

---

[9] For this reason, I cannot go along with Matthiessen who holds that Ahab "suffers, but . . . remains damned." But Auden overstates the case when he calls Ahab "the Christian tragic hero," who "like the saint . . . wills one thing," for which he gives up everything.

[10] Fedallah is not Ahab's evil spirit, as Sedgwick and other critics maintain. Fedallah dies; however, his death does not temper but, if anything, intensifies Ahab's demonic drive. More is made of Fedallah than the story as such justifies. What appears to have been Melville's *intention* was to make Fedallah's passive, self-contained, speechless impersonality the Eastern counterpart to Ahab's Western rhetorical and willful individualism. But this is not executed. Fedallah remains a "shadow" as a literary character as well.

[11] Melville "tacks on" a hopeful portent: The sky-hawk is nailed to the Pequod by Tashtego's hammer. The bird goes down with the ship which, "like Satan would not sink to hell till she had dragged a living part of heaven with her, and helmeted herself with it." Joseph Campbell's *The Hero With A Thousand Faces* notes that in many myths, the birds rescue the hero from the whale by pecking open the side of the whale's belly.

of the liberties of the world." But Whitman's ideal of fraternity, which was to replace the European notion of paternity, is a whole composed of equally important "leaves of grass," and Sandburg's "people" are a like procession of interchangeable parts. Perhaps we have here the morality of a technical civilization. The efficiency of technics depends on reduction to a common "democratic" denominator, on streamlined coordination. This threatens to obliterate the varieties of folkways which provide the substance of the living myth. Theodore Dreiser's *The Bulwark* warns that the earlier American tradition of brotherly linkage ("religion") is being supplanted by a religion of gadgets and of gambling freedom.

Yet, our American beginnings contain the elements of the universal myth. We began as an interracial commune and with the need for reconstructing old forms. There is danger that our unity will become petrified into airless conformity and that our freedom will disintegrate into capriciousness. But there is promise in their harmonious interplay. And this American promise is great.

Alfred Kazin

An Introduction to *Moby-Dick*

Moby-Dick is not only a very big book; it is also a peculiarly full and rich one, and from the very opening it conveys a sense of abundance, of high creative power, that exhilarates and enlarges the imagination. This quality is felt immediately in the style, which is remarkably easy, natural and "American," yet always literary, and which swells in power until it takes on some of the roaring and uncontainable rhythms with which Melville audibly describes the sea. The best description of this style is Melville's own, when he speaks of the "bold and nervous lofty language" that Nantucket whaling captains learn straight from nature. We feel this abundance in heroic types like the Nantucketers themselves, many of whom are significantly named after Old Testament prophets and kings, for these, too, are mighty men, and the mightiest of them all, Captain Ahab, will challenge the very order of the creation itself. This is the very heart of the book—so much so that we come to feel that there is some shattering magnitude of theme before Melville as he writes, that as a writer he had been called to an heroic new destiny.

It is this constant sense of power that constitutes the book's appeal to us, that explains its hold on our attention. *Moby-Dick* is one of those books that try to bring in as much of life as a writer can get both hands on. Melville even tries to create an image of life itself as a ceaseless creation. The book is written with a personal force of style, a passionate learning, a steady insight into our forgotten connections with the primitive. It sweeps everything before it; it gives us the happiness that only great vigor inspires.

If we start by opening ourselves to this abundance and force, by welcoming not merely the story itself, but the manner in which it speaks to us, we shall recognize in this restlessness, this richness, this persistent atmosphere of magnitude, the essential image on which the book is founded. For *Moby-Dick* is not so much a book *about* Captain Ahab's quest for the whale as it is an experience *of* that quest. This is only to say, what we say of any true poem, that we cannot reduce its essential substance to a subject, that we should not intellectualize and summarize it, but that we should recognize that its very force and beauty lie in the way it is conceived and written, in the qualities that flow from its being a unique entity.

In these terms, *Moby-Dick* seems to be far more of a poem than it is a novel, and since it is a narrative, to be an epic, a long poem on an heroic theme, rather than the kind of realistic fiction that we know today. Of course Melville did not deliberately set out to write a formal epic; but half-consciously, he drew upon many of the traditional characteristics of epic in order to realize the utterly original kind of novel *he* needed to write in his time—the spaciousness of theme and subject, the martial atmosphere, the association of these homely and savage materials with universal myths, the symbolic wanderings of the hero, the indispensable strength of such a hero in Captain Ahab. Yet beyond all this, what

This essay is the Introduction to the Riverside Edition of *Moby-Dick*, edited by Alfred Kazin (Boston: Houghton Mifflin Company, 1956); reprinted in the *Atlantic Monthly*, CXCVIII (1956), 81–85. Used by permission of the author and Houghton Mifflin Company.

distinguishes *Moby-Dick* from modern prose fiction, what ties it up with the older, more formal kind of narrative that was once written in verse, is the fact that Melville is not interested in the meanness, the literal truthfulness, the representative slice of life, that we think of as the essence of modern realism. His book has the true poetic emphasis in that the whole story is constantly being meditated and unravelled through a single mind.

"Call me Ishmael," the book begins. This Ishmael is not only a character in the book; he is also the single voice, or rather the single mind, from whose endlessly turning spool of thought the whole story is unwound. It is Ishmael's contemplativeness, his *dreaming,* that articulates the wonder of the seas and the fabulousness of the whale and the terrors of the deep. All that can be meditated and summed up and hinted at, as the reflective essence of the story itself, is given us by Ishmael, who possesses nothing but man's specifically human gift, which is language. It is Ishmael who tries to sum up the whole creation in a single book and yet keeps at the center of it one American whaling voyage. It is Ishmael's gift for speculation that explains the terror we come to feel before the whiteness of the whale; Ishmael's mind that ranges with mad exuberance through a description of all the seas; Ishmael who piles up image after image of "the mightiest animated mass that has survived the flood." It is Ishmael who, in the wonderful chapter on the masthead, embodies for us man as a thinker, whose reveries transcend space and time as he stands watch high above the seas. And of course it is Ishmael, both actually and as the symbol of man, who is the one survivor of the voyage. Yet utterly alone as he is at the end of the book, floating on the Pacific Ocean, he manages, buoyed up on a coffin that magically serves as his life-buoy, to give us the impression that life itself can be honestly confronted only in the loneliness of each human heart. Always it is this

emphasis on Ishmael's personal vision, on the richness and ambiguity of all events as the sceptical, fervent, experience-scarred mind of Ishmael feels and thinks them, that gives us, from the beginning, the new kind of book that *Moby-Dick* is. It is a book which is neither a saga, though it deals in large natural forces, nor a *classical* epic, for we feel too strongly the individual who wrote it. It is a book that is at once primitive, fatalistic, and merciless, like the very oldest books, and yet peculiarly personal, like so many twentieth-century novels, in its significant emphasis on the subjective individual consciousness. The book grows out of a single word, "I," and expands until the soul's voyage of this "I" comes to include a great many things that are unseen and unsuspected by most of us. And this material is always tied to Ishmael, who is not merely a witness to the story—someone who happens to be on board the *Pequod*—but the living and germinating mind who grasps the world in the tentacles of his thought.

The power behind this "I" is poetical in the sense that everything comes to us through a constant intervention of language instead of being presented flatly. Melville does not wish, as so many contemporary writers do, to reproduce ordinary life and conventional speech. He seeks the marvellous and the fabulous aspects that life wears in secret. He exuberantly sees the world through language—things exist as his words for them—and much of the exceptional beauty of the book lies in the unusual incidence of passages that, in the most surprising contexts, are so piercing in their poetic intensity. But the most remarkable feat of language in the book is Melville's ability to make us see that man is not a blank slate passively open to events, but a mind that constantly seeks meaning in everything it encounters. In Melville the Protestant habit of moralizing and the transcendental passion for symbolizing all things as examples of "higher laws" combined to make a mind that instinctively brought an inner significance to each episode. Everything in *Moby-Dick* is saturated in a mental atmosphere. Nothing happens for its own sake in this book, and in the midst of the chase, Ishmael can be seen meditating it, pulling things apart, drawing out its significant point.

But Ishmael is not just an intellectual observer; he is also very much in the story. He suffers; he is there. As his name indicates, he is an estranged and solitary man; his only friend is Queequeg, a despised heathen from the South Seas. Queequeg, a fellow "isolato" in the smug world of white middle-class Christians, is the only man who offers Ishmael friendship; thanks to Queequeg, "no longer my splintered heart and maddened hand were turned against the wolfish world. This soothing savage had redeemed it." Why does Ishmael feel so alone? There are background reasons, Melville's own: his father went bankrupt and then died in debt when Melville was still a boy. Melville-Ishmael went to sea—"And at first," he tells us, "this sort of thing is unpleasant enough. It touches one's sense of honor, particularly if you come of an old established family in the land." But there is a deeper, a more universal reason for Ishmael's apartness, and it is one that will strangely make him kin to his daemonic captain, Ahab. For the burden of his thought, the essential cause of his estrangement, is that he cannot come to any conclusion about anything. He feels at home with ships and sailors because for him, too, one journey ends only to begin another; "and a second ended, only begins a third and so on, for ever and for aye. Such is the endlessness, yea, the intolerableness of all earthly effort."

Ishmael is not merely an orphan; he is an exile, searching alone in the wilderness, with a black man for his only friend. He suffers from doubt and uncertainty far more than he does from homelessness. Indeed, this agony of disbelief *is* his homelessness. For him nothing is ever finally settled and decided; he is man, or as we like to think, modern man, cut off from the certainty that was once his inner world. Ishmael no longer has any sure formal belief. All is in doubt, all is in eternal flux, like the sea. And so condemned, like "all his race from Adam down," to wander the seas of thought, far from Paradise, he now searches endlessly to put the whole broken story together, to find a meaning, to ascertain—where but in the ceaselessness of human thought?—"the hidden cause we seek." Ishmael does not perform any great actions, as Ahab does; he is the most insignificant member of the fo'c'sle and will get the smallest share of the take. But his inner world of thought is almost unbearably symbolic, for he must think, and think, and think, in order to prove to himself that there is a necessary connection between man and the world. He pictures his dilemma in everything he does on board the ship, but never so clearly as when he is shown looking at the sea, searching a meaning to existence from the inscrutable waters.

What Melville did through Ishmael, then, was to put man's distinctly modern feeling of "exile," of abandonment, directly at the center of his stage. For Ishmael there are no satisfactory conclusions to anything; no final philosophy is ever possible. All that man owns in this world, Ishmael would say, is his insatiable mind. This is why the book opens on a picture of the dreaming contemplativeness of mind itself: men tearing themselves loose from their jobs to stand "like silent sentinels all around the town . . . thousands of mortal men fixed in ocean reveries." Narcissus was bemused by that image which "we ourselves see in all rivers and oceans," and this, says Ishmael when he is most desperate, is all that man ever finds when he searches the waters—a reflection of himself. All is inconclusive, restless, an endless flow. And Melville's own style rises to its highest level not in the neo-Shakespearean speeches of Ahab, which are sometimes bombastic, but in those amazing prose flights on the whiteness of the whale and on the Pacific where Ishmael reproduces, in the rhythms of the prose itself, man's brooding interrogation of nature.

II

But Ishmael is a witness not only to his own thoughts, but also a witness to the actions of Captain Ahab. The book is not only a great skin of language stretched to fit the world of man's philosophic wandering; it is also a world of moral tyranny and violent action, in which the principal actor is Ahab. With the entry of Ahab a harsh new rhythm enters the book, and from now on two rhythms—one reflective, the other forceful—alternate to show us the world in which man's thinking and man's doing each follows its own law. Ishmael's thought consciously extends itself to get behind the world of appearances; he wants to see and to understand everything. Ahab's drive is to *prove*, not to discover; the world that tortures Ishmael by its horrid vacancy has tempted Ahab into thinking that he can make it over. He seeks to dominate nature, to impose and to inflict his will on the outside world— whether it be the crew that must jump to his orders or the great white whale that is essentially indifferent to him. As Ishmael is all rumination, so Ahab is all will. Both are thinkers, the difference being that Ishmael thinks as a bystander, has identified his own state with man's utter unimportance in nature. Ahab, by contrast, actively seeks the whale in order to assert man's supremacy over what swims before him as "the monomaniac incarnation" of a superior power:

"If man will strike, strike through the mask! How can the prisoner reach outside except by thrusting through the wall? To me, the white whale is that wall, shoved near to me. Sometimes I think there's naught beyond. But 'tis enough. He tasks me; he heaps me; I see in him outrageous strength, with an inscrutable malice sinewing it. That inscrutable thing is chiefly what I

hate; and be the white whale agent, or be the white whale principal, I will wreak that hate upon him. Talk not to me of blasphemy, man; I'd strike the sun if it insulted me. For could the sun do that, then could I do the other; since there is ever a sort of fair play herein, jealousy presiding over all creations. But not my master, man, is even that fair play. Who's over me? Truth hath no confines."

This is Ahab's quest—and Ahab's magnificence. For in this speech Ahab expresses more forcibly than Ishmael ever could, something of the impenitent anger against the universe that all of us can feel. Ahab may be a mad sea captain, a tyrant of the quarter deck who disturbs the crew's sleep as he stomps along on his ivory leg. But this Ahab does indeed speak for all men who, as Ishmael confesses in the frightening meditation on the whiteness of the whale, suspect that "though in many of its aspects this visible world seems formed in love, the invisible spheres were formed in fright." So man, watching the sea heaving around him, sees it as a mad steed that has lost its rider, and looking at his own image in the water, is tortured by the thought that man himself may be an accident, of no more importance in this vast oceanic emptiness than one of Ahab's rare tears dropped into the Pacific.

To the degree that we feel this futility in the face of a blind impersonal nature that "heeds us not," and storm madly, like Ahab, against the dread that there's "naught beyond"—to this extent all men may recognize Ahab's bitterness, his unrelentingness, his inability to rest in that uncertainty which, Freud has told us, modern man must learn to endure. Ahab figures in a symbolic fable; he is acting out thoughts which we all share. But Ahab, even more, is a hero; we cannot insist enough on that. Melville believed in the heroic and he specifically wanted to cast his hero on American lines—someone noble by nature, not by birth, who would have "not the dignity of kings and robes, but that abounding dignity which has no robed investiture." Ahab sinned against man and God, and like his namesake in the Old Testament, becomes a "wicked king." But Ahab is not just a fanatic who leads the whole crew to their destruction; he is a hero of thought who is trying, by terrible force, to reassert man's place in nature. And it is the struggle that Ahab incarnates that makes him so magnificent a *voice*, thundering in Shakespearean rhetoric, storming at the gates of the inhuman, silent world. Ahab is trying to give man, in one awful, final assertion that his will *does* mean something, a feeling of relatedness with his world.

Ahab's effort, then, is to reclaim something that man knows he has lost. Significantly, Ahab proves by the bitter struggle he has to wage that man is fighting in an unequal contest; by the end of the book Ahab abandons all his human ties and becomes a complete fanatic. But Melville has no doubt—nor should we!—that Ahab's quest is *humanly* understandable. And the quest itself supplies the book with its technical *raison d'être*. For it leads us through all the seas and around the whole world; it brings us past ships of every nation. Always it is Ahab's drive that makes up the *passion* of *Moby-Dick*, a passion that is revealed in the descriptive chapters on the whale, whale-fighting, whale-burning, on the whole gory and fascinating industrial process aboard ship that reduces the once proud whale to oil-brimming barrels in the hold. And this passion may be defined as a passion of longing, of hope, of striving: a passion that starts from the deepest loneliness that man can know. It is the great cry of man who feels himself exiled from his "birthright, the merry May-day gods of old," who looks for a new god "to enthrone . . . again in the now egotistical sky; in the now unhaunted hill." The cry is Ahab's—"Who's to doom, when the judge himself is dragged to the bar?"

Behind Ahab's cry is the fear that man's covenant with God has been broken, that there is no purpose to our existence. The *Pequod* is condemned by Ahab to sail up and down the world in search of—a symbol. But this search, mad as it seems to Starbuck the first mate, who is a Christian, nevertheless represents Ahab's real humanity. For the ancient covenant is never quite broken so long as man still thirsts for it. And because Ahab, as Melville intended him to, represents the aristocracy of intellect in our democracy, because he seeks to transcend the limitations that good conventional men like Starbuck, philistine materialists like Stubb, and unthinking fools like Flask want to impose on everybody else, Ahab speaks for the humanity that belongs to man's imaginative vision of himself.

Yet with all this, we must not forget that Ahab's quest takes place, unceasingly, in a very practical world of whaling, as part of the barbaric and yet highly necessary struggle by man to support himself physically in nature. It is this that gives the book its primitive vitality, its burning authenticity. For *Moby-Dick*, it must be emphasized, is not simply a symbolic fable; nor, as we have already seen, can it possibly be construed as simply a "sea story." It is the story of agonizing thought in the midst of brutal action, of thought that questions every action, that annuls it from within, as it were—but that cannot, in this harsh world, relieve man of the fighting, skinning, burning, the back-breaking row to the whale, the flying harpoons, the rope that can take you off "voicelessly as Turkish mutes bowstring their victims." *Moby-Dick* is a representation of the passionate mind speaking, for its metaphysical concerns, out of the very midst of life. So, after the first lowering, Queequeg is shown sitting all night in a submerged boat, holding up a lantern like an "imbecile candle in the heart of that almighty forlornness . . . the sign and symbol of a man without hope, hopelessly holding up hope in the midst of despair." Melville insists that our thinking is *not* swallowed up by practical concerns, that man constantly searches for a reality equal to his inner life of thought—and it is his ability to show this in the midst of a brutal, dirty whaling voyage that makes *Moby-Dick* such an astonishing book. Just as Ahab is a hero, so *Moby-Dick* itself is a heroic book. What concerns Melville is not merely the heroism that gets expressed in physical action, but the heroism of thought itself as it rises above its seeming insignificance and proclaims, in the very teeth of a seemingly hostile and malevolent creation, that man's voice *is* heard for something against the watery waste and the deep, that man's thought has an echo in the universe.

III

This is the quest. But what makes *Moby-Dick* so fascinating, and in a sense even uncanny, is that the issue is always in doubt, and remains so to the end. Melville was right when he wrote to Hawthorne: "I have written a wicked book, and feel as spotless as the lamb." And people who want to construe *Moby-Dick* into a condemnation of mad, bad Ahab will always miss what Melville meant when he wrote of his book: "It is not a piece of fine feminine Spitalfields silk—but it is of the horrible texture of a fabric that should be woven of ships' cables & hawsers. A Polar wind blows through it, & birds of prey hover over it." For in the struggle between man's effort to find meaning in nature, and the indifference of nature itself, which simply eludes him (nature here signifies the whole external show and force of animate life in a world suddenly emptied of God, one where an "intangible malignity" has reigned from the beginning), Melville often portrays the struggle from the side of nature itself. He sees the whale's view of things far more than he does Ahab's: and Moby-Dick's milk-white head, the tail feathers of the sea birds streaming from his back like pennons, are described with a rapture that is like the adoration of a god. Even in the most terrible scenes of the shark massacre, where the sharks bend

around like bows to bite at their own entrails, or in the ceaseless motion of "my dear Pacific," the "Potters' fields of all four continents," one feels that Melville is transported by the naked reality of things, the great unending flow of the creation itself, where the great shroud of the sea rolls over the doomed ship "as it rolled five thousand years ago." Indeed, one feels in the end that it is only the necessity to keep one person alive as a witness to the story that saves Ishmael from the general ruin and wreck. In Melville's final vision of the whole, it is not fair but it is entirely *just* that the whale should destroy the ship, that man should be caught up on the beast. It is just in a cosmic sense, not in the sense that the prophet (Father Mapple) predicts the punishment of man's disobedience in the telling of Jonah's story from the beginning, where the point made is the classic reprimand of God to man when He speaks out of the whirlwind. What Melville does is to speak for the whirlwind, for the watery waste, for the sharks.

It is this that gives *Moby-Dick* its awful and crushing power. It is a unique gift. Goethe said that he wanted, as a writer, to know what it is like to be a woman. But Melville sometimes makes you feel that he knows, as a writer, what it is like to be the eyes of the rock, the magnitude of the whale, the scalding sea, the dreams that lie buried in the Pacific. It is all, of course, seen through human eyes—yet there is in Melville a cold, final, ferocious hopelessness, a kind of ecstatic masochism, that delights in punishing man, in heaping coals on his head, in drowning him. You see it in the scene of the whale running through the herd with a cutting spade in his body, cutting down his own; in the sharks eating at their own entrails and voiding from them in the same convulsion; in the terrible picture of Pip the cabin boy jumping out of the boat in fright and left on the Pacific to go crazy; in Tashtego falling into the "honey head" of the whale; in the ropes that suddenly whir up from the spindles and carry you off; in the final awesome picture of the whale butting its head against the *Pequod*. In all these scenes there is an ecstasy in horror, the horror of nature in itself, nature "pure," without God or man: the void. It is symbolized by the whiteness of the whale, the whiteness that is not so much a color as the absence of color. "Is it that by its indefiniteness it shadows forth the heartless voids and immensities of the universe, and thus stabs us from behind with the thought of annihilation, when beholding the white depths of the milky way?" And it is this picture of existence as one where man has only a peep-hole on the mystery itself, that constitutes the most remarkable achievement of Melville's genius. For as in the meditation on the whiteness of the whale, it becomes an uncanny attempt to come to grips with nature as it might be conceived with man entirely left out; or, what amounts to the same thing, with man losing his humanity and being exclusively responsive to primitive and racial memories, to the trackless fathomless nothing that has been from the beginning, to the very essence of a beginning that, in contradiction to all man's scriptures, had no divine history, no definite locus, but just *was*—with man slipped into the picture much later.

This view of reality, this ability to side with nature rather than with man, means an ability to love what has no animation, what is inhumanly still, what is not in search, as man himself is—a hero running against time and fighting against "reality." Here Melville puts, as it were, his ear to reality itself: to the rock rather than to the hero trying to get his sword out of the rock. He does it by constantly, and bitterly, and savagely, in fact, comparing man with the great thing he is trying to understand. Ahab may be a hero by trying to force himself on what is too much for him, but Melville has no doubt that man is puny and presumptuous and easily overwhelmed

—in short, drowned—in the great storm of reality he tries to encompass.

This sense of scale lies behind the chapters on the natural history of the whale, and behind the constant impressing on our minds of the contrast between man and the whale—man getting into a small boat, man being overwhelmed by his own weapons. The greatest single metaphor in the book is that of bigness, and even when Melville laughs at himself for trying to hook this Leviathan with a pen—"Bring me a condor's quill! Bring me Vesuvius' crater for an inkstand!"—we know that he not merely feels exhilaration at attempting this mighty subject, but that he is also abashed, he feels grave; mighty waters are rolling around him. This compelling sense of magnitude, however, gets him to organize the book brilliantly, in a great flood of chapters —some of them very small, one or two only a paragraph long, in the descriptive method which is the great homage that he pays to his subject, and which so provides him with an inexhaustible delight in devoting himself to every conceivable detail about the whale. And, to go back to a theme mentioned earlier, it is this sense of a limitless subject that gives the style its peculiarly loping quality, as if it were constantly looking for connectives, since on the subject of the whale no single word or statement is enough. But these details tend, too, to heap up in such a staggering array as to combine into the awesomeness of a power against which Ahab's challenge is utterly vain, and against which his struggle to show his superiority over the ordinary processes of nature becomes blasphemous. The only thing left to man, Melville seems to tell us, is to take the span of this magnitude—to feel and to record the power of this mighty torrent, this burning fire.

And it is this, this poetic power, rather than any specifically human one, this power of transcription rather than of any alteration of life that will admit human beings into its tremendous scale, that makes up the greatness of the book—by giving us the measure of Melville's own relation to the nature that his hero so futilely attempts to master or defy. For though Melville often takes a grim and almost cruel pleasure in showing man tumbling over before the magnitude of the universe, and though much of the book is concerned, as in the sections on fighting and "cooking" the whale, with man's effort to get a grip on external nature, first through physical assault and then by scientific and industrial cunning, man finds his final relatedness to nature neither as a hero (Ahab) nor by heeding Father Mapple's old prophetic warning of man's proper subservience to God. Though all his attempted gains from nature fail him, and all goes down with the *Pequod*—all man's hopes of profit, of adjustment to orthodoxy (Starbuck), even

of the wisdom that is in madness (Pip)— man, though forever alien to the world, an Ishmael, is somehow in tune with it, with its torrential rhythms, by dint of his art, by the directness with which his words grasp the world, by the splendor of his perceptions, by the lantern which he holds up "like a candle in the midst of the almighty forlornness." Man is not merely a waif in the world; he is an ear listening to the sea that almost drowns him; an imagination, a mind, that hears the sea in the shell, and darts behind all appearance to the beginning of things, and runs riot with the frightful force of the sea itself. There, in man's incredible and unresting mind, is the fantastic gift with which we enter into what is not our own, what is even against us—and for this, so amazingly, we can speak.

Charles H. Cook, Jr.

Ahab's "Intolerable Allegory"

IN CHAPTER XLV of *Moby-Dick* appears Herman Melville's well-known admonition against scouting at the white whale as a fable or an allegory: "So ignorant are most landsmen of some of the plainest and most palpable wonders of the world, that without some hints touching the plain facts, historical and otherwise, of the fishery, they might scout at Moby Dick as a monstrous fable, or still worse and more detestable, a hideous and intolerable allegory." [1] Although occasionally misinterpreted as a blanket condemnation of allegorical literature,[2] this passage is for the most part rightly understood as Melville's (or Ishmael's) protest that white whales are realities, not imaginary sea-monsters. But scholars and critics have not yet exploited the possibility that this "intolerable allegory" statement may have much deeper significance. May it even be the key to the main theme of the novel and to the tragic flaw in Ahab's character? Aware of the human temptation to project simple, personal meanings upon things which are formless or incomprehensible, Melville may be giving us the tragedy of a man who yields his whole soul to this temptation, who inflates his own private hurt into the hurt of all mankind, and who allegorizes the inflictor of this hurt as the dwelling place of all human evil. Is Ahab an example of that deadly brand of reformer whose obsession with one evil blinds him to the enigmatic ambiguity of the moral world? Is he the creator of a hideous and intolerable allegory?

Circumstances and facts favoring this interpretation of *Moby-Dick* are plentiful. Events in the main action of the story, the symbolism of the white whale, details of Ahab's character, and the numerous cetological digressions all support the idea. Moreover, this interpretation provides a defense for Melville against the frequent charge of vagueness. This apparent vagueness is actually an effect painstakingly cultivated by the author. By this means the reader is made to feel the baffling multiplicity and incomprehensibility of the universe which confronts the characters of the novel. The only character in *Moby-Dick* who succeeds in eliminating all vagueness from his mind is the monomaniacal Ahab. He discovers only a false and treacherous oneness focused upon the symbol of the white whale.

A quick review of the main story reveals the intolerable-allegory interpretation to be compatible with the main events of the plot. Ishmael, a man never entirely sure of anything but fairly respectful toward all possibilities, ships upon a whaler whose cosmopolitan crew cannot fail to suggest the varied races, nationalities, and classes of mankind. As the narrative voice of the author, Ishmael stands like a philosophical question mark, absorbing, experiencing, commenting, explaining, but always wondering and never imposing final meaning upon the enigmas that confront him. The other members of the crew have more

[1] *Moby-Dick*, ed. Willard Thorp (New York: Oxford University Press, 1947), p. 193. All subsequent *Moby-Dick* references indicate this edition.

[2] A recent example of this error is to be found in Edward Bloom, "The Allegorical Principle," *ELH*, XVIII (1951), 163–190.

Reprinted by permission from *Boston University Studies in English*, I (1955–56), 45–52.

definite but more limited personalities than Ishmael. Over them all reigns Ahab, obsessed, leading and driving his crew toward the habitat of Moby Dick, the ferocious white whale who has previously bitten off the captain's leg. But Ahab's original motive of personal revenge has already turned into something much more grand and weird. The whale has become, in Ahab's mind, an incarnation of the world's evil. Out of himself Ahab has projected upon the whale the evil inherent in mortality. By killing this monster he would bring mankind into the millennium. In his desperate pursuit, intent upon what he supposes to be the greatest boon to humanity, he surrenders human values and enlists the aid of evil in its own pursuit. He obtains his crew by deception, leading the members to believe that they are embarking on a regular whaling expedition to seek oil for the lamps of mankind. When the men comprehend the true purpose of the voyage and develop an obvious reluctance, Ahab leads them on by sheer power of will, by promises, and by trickery. Employing the mass-psychology of a Hitler and the scientific deception of a magician, he awes the men by converting a sailmaker's needle into a pointer for the ship's compass.[3] At last he plunges to the depths of inhumanity when, for fear of losing the hot track of Moby Dick and consequently the chance of blasting evil from the world, he refuses to join the search for the lost sons of the captain of the *Rachel*. He refuses to respond to the exhortations of the golden rule. "Do to me as you would have me do to you in like case," pleads the *Rachel's* commander. " 'Avast,' cried Ahab—'touch not a rope-yarn'; then in a voice that prolongingly moulded every word—'Captain Gardiner, I will not do it. Even now I lose time. Good bye, good bye.' "[4] The outcome of this madness is the destruction by the angered

whale of boat, crew, captain—all except Ishmael, whose survival is justified partly by the practical necessity of saving the narrator of the story but also by the questioning humility of his personality, which prevents him from committing Ahab's tragic error of allegorizing. To Ishmael the whale is doubtless a symbol, but a symbol of infinitely multiple significance beyond the full comprehension of any man. To Ahab, filled with monomaniacal egotism, the whale is an unmixed incarnation of evil and therefore, by Melville's standards, a hideous and intolerable allegory.

As the reader can see, the validation of this interpretation calls for evidence that the whale holds one kind of meaning for Melville and Ishmael and a different and more specific meaning for Ahab.[5] Such evidence is abundantly and pointedly supplied within the novel.

First, Melville is eager that his readers should recognize the flesh-and-blood reality of creatures like Moby Dick—whales whose unusual strength, appearance, and behavior have won them individual recognition. The point of the chapter entitled "The Affidavit," and in fact of most of the cetological material throughout the book, is that whales are not fictional or mythical creatures, but completely real. Evidence is desirable, Melville explains, to establish the "reasonableness of the whole story of the White Whale." Where wonders of the natural world are concerned, truth may require "as much bolstering as error." Without facts and statistics, "ignorant landsmen might scout at Moby Dick as a monstrous fable, or . . . a hideous and intolerable allegory."[6] However, Melville is certainly not denying that the white whale has symbolic significance. Because of the vagueness of contemporary cetological information, and because of the many myths al-

[3] *Moby-Dick*, p. 481.
[4] *Moby-Dick*, p. 492.

[5] Although the author does not go so far as to say that Ishmael represents Melville, it is evident that Ishmael is Melville's device for getting the story told.
[6] *Moby-Dick*, pp. 192–193.

ready associated with whales, Moby Dick provides an almost ideal symbol for the author's purposes.

Of what, then, is the whale a symbol? The novel provides a multitude of hints, but they are often contradictory. The author refuses to give his sanction to any one meaning. Ahab, to be sure, thinks that he has the whole enigma figured out, but his presumption is a major part of Melville's theme. Out of the tantalizing multiplicity of significances offered in the novel, the reader, like Ahab, can easily be misled into the error of choosing some specific *one*. To avoid this error, the reader should consider especially the chapter on "The Whiteness of the Whale." There it is made clear that whiteness, in various associations, can symbolize goodness, chastity, magnificence, supremacy, joy, innocence, religious purity, divinity, terror, ghastliness, ill omen, death, and the immense void of the universe. "And of all these things," Melville concludes, "the Albino Whale was the symbol. Wonder ye then at the fiery hunt?" [7] The stress is upon no single meaning but upon the infinity of possibilities, upon man's bafflement in the face of that infinity.

Along with this multiplicity of meaning there appears to be an intentionally confused duality suggestive of good and evil. In a style characteristic of Melville, we are informed that the whale's eyes, placed on diametrically opposite sides of his head, force him to contemplate two different pictures simultaneously. As a result, there must exist within the whale's brain at any one time a confusion of opposites. Melville depicts the whale as an essentially dualistic creature, a being whose enigmatic motives may somehow be related to this dualism.[8] Obviously, any human attempt to understand the whale must take into consideration this doubleness.

However, because of their basic nature human beings experience overwhelming difficulty in their attempts to reconcile op-

[7] *Moby-Dick*, pp. 176–184.
[8] *Moby-Dick*, pp. 311–312.

posites or to contemplate opposing concepts simultaneously. To comprehend such opposites inter-extant in a single nature is almost beyond human capability.

Anyone's experience will teach him that though he can take in an undiscriminating sweep of things at one glance, it is quite impossible for him, attentively, and completely, to examine any two things—however large or however small—at one and the same instant of time; never mind if they lie side by side and touch each other. But if you now come to separate these two objects, and surround each with a circle of profound darkness; then, in order to see one of them, in such a manner as to bring your mind to bear on it, the other will be utterly excluded from your contemporary consciousness.[9]

Man, then, has an essentially monistic nature. To attempt to interpret the whale in terms of the essentially monistic human intelligence is a dangerous business. But when the natural human monism becomes obsessive, it turns into monomania and the result is the tragic fate of Ahab.[10]

Melville and Ishmael know only this of the white whale: it is a real and living part of our world, and its incomprehensibility lures man to seek in it some tremendous philosophical significance. Whether any such significance actually inheres in the whale is a question that Melville carefully avoids answering in any final form. Philosophical significance is chiefly a matter of human creativity. The meanings which most men find in the whale are actually in the beholders themselves. Even at best these meanings are apt to be monstrous oversimplifications of life. At worst they are madness. The white whale is (to quote the novel) "physiognomically a Sphinx," his brain "that geometrical circle which it is

[9] *Moby-Dick*, p. 311.
[10] The author is aware that this is not the meaning usually ascribed to *monomania*. However, it appears probable that Melville had this second meaning in mind when he employed the word in connection with Ahab. In this new sense, *monomania* signifies the natural human monism gone berserk.

impossible to square," his head "an entire delusion." [11]

To Job, out of the whirlwind, came the questioning voice of the Lord:

Canst thou draw out leviathan with an hook? or his tongue with a cord which thou lettest down? Canst thou put an hook into his nose? or bore his jaw through with a thorn? Will he make supplications unto thee? will he speak soft words unto thee? Will he make a covenant with thee? wilt thou take him for a servant for ever? [12]

Confronted by these inquiries, Job (that Everyman of the Old Testament) sank humbled. These questions, presented in a different symbolic context, are the same ones posed in *Moby-Dick*. Never at any time does Melville imply that he has the answers. The wisest course for critics would probably be to follow Melville's example and refrain from applying any specific abstract term to the mystery symbolized by the white whale. Melville confronts us with the unreadable face of the whale and hurls at us the playfully wicked challenge to "read it if you can." [13] He also confronts us with a series of warnings, including the admonition against allegorizing Moby Dick and the example of Ahab's tragic fate. In the words of Ishmael, he tells us point-blank that the whale's face is a *tabula rasa* or a white screen. Any pictures that we see there must be projected from our own imaginations:

Dissect him how I will, I go but skin deep; I know him not, and never will. But if I know not even the tail of this whale, how understand his head? much more, how comprehend his face, when face he has none? Thou shalt see my back parts, my tail, he seems to say, but my face shall not be seen. But I cannot completely make out his back parts; and hint what he will about his face, I say again he has no face. [14]

Captain Ahab commits the tragic error which Ishmael avoids. He converts this

[11] *Moby-Dick*, p. 327.
[12] Job. XLI. 1–4.
[13] *Moby-Dick*, p. 326.
[14] *Moby-Dick*, p. 356.

facelessness into an intolerable allegory. The evil which surges within his own heart is externalized and fastened upon the white whale, which is all-embracing and all-receiving in its incomprehensibility. Under the illusion that he has shoved the world's evil beyond arm's length, where it can be hacked out of existence without simultaneous expungement of the attacker himself, Ahab undertakes his mad venture.

The White Whale swam before him as the monomaniac incarnation of all those malicious agencies which some deep men feel eating in them, till they are left living on with half a heart and half a lung. That intangible malignity which had been from the beginning; to whose dominion even the modern Christians ascribe one-half of the worlds; which the ancient Ophites of the east reverenced in their statue devil;—Ahab did not fall down and worship it like them; but deliriously transferring its idea to the abhorred White Whale, he pitted himself, all mutilated, against it. . . . All the subtle demonisms of life and thought; all evil, to crazy Ahab, were visibly personified, and made practically assailable in Moby Dick. [15]

Ahab's error of allegorizing is partly the result of his having erred in a much more fundamental way. He has failed to comprehend what Melville, along with Milton, held to be the basic truth of the moral universe: that good and evil are inextricably involved with one another in realms of mortality. As Milton pointed out in *Areopagitica*, [16] and as Melville implies by

[15] *Moby-Dick*, pp. 172–173.
[16] See *Areopagitica*, Everyman's Library Edition (London and New York: J. M. Dent and E. P. Dutton, 1927), especially p. 13: "Good and evil we know in the field of this world grow up almost inseparably; and the knowledge of good is so involved and interwoven with the knowledge of evil . . . that those confused seeds that were imposed upon Psyche as an incessant labor to cull out, and sort asunder, were not more intermixed," etc. There is a slight possibility that Melville received the basic philosophic premise of his major works, plus the idea of whiteness as a symbolic color, from *Areopagitica*. Henry F. Pommer, in his *Milton and Melville* (Pittsburgh: University of Pittsburgh Press, 1950), has called attention to many evidences of influence but neglects to bring

the ambiguous duality of his symbolism and by the tragic outcome of *Moby-Dick*, any attempt to eradicate evil by external injunction or attack must, if it is pursued strongly, simultaneously eradicate the good which is involved with the evil. Virtue, as Milton viewed it, constitutes a dynamic victory of good over evil *within the individual soul*. When, in order to externalize his own portion of evil, Ahab ignored the external involvement of good and evil and made an allegory of the white whale, he surrendered his own opportunity for virtue. His degeneration is obvious and at last complete. He recruits his whalers by deception, allies himself with evil, and in the end flaunts the basic moral guide of humanity, the golden rule. And, irony of ironies, he supposes that he is doing all this *for* humanity, to rid the world of the very evil which he enlists in the attack upon his own allegory of evil. When the evil which Ahab envisions is finally blotted out, the means of its extinction is not the death of the whale but the death of Ahab himself.

Ahab's ignorance of the mortal entanglement of good and evil and his consequent tendency to allegorize are depicted by Melville as deeply ingrained traits of Ahab's character rather than mere latter-day acquisitions. As Charles C. Walcutt suggests in his article on the fire symbolism in *Moby-Dick*, Ahab had indulged his folly in connection with his earlier Zoroastrianism. As a worshipper of fire, Ahab had adored the flame. When, during the ritual, a tongue of fire accidentally leaped out at him and branded him with the ghastly white scar so often mentioned in the novel, he entirely reversed his former attitude and made of the

flame a symbol of unmixed evil.[17] Monomania—the obsessive propensity to see things as single rather than multiple, as all good or all bad rather than as a mixture of the two—was a very early part of Ahab's character. The making of "hideous and intolerable allegory" is just another way of designating the same process.[18]

Possibly in the example of Ahab there lies a warning, unintentional on Melville's part, for those ingenious critics who try to impose contrived allegorical systems on Moby Dick, who dart their Freudian or Swedenborgian harpoons at the great white whale.[19] Might the book even serve as a warning for man in the twentieth century? Slightly giddy with scientific success, a little blear-eyed from our mad glimpse into the atomic nature of things, we presume a capacity to see eventually into the heart of *all* things—even to untangle, perhaps, the intricate knot of good and evil. In a sense it is a noble presumption, as was Ahab's. But it is a supremely dangerous one, for the rope has a way of tightening around the

---

out the possibilities surrounding the Miltonic prose works in general and *Areopagitica* in particular. Consider, for example, Milton's words about virtue: "That virtue therefore which is but a youngling in the contemplation of evil, and knows not the utmost that vice promises to her followers, and rejects it, is but a blank virtue, not a pure; her whiteness is but an excremental whiteness" (*Areopagitica*, p. 13).

[17] "The Fire Symbolism in *Moby-Dick*," MLN, LIX (1944), 304–310.

[18] Melville's other works display other aspects of the human tendency to create allegorical oversimplifications. In *Mardi*, the hero makes of Yillah an allegory of heavenly, or ideal, beauty. Yillah's perfection is a projection from the mind of Taji, not an actuality. Consequently, she becomes lost to him as soon as he attempts to possess her in the flesh. He sails off into trackless oceans in a futile search for something which exists only within his own mind. Pierre, likewise, refuses to accept the facts which reality presents. All he *knows* of Isabel, is that she is a woman, just as all that Ahab knows of Moby Dick is that he is a whale. But Pierre builds around Isabel an intricate fabric of allegory and self-projection. He attempts to effect heavenly righteousness upon earth, but ironically his means include human subterfuge. His ambiguous brother-husband relationship with Isabel involves him in some of the world's worst sins. Taji, Ahab, and Pierre are all victims of a similar thought-malady: they try to circumvent the inherent ambiguities of life by oversimplification, projection, and allegorizing.

[19] For an early and ingenious example of this type of interpretation, see W. S. Gleim, "A Theory of *Moby-Dick*," NEQ, II (1929), 402–419.

neck of the operator even as he is intent upon loosening the strands of the main knot:

Ahab's harpoon was darted; the stricken whale flew forward; with ignited velocity the line ran through the groove;—ran foul. Ahab stooped to clear it; but the flying turn caught him round the neck, and voicelessly as Turkish mutes bowstring their victim, he was shot out of the boat, ere the crew knew he was gone. Next instant, the heavy eye-splice in the rope's final end flew out of the stark empty tub, knocked down an oarsman, and smiting the sea, disappeared in its depths.[20]

[20] *Moby-Dick*, p. 530.

John Parke

Seven *Moby-Dicks*

"Hark ye yet again,—the little lower layer."—AHAB

Moby-Dick has been justly and sufficiently acclaimed as a peerless saga of physical adventure, appealing to young and old just like any other good yarn. Its external action takes place in a world of athletic heroism, the kind of man's world that many girls at one time or another and all boys fervently wish to enter. It is filled with boasting talk, odd characters, rough deeds, alarums, accidents, mysteries, and narrow escapes. The exciting paradox of the fragility of men's bodies and the sturdiness of their ingenuities is vividly present; and the technical descriptions—of the process of killing a whale, for instance—with their robustly metaphoric picturization and their hallmark of cleanly observant intimacy with materials and elements, arouse the most imaginative sort of manipulative interest. Merely as marine exposition the book is expert; merely as action narrative the story is a good one, as the frequent appearance of "The Chase" in anthologies and school readers attests.

But let us descend one layer. Mere good narrative or exposition is exhaustible. Even those readers least disposed or equipped to interpret *Moby-Dick* metaphorically often feel its power as something strange and haunting. This phenomenon did not escape critical notice even prior to the Melville renaissance of the 1920's; Melville's version of the old struggle with the sea and monsters simply seems to excel as a producer of what might be called the spiritual sensation of marine adventure. For here the

sea and the universe are perhaps most unconquerable (and does man not tire of "conquests" over nature at last?). Here civilized insulation from the cosmos is least purchasable; the very fierceness with which it is scorned should challenge the creeping spirit of the most troglodytic reader. "The Lee Shore," an early heroic chapter, sets this spiritual tone (if Chapter I has not already), vigorously lifting the adventure story to a supraphysical level; and though from here on the central narrative and theme go in a morally oblique direction (or does Bulkington? and would *he* have bent to Ahab's will?), this "six-inch chapter" is as it were a harmonic which vibrates again and again throughout the book, particularly in relation to the landlessness of Ahab, and the crew's gradual involvement in it, on the one hand, and the far-voyaging speculations of the narrator-adventurer on the other. And when the majesty of the antagonist whale, or the alluring terror of the putative drop from masthead to water, is dramatized against such a background of material observation, we surely have adventure writing of the highest order, even as we do in the fight with Grendel's mother or the escape from Circe.

But leaving behind that self-limiting view which is pleased to regard *Moby-Dick* as a mere physical adventure story with a certain exotic spiritual tonality, we can proceed to discover next a sort of emblem-story of man and nature, in which are revealed certain accumulated meanings of an age-long struggle. Several generations of readers have seen in these emblems, the more obvious ones at least, what man does to nature and nature to man—the imprint

Reprinted by permission from the *New England Quarterly*, XXVIII (1955), 319–338.

left on each by the other. At times, as in the descriptions of Flask's pugnacity concerning whales or of Moby Dick's accumulated tangle of barbs and line, they are presented in fairly literal terms—so literal, in fact, that the reader predisposed to literalness will contend, again, that they are nothing more than what they seem. At other times, as with the albatross, the mat-weaving, or the final vignette of the flag, the hammer, and the bird, they are in more figurative, and hence more suggestive and extendible, terms. (We except here the more dramatic metaphors or symbolic constructions which relate directly to dynamic aspects of the theme, such as Ishmael's hallucination at the helm when he gazes into the nocturnal try-works, or Ahab's magnetizing of the needle.) These symbolic vignettes, often explicitly—even heavily—interpreted by the author, were Melville's delight; indeed, he had a connoisseur's penchant for them. This is held against him by readers unreceptive to the central symbolism of *Moby-Dick;* and if the subject-matter exclusive of strict narration consisted largely of a heavy sprinkling of unrelated emblematic tableaux, they would have solid grounds for objection. But such is not the case. The various symbols, static and otherwise, do indeed "add up"; they are, ultimately, part of the tissue of drama and inner theme. These latter elements must now be dealt with on their own proper level.

For Ahab's wound and mania, the preternatural Fedallah, Starbuck's tense and ambivalent relation to his captain, the prophetic soliloquies, Pip, and the "Whiteness of the Whale"—these are entities of another sort. When we examine the complicated moral drama, with the much disputed theme —that "hideous and intolerable allegory" which Melville more than half facetiously disavowed—we are indeed working on a much "lower layer," or series of layers. In the story of Ahab and his crew, and the one articulate antagonist, Starbuck, we discover a grimly joined inner battle, a searing and terrible symbolic representation of a pro-

found conflict in the soul of man. There is no mistaking Melville's intent so to generalize. There is only the necessary search for applicability.

As with *Hamlet,* where three hundred years have not sufficed for the emergence of a definitive thematic interpretation, we have here a host of contenders for authoritative explication. This can mean one of two things: that the text, due to confusion in concept or execution, is at fault; or that, as a sort of master metaphor, it embodies an archetypal situation capable of a considerable variation of perfectly relevant responses or "meanings." Of course, this state of affairs always produces at some time a school of critics whose compulsion is to debunk all symbolic interpretations and to deny all levels of meaning in the work except the "factual" or phenomenal. It is our privilege to ignore these dogmatic skeptics and to assume, pending close examination, that the second alternative above fairly describes the novel. It is our further privilege to work for as specific an interpretation as possible according to our own lights, in the hope that all thoughtful contributions to an understanding of the work may enrich the experience of its readers, whether or not final agreement is yet— or ever—possible.

The primary and indisputable fact of the inner drama is that Captain Ahab has been led to attribute deliberation ("inscrutable malignity") on the part of the universe against himself. Thereafter, instead of minding his whaling business prudently, as Starbuck or any good Quaker would, he conjured up a soul's antagonist in The Whale. With this phantasm he then had to do unceasing battle, magnifying it to the proportions of a life-usurping fetish, until its power over his soul destroyed him, just as the actual whale sank his ship and left him to drown. This inner human destruction is the core of the drama, as two utterances by Ahab at the denouement show: "For the third time my soul's ship starts upon this voyage, Starbuck"; and finally:

Oh, now I feel my topmost greatness lies in my topmost grief. Ho, ho! from all your furthest bounds, pour ye now in, ye bold billows of my whole foregone life, and top this one piled comber of my death! Towards thee I roll, thou all-destroying but unconquering whale; to the last I grapple with thee; from hell's heart I stab at thee; for hate's sake I spit my last breath at thee. Sink all coffins and all hearses to one common pool! and since neither can be mine, let me then tow to pieces, while still chasing thee, though tied to thee, thou damned whale! *Thus*, I give up the spear!

Now, what brought about this titanic nemesis? What is at issue in the conflict within the particular man Ahab, and between him and Starbuck? What is Melville's "mighty theme" for which the drama serves as vehicle? What is the archetypal situation?

The title points to The Whale as chief protagonist, not to Ahab; The Whale was there before Ahab, and outlived him, so we had best find out about it. Moby Dick, with his ambivalent whiteness, his solitariness, his mildness and transient fury, his ubiquitousness and his scars, is, as more than one critic has suggested, the noumenon of nature itself—a comprehensive dynamic symbol for the whole immense, riddling, uncaring cosmos in which man finds himself nurtured, stunned, challenged, and (if he choose and can) at home. The *uncaringness* is the point. A significant part of the thematic framework of the book is the strong auctorial suggestion that the universe is neutral and unpurposeful in terms of human values and purposes. From this it follows that man's adaptation to the universe, to the limitations, opportunities, and destiny (favorable or otherwise) with which it presents him, shapes his whole concept of it.

For, if external nature simply does not concern itself with man's destiny, the malevolence or benevolence he attributes to it is obviously a mere projection of his own hate or love, fear or faith. But if he believes it malevolent—i.e., cannot accept whatever is accorded him of fate—and attacks it, it will prove malevolent, or prove to seem so, and expertly accommodate him in his own undoing—either physically, or inwardly through upheaval in his own nature, or both. Melville drives home this neutrality of nature in the chapter on The Whale's mysterious whiteness, where the ambivalence (to man) is marvelously exhibited through countless and ageless instances: the evil white and the beneficent white in man's vision, but always the irresistible white, the dazzling summit of all colors, the emblem of his most intense spiritual energy. The energy, in man and outside him, is impersonal and neutral: it is man personally or collectively who, by free choice or inward compulsion, turns it to destructive or creative ends in himself and so sees it in malevolent or benevolent aspects outside him.

It is further evident that man in this universe is equipped to observe, marvel, deduce; that he can minutely and partially manipulate, deflect, exploit; but that he cannot influence the power of created life at its source; and, strangely, that he cannot even attempt this with impunity. The mighty Whale is content to let Ahab and other men live, so long as they do not seek power over the principle of nature itself, the "phantom of life"; so long as they attack only whales and not The Great Whale of the Universe.

"Oh! Ahab," cried Starbuck, "not too late is it, even now, the third day, to desist. See! Moby Dick seeks thee not. It is thou, thou, that madly seekest him!"

Consider normal man (Starbuck), rational and sane, submitting his heart and his behavior not only to those natural forces far beyond his control but to a traditional *ethos*, acknowledging both his relatedness and his obligation to his kind (Ahab cannot endure obligation: "Cursed be . . . mortal inter-indebtedness . . ."). Encountering the raw power of physical nature, he can maintain his livelihood and his equanimity by ingenuity, patience, submission to necessity, and the fulfilment of his sense of responsibility. But let some traumatic experience or historical upheaval upset his sense of cosmic and social proportion, his humanity, and his proper respect toward immensity and careless omnipotence; above all, let him then indulge in vindictiveness toward that which is incapable of charity, justice, and premeditated animosity alike, and he is lost. His presumption ("I'd strike the sun if it insulted me"), violating a law of his own nature, will ignite a conflict in his soul so abrasive that he will gradually wear away a lung and half a heart (yet possibly become great in the process—". . . all mortal greatness is but disease," says Melville; the trauma is perhaps the grain which stings the pearl into being); he will become an unconsciously eager victim of a catastrophe which will seem to him in his phantasm the working of a purposeful external vengeance.

So with Ahab. In him nature's mold has cracked, and so the universe seems to have turned against him. As in the opening of *King Lear,* the loyal and wholly human man (Kent, Starbuck) is impotent; the runaway fragment holds mad sway. What such a desperate man, who would be whole and reign within himself, has then to contend with is something in the nature of an autonomous complex: Ahab's "purpose, by its own sheer inveteracy of will, forced itself against gods and devils into a kind of self-assumed, independent being of its own." Now, the conflict between Ahab and Starbuck is the direct reflection of this conflict within Ahab; Starbuck submits to an *ethos,* a job, and an emotional responsibility to his family, accepting any disproportion "between his just deserts and what he gets"; Ahab, on the other hand, profoundly sensitive enough to have been hurt by life, identifying his whole being with an injured part that will not heal, and rationalizing his consequent derangement, sets himself up above the *ethos,* denies his obligations and his human feeling, and opposes

his personal conscious will to destiny. And this, of course, is the *hubris;* oversimplified, it is the sin of pride. Here is a basic thematic interpretation.

But again, "the little lower layer." More than the pride of a particular man is involved, both initially and ultimately, and more than trauma. Melville's intention was not nearly so simple, and part of the novel's durable fascination is the fact that the *hubris* is less readily apparent, in its precise nature, than the nemesis. In fact, it is both deeply subtle and extremely complex.

Mankind itself (all races and important nationalities are represented in the crew of the *Pequod*) is fatefully embarked on a pursuit which is, as we have seen, a titanically malicious attack on nature itself. (Ahab's malice is partly intellectual—more of that anon—while the crew's is blindly instinctive.) Now, while it is of course fitting, or at least traditional, that hazardous expeditions are for men, the absence of women and their influence from the crew and, generally speaking, from the story, may be taken as symbolic. For not merely humanity (the moral quality) is left ashore, but the specific feminine principle of relatedness, of nurturing, of instinctive affection, is implicitly and expressly denied. Even the comradeship of Ishmael and Queequeg, so intimate in the early chapters, is dropped. Pip, the most defenseless and lovable creature imaginable, is deranged by being abandoned in the water and is later agonized by the crew's denial of the security which he needs and which, paradoxically, it becomes Ahab's particular joy to give him. Ahab cancels his ties with his new wife and babe. Masculinity is isolated; life is unbalanced. Only Starbuck, among the active characters, remains whole, despite his limitations, and truly human—that is, both masculine and potentially feminine.

The denouement is thus made psychologically inevitable, since self-mutilation can result only in disaster; Melville hints at it many times in advance. The sexless, inhuman symbol Fedallah (identified with the devil, for he casts no shadow) is an early harbinger of what is to come. From the moment of embarkation at Nantucket there is an insidious presence and a tension on board, manifested in all sorts of external omens and symbols; these are a sort of ground bass for the gradual revelation of the core of evil in Ahab's soliloquies, colloquies, and actions.

Vast destructive powers are loosed as Ahab and the opposing forces converge; despite the integrity and sanity and (in normal human measure) the considerable strength of Starbuck, despite his protests to the captain, despite Ahab's intense struggle with himself and his long surviving ability to feel sympathy and pain, the captain totally rejects his instincts, casts off his humanity, even the tool of his craft of navigation; he resolves on his own destruction. As his mania gathers the support of all his faculties, his fervor and his will catch up all the other men (but Starbuck) in a great bonfire of destructive energy. All values are inverted—note Ishmael's sense of psychic inversion in "The Try-Works"; there are no laws to hold to when man sets himself to wreak vengeance on the nameless phantom life itself, on the universe, on himself. And, inevitably, all is lost in the grand debacle of such a paranoiac orgy.

Justice poetic enough, and righteous enough even for the orthodox Christian of Melville's day. The sins of pride and self-mutilation are fittingly punished. May we not now sum up the theme and extend it to a universal moral? Ahab's intellectual presumption, his denial of humanity, his identification of his entire personality with his injured pride and towering conscious will, is in every one of us who seeks knowledge of all mysteries, who seeks total power over circumstance, and who would refuse submission to the law of personal integration, who would reject that which is greater than personality and beyond the human. This it is to be a renegade. The dramatization of the issue is, of course, out of all proportion to our individual variant experiences; but that is precisely why it so affects us. It is as if one of our own little inward battles against super-personal necessity were projected on a screen in dimensions and social ramifications a thousand times beyond the scope of our insignificance. *Moby-Dick* is a huge nightmare of ourselves at war with fate and the universe, one which we would do well to contemplate—Americans particularly, who have yet, in all their scientific plundering and tinkering, to learn respect for nature and the cosmos, for life and death, and for themselves.

But, once more, the situation is not so simple. There is another "lower layer." For Ahab voluntarily and deliberately places himself outside the pale of Christendom; *and yet he dies a hero of a sort.* Renegade though he is, it is he, not Starbuck, who excites our admiration and our vicarious participation, and is meant to. Starbuck is by contrast simply too human, too normally proportioned. ("Thou art but too good a fellow, Starbuck," says Ahab.) Let us consider Ahab as a hero, and let us see the way in which Melville presents him to us.

Just as Hawthorne's too masculine Ethan Brand embodies the destructive aspect of the pride of knowledge, Ahab, in our initial oversimplification, embodies the pride of will. He must overcome destiny. But he is presented far more effectively than Hawthorne's character, with far more of revelation, for Melville is magnanimous and daring enough to force us to admire Ahab and to pity him, to make us feel the pull of his electric leadership, to have us see for ourselves what it is to become exalted and then overwhelmed in the identification with maimed and self-maimed, vengeful masculinity ("I, Ishmael, was one of that crew; my shouts had gone up with the rest . . ."). In the Hawthorne tale (as in many of his others) it is hard for us to embed the author's implied judgment very deep in our feeling, however much we may intellectually agree, for the protagonist is too black and furtive, too repugnant, too pitiless toward himself, for us to see readily in him a reflection of any part of ourselves. But Ahab, figurehead of the independent mind, scorning to reconcile himself to a fate he can neither control nor avoid, much less understand; Prometheus-like refusing (in Elizabethan rhetoric!) to acknowledge the everlasting superiority of the cosmic forces concentrated against his brittleness like an immense, careless army; above all, knowing his own madness, his pain, and his humanity: this is irresistible. Though we quit and condemn his presumptuous folly at last, even as Ishmael escapes the wreck of the *Pequod,* we do so with intimate knowledge and with profit; for Melville, instead of reading us a homily, has made us participants. If nothing else in the book will do it, the titanic pathos of the "Sunset" chapter, or the heartrending gibberish of Pip (Lear's fool's descendant), or the tremendous climactic antiphony of "The Symphony," will implicate us in pity for the part of ourselves that has been wrenched from us in the magnificently demented Ahab. Perhaps not even Lear, who cracks too easily and whose fault is so much more trivial, can stir us so.

For Ahab is tragic, not just pathetic or grotesque. He has the courage to face what he fears, the inner nemesis he knows he has prepared for himself; and he finds he must constantly fight his own humanity to keep that courage. The sacrifice is not easy. This is made especially convincing in the two chapters last named above. At the same time that he misdirects his great spiritual energies to a suicidal as well as homicidal end, he becomes fully, painfully aware of what he has sacrificed in himself and in others. (His ordering Starbuck to keep to the ship at the end is profoundly humane as well as self-propitiatory.) If he is not finally master of himself or of the situation he finds himself in, not able to balance values and create himself anew at his death, he at least has the courage and far exceeds the vision of Milton's Satan, who has been more than sufficiently admired as a "tragic hero." And if, like Conrad's

Kurtz, he dies unreconstructed despite his at times prayerful awareness of the moral and psychic horror in which he has become involved, he has the decency to outlive his moment of pause and to die unself-forgiving and with harness on his back. Satan's end is repulsive, Kurtz's pathetic; Ahab's, though like the others' morally repugnant, is paradoxically magnificent. The ambivalence, as in *Macbeth,* makes this a doubly stirring, if disconcerting, denouement for modern readers.

Now, the nature of the theme on this sixth layer will become evident if we examine the situation which calls forth heroic action. This tragedy is neither Aristotelian nor, in the Elizabethan sense, personally or politically ethical, nor, in the Thomas Hardy sense, psychologically deterministic. Ahab's downfall carries with it far more than the undoing of one man and his accomplices. The tone of the ending, to take one of the many indications, is epically grand and out of all proportion to Ahab's immediate significance as a mere individual. It does indeed, in spite of Melville's scornful disclaimer, suggest an allegory of man in a historical predicament.

The plain fact is that Melville, in dealing with the problem of fate, is doing so completely outside the Christian frame of reference. "I have written a wicked book, and feel spotless as a lamb," he wrote Hawthorne after finishing *Moby-Dick.* His depiction of a *universe both godless and purposeless,* was, and he knew it, in effect a blasphemy from the point of view of orthodoxy and transcendentalism alike. The shock upon his contemporary public (if they had widely understood) could be compared to the effect that Robinson Jeffers' theology might have had upon Queen Victoria.

Now we see why Melville left his hero unredeemed and apparently uncondemned (note the final helplessness of the godly Starbuck), dying in a black destructive fury of pride and negation—yet, paradoxically, still heroic. For Ahab's tragic predicament is the result of his own heroic temper and special personality *plus* this philosophical or theological condition: the removal of God and Providence from the universe. If the universe is ethically ungoverned and purposeless, the apparent corollary is the absence of any principle of fatal justice, and so the stultification of human ethical norms and social laws. No wonder Ahab sought his own death and met it with a curse! No wonder Melville felt socially "guilty," for he was cutting himself loose from all the bulwarks of ethical and theological thought familiar and normal in his day. He was heading into a dangerous open sea, and he knew it.

Interestingly enough, the process seems to have begun during the writing of the book. In the early chapters, before Ishmael and Queequeg reach Nantucket, there are no eschatological undertones, and the frame of reference is specifically Protestant: both Father Mapple's austere but genuine kindliness and evangelism, and the brotherly rapport between the self-respecting New Englander and the pagan harpooneer embody this. All is black and white. But these are points of departure only, for we soon move on into an already senile, partly blasphemous world of Quaker commercialism at Nantucket, which in its decadence is threatened by Elijah's prophecy and the mysterious embarkation of the apostate Ahab's boat crew. Next Bulkington, the unaffiliated man of pure, unquestioning spirituality, is swept overboard at the start of the voyage (how isolated he would have been among the *Pequod's* crew!) Then the comradeship of Ishmael and Queequeg is quietly dropped, as Ishmael becomes less a character and more a device; and the whole focus of the book ("WHALING VOYAGE BY ONE ISHMAEL"?) seems to change as Melville becomes caught up in an immense superpersonal theme.

Ultimately, in *Moby-Dick*, we find ourselves involved in a sort of apocalypse: "This is the way the world ends." (At least there's a bang to it in nineteenth-century America!) This, Melville's prophetic intuition seems to tell him, is the only at-present-conceivable result of the collision between the wayward spirit and intellect of man (with all his inherited ideals of justice) and the un-Providential, unjudicial, uncaring universe empty of God. Note that Melville wastes no love upon his steadfast Christian, Starbuck: the mate is, in the moral climate of the story, an anachronism: he lives on, secure and unshakable, in a world whose illusions are irreparably shattered for Ahab. When Starbuck at the height of the typhoon says, "God, God is against thee, old man, . . ." and the superstitious crew falter before the corposants, we can only laugh, not at the fear but at the terms in which it is articulated by the mate; for the poetry has converted us already to Ahab's fierce animism, as our identification with him (so carefully and gradually developed by Melville) had previously made us atheists. Though we cannot but respect Starbuck's uprightness, his humanitarian goodness, his steadfastness, we can only scorn his prosaic mildness beside the splendid vigor of Ahab.

True, Ahab is a fated loser; even at his most admirable, when he is struggling most awarely and more feelingly to preside over his own experience and salvage his soul, he is damned. Melville never lets us forget or doubt this. He carries his personal doom with him, and loves it, for in a collapsing moral creation its grandeur is all he has left. But, *natural* laws are still in operation: Ahab, by the nature of his reaction to the void with which his time, his misfortune, and his personal disposition confront him, seals his own fate. Hate still does not, cannot, triumph over nature, but over the hater at last; Moby Dick goes free, immortal, and essentially invulnerable, while Captain Ahab and his accomplices are unmercifully drowned. As Lewis Mumford has said, Ahab "becomes the image of the thing he hates; he has lost his humanity in the very act of vindicating it."

If he is heroic, it is because of his intellectual and spiritual fortitude as a mere human being in confronting chaos—physical, ethical, metaphysical chaos, the long displaced but never extinguished old deity of the myths. How, indeed, when God and the comforting concepts of Providence, divine justice, and salvation are lost, does man reconcile himself to his fate? Ahab, born into the story scarred and godless, most nakedly exposed to the apparent nihilism of the universe, faces this challenge alone. The others do not see it; he is their superior. The fact that from the outset he takes a course which dooms him to frustration and madness makes him no less heroic, and no less pitiable. Finding in the cosmos indifference, injustice, even (apparently) total depravity, he determines to make it bow to his personal need for revenge—an attempt at restoration of order—or know the reason why. It is a blind, typically human reaction, stirring because of the preterhuman stature and intellectual power of the man who embodies it, and because of his abiding sense of alternatives. The fact that his personality is still inadequate to embrace a resolution that is not self-destructive suggests Melville's, the prophet's, terror before the looming problem—and his courage in revealing its direct and present threat.

Having progressed through so many levels of interpretation to this exposition of a theological allegory, we might think we had reached the full depth, the quintessence, of Melville's "mighty theme." This, indeed, is as mighty as the story of Job himself: the confrontation of chaos by man —Chaos, the old god of the Mediterranean, so frighteningly depicted by Milton as waiting, though in abeyance, outside the framework of the created universe, where he waits still, no doubt, for modern man, beyond the crumbling pale of the Christian citadel and the evaporating heavenly city of rationalism, close beneath the flimsy suburban scaffolding of scientific relativism. But, "Hark ye yet again . . ."—there is more.

The chaos, says Melville, is not merely around man; it is in him. For, after the dissipation of the Christian theology, the heart of man is still found to be literally writhing with evil. In fact, the evil in man is the cause of the apparent outer chaos ("Moby Dick seeks thee not . . ."). Perhaps our author would have liked to be a humanist; but his insight into human nature would not let him! For, in one telling passage (buttressed by many others), he indisputably objectifies and points up for us the eternal problem of human evil and man's bewilderment before it as the basis of Ahab's preoccupation and therefore as the inmost core of the book's theme:

The White Whale swam before him as the monomaniac incarnation of all those malicious agencies which some deep men feel eating in them. . . . That intangible malignity which has been from the beginning . . . deliriously transferring its idea to the abhorred white whale, he pitted himself, all mutilated, against it. . . . all the subtle demonisms of life and thought; all evil, to crazy Ahab, were visibly personified and made practically assailable in Moby Dick. He piled upon the whale's white hump the sum of all the general rage and hate felt by his whole race from Adam down; and then, as if his chest had been a mortar, he burst his hot heart's shell upon it.

Moby-Dick, then, is ultimately a study of evil. But what sort of evil? What is Melville's notion of evil? Evil's first apparent manifestation (or so it is interpreted by Ahab) is the White Whale's mutilation of his leg. But the *Pequod* meets an English whaler whose captain has had his arm torn off by the same whale; this man is not maddened, nor does he regard the event as more than a perfectly natural, though fearful, accident incurred in the routine business of whaling. His sensible conclusion is that, as far as he and his men are concerned, this particular whale is best let alone. Now, Ahab, a deeper man by far, is obsessed not only with what seems the injustice of the excruciating treatment accorded him (he was delirious for days after the accident, and convalescent for months) ; he is obsessed too, as we have seen, with the notion of hidden forces in the universe. More than this, he is a sinisterly marked man, with a long, livid, probably congenital scar (an emblem, surely, of original sin) ; with a record of blasphemy and certain peculiar, darkly violent deeds; with a series of evil prophecies hanging over him; and with the given name of an idolatrous and savage king.

All this is fittingly suggestive preparation for the complete deliverance of Ahab's soul to evil through obsession and revenge. But his motive for revenge is not simple, not merely wicked. His quest for Moby Dick is in part a metaphysical one, for he is *in revolt against the existence of evil itself*. His vindictiveness, blind as it is, and motivated by personal hurt, is nevertheless against the eternal fact of evil. He thinks "the invisible spheres were formed in fright," feels his burden is that of all mankind (". . . as though I were Adam, staggering beneath the piled centuries since Paradise"), thinks the White Whale either the "principal" or the agent of all evil. He, Ahab, is evil, Melville seems to say (through Starbuck and Ahab both), because he seeks to overthrow the established order of dualistic human creation; and yet he is admirable, for he has gone over to evil not merely, like Faustus, for purposes of self-gratification, but in angry and misguided protest aganst its existence and its ravages in him.

What inevitably happens is that, in casting himself as the race-hero opposing the existence of the principle of evil, he but projects his own evil outward ("deliriously transferring its idea to the abhorred white whale") and so becomes all the more its avatar and its prey. He would "strike through the mask" of the visible object (the agent of evil), hoping there to find the key to the riddle. His occasional suspicion ("Sometimes I think there's naught

beyond") that this will not result in any discovery whatsoever, and so not in an effective revenge, deters him not at all, though it drives him ever in upon himself as his fatal hour approaches, till, near the end, he does see the working of evil in himself— and yet dies its avowed agent. For he is mad; he is "madness maddened," quite conscious of his own derangement, and obsessed with it. The final, terrifying chaos, then, is that which he discovers within himself as his vestigial sanity contemplates his madness and its futility, as he admits his incomprehension of the thing that has driven him to irreparable folly and has lost him his very identity ("Is Ahab, Ahab?") :

"What is it, what nameless, inscrutable, unearthly thing is it (the very language used earlier to describe evil) ; what cozening, hidden lord and master, and cruel, remorseless emperor commands me; that against all natural lovings and longings, I so keep pushing, and crowding, and jamming myself on all the time? . . ."

Here is raised even the question of whether man, this proud and splendid aristocrat of the spirit, is indeed a free agent; Ahab, having at other times defied all the gods and called them cricket players, having assumed and never doubted that he could have made himself lord of creation, now turns (in "The Symphony") from Edmund's flouting, free-will cynicism to Gloucester's craven determinism: "By heaven, man, we are turned round and round in this world, like yonder windlass, and Fate is the handspike." He is not captain of his soul after all.

Ahab knows, then, everything about his predicament except its cause in himself— and so its solution. He feels the cause to be an immemorial curse visited upon all men. An exile from Christendom, he yet perceives and abhors the existence of evil. Worse still, he resists it; he will not come to terms with it. He wishes it could simply be swept away, or covered over: "Man, in the ideal, is so noble and so sparkling, such a grand and glowing creature, that over any ignominious blemish 'in him all his fellows should run to throw their costliest robes." But the dark side (which cannot be concealed) cannot be explained or avoided, either. And the most maddening thing of all about it—this is a constant refrain throughout the book—is the deceptive way it lurks beneath a smiling and lovely exterior. ("These temporary apprehensions, so vague but so awful, derived a wondrous potency from the contrasting serenity of the weather . . ." ". . . Fate is the handspike. And all the time, lo! that smiling sky, and this unsounded sea!' And on the very morning of the last terrible day of The Chase—

"What a lovely day again! were it a new-made world, and made for a summer-house to the angels, and this morning the first of its throwing open to them, a fairer day could not dawn upon that world.")

Ahab's tragedy (and, on this final level, the book's theme) is, then, his inability to locate and objectify evil in himself, or to accept it and deal with it prudently as part of the entire created world, and so to *grow* despite it and because of it; it is his own fated indenture to evil while he seeks to destroy it, and his more and more precise knowledge of what is happening to him. It is the magnificence and yet the futility of his attempt. "I know that of me, which thou knowest not of thyself, oh, thou omnipotent," he cries to the great impersonal spirit of fire which he acknowledges as his maker and which, as its individualized creation, he defies. He defies his paternal maker, light, because, discovering his own dual nature (he says he never knew his mother), he has revolted and leagued himself now with darkness (the unrecognized mother-symbol, standing here for a regressive identification, which is of course what supplies the destructive energy). Then, "I am darkness leaping out of light," and "cursed be all the things that cast man's eyes aloft to that heaven, whose live vivid-

ness but scorches him. . . ." "So far gone am I in the dark side of earth, that its other side, the theoretic bright one, seems but uncertain twilight to me." And at his death, the magnificent line—as great and moving in its utter verbal simplicity, and yet as fraught with complex resignation as Edgar's "Ripeness is all": "I turn my body from the sun"—a line whose full and exact significance has been specifically constellated in advance by his own apostrophe to the dying whale in Chapter CXVI.

Ahab is no Faustus. He always has a choice. Many are the times he backslides; the tension between humanity and will is constantly active. Pip, the piteous embodiment of warmly instinctive human nature, of all that Ahab must tread on in himself, acts several times as the unwitting touchstone of that humanity. "Hands off from that holiness!" But, "There is that in thee, poor lad, which I feel too curing to my malady . . . and for this hunt, my malady becomes my most desired health." Starbuck too again and again is the foil and the polar opposite; and once Ahab even finds it good to feel dependence on human aid, for when the White Whale has crushed his ivory leg in the "Second Day," he exclaims while half hanging on the shoulder of his chief mate, "Aye, aye, Starbuck, 'tis sweet to lean sometimes . . . and would old Ahab had leaned oftener than he has." And just once, in "The Symphony," "Ahab dropped a tear into the sea; nor did all the Pacific contain such wealth as that one wee drop."

He must remain, for the brooding Melville apparently and for us, a symbol of that independent spirit and will which, scorning all "lovely leewardings," pushes off from the haven of all creeds to confront an ultimate chaos in the human soul; admirable, perhaps, beyond all flawed heroes (Bulkington was too simple an embodiment—pure essence, he was fit only for deification) in his energy and his courage, but condemned to split at last on the rock of evil, the very thing he willed out of existence; fated—and magnificently, agonizingly willing—to become the pawn (no, the prince, the king) of evil in consequence of his misguided revolt, to lose his identity in the end because he sought to exalt it against the immutable principles of its creation.

Here is our many-layered theme—a Protean archetype indeed! The physical adventure, the spiritual exaltation of hazardous voyaging, the interaction of husbandmen and nature, are there as fresh and valid as ever. The pride and retribution thesis still stands, and the nemesis of self-mutilation through the exalting of will at the expense of instinct. On the meta-physical level, however, chaos, even if thought of only as externally cosmic, is an old, old image of man's, the adversary of all enshrined deities; its confrontation by man is fit matter for grand tragedy. But as an internal moral and emotional predicament the chaos of evil and idealism and madness in the individual is certainly the most compelling phase of the archetype, and the one which evokes more and deeper echoes than any other.

For Melville's grand implication seems to be that all attempts to resist or deny evil, no matter how they are rationalized, are maddeningly futile. Christianity may be gone, he says in effect, but evil is here to stay; no use trying to idealize it out of existence, or conceal it with "costliest robes" or annihilate it by main strength of will and resentment. It will abide and elude; and it must be reckoned with. It is in us, even the deepest of us. Melville cites no text; he preaches no sermon on this head; he merely enunciates as best he can the critical moral predicament which his prophetic imagination apprehends.

Part of the extendibility of Melville's theme on this final level, of course, is due to the fact that he was truly prophetic, both in the sense of apprehending an incipient but suppressed conflict and dilemma of his own day (which only Hawthorne among his American contemporaries honestly confronted in his writings), and in the sense that historically the full reckoning with the problem was yet to come—*and just such an ill-starred solution was to be attempted* by modern man, who has tried philosophically and pragmatically to dismiss the notion of evil.

The problem has been with us now so long that there are many who have lost the capacity to be terrified by it; if an ever richer general response to this tragic novel can help us today or tomorrow to grasp and hold the reality of evil in our imagination, the book will have served as high a human purpose as any less "wicked" book in a time of more stable values. And if Ahab is to be the last of the race of great literary heroes (fittingly embodying the evil of evils and the highest spiritual splendor of man), why, even in the decline of our culture our pleasure in reading *Moby-Dick,* mixed with pain in a true purgation, will come in large part from our sense of participation in the magnificence and the richly deserved doom.

How it could be avoided, Melville does not tell us. Could we tell him?

R. E. Watters

The Meanings of the White Whale

"To PRODUCE a mighty book," wrote Herman Melville, "you must choose a mighty theme. No great and enduring volume can ever be written on the flea, though many there be who have tried it" (452).[1] Everybody will now grant that *Moby Dick* is a mighty book on a mighty theme—even though there is little agreement about the definition of that theme.

At the core of the problem is the interpretation of the white whale himself. Every reader capable of seeing more in the book than an exciting adventure story or a treatise on an extinct maritime industry soon becomes an enthusiastic fisherman, endeavouring "to hook the nose of this leviathan" (131). Not all such enthusiasts are sufficiently impressed by Ishmael's warning that the undertaking is a ponderous task: "To grope down into the bottom of the sea after them [the whales]; to have one's hands among the unspeakable foundations, ribs, and very pelvis of the world; this is a fearful thing. What am I that I should essay to hook the nose of this leviathan! The awful tauntings in Job might well appal me. 'Will he (the leviathan) make a covenant with thee? Behold the hope of him is vain!' But I have swam through libraries and sailed through oceans . . . I am in earnest; and I will try" (131). And much later Ishmael cries out that "in the mere act of penning my thoughts of this Leviathan, they weary me, and make me faint with their out-

reaching comprehensiveness of sweep, as if to include the whole circle of the sciences, and all the generations of whales, and men, and mastodons, past, present, and to come, with all the revolving panoramas of empire on earth, and throughout the whole universe, not excluding its suburbs. Such, and so magnifying, is the virtue of a large and liberal theme!" (452) If Melville himself, through Ishmael, could declare that his "whole book is a draught—nay, but the draught of a draught" (142), it at least behooves all commentators to avoid easy and superficial interpretations.

Nevertheless, the very disagreement of the critics may indicate something of value. Perhaps we might take a hint from Ahab and dive to "a little lower layer" for the universal principle which may be putting "forth the mouldings of its features" (162) through the different white whales. Might it not have been Melville's own intention to invest his great symbolic leviathan with a plurality of meanings?

Simultaneously with his posing the problem, Melville created a formidable body of conflicting interpretations. The whalers on board the *Pequod* and the other whaling ships differed about the meaning of the white whale. At least, they differed when they were not hypnotized by Ahab's "evil magic," as Ishmael calls it, into accepting Ahab's interpretation that the whale was "in some dim, unsuspected way . . . the gliding great demon of the seas of life" (186). Many readers are similarly hypnotized into accepting one or more of Ahab's views; Ahab, be it noted, had more than one.

[1] Numbers following quotations indicate pages in the "Modern Library" edition of *Moby Dick*. Any quotations from other books will be indicated by standard footnotes.

Reprinted by permission from the *University of Toronto Quarterly*, XX (January, 1951), 155–168, with a few changes by the author.

In *Pierre*, the novel written immediately after *Moby Dick*, Melville writes: "Say what some poets will, Nature is not so much her own ever-sweet interpreter, as the mere supplier of that cunning alphabet, whereby selecting and combining as he pleases, each man reads his own peculiar lesson according to his own peculiar mind and mood." [2] In *Moby Dick* Melville may have followed Nature in supplying, in the white whale, a "cunning alphabet" for each of us to read his own lesson.

One doesn't have to read *Pierre* to obtain this clue to the riddle of Melville's greatest book. *Moby Dick* can live without help. There is a clear hint in the very chapter of *Moby Dick*, where Melville, discussing the fascination exercised on men by water, says: "Surely all this is not without meaning. And still deeper the meaning of that story of Narcissus, who because he could not grasp the tormenting, mild image he saw in the fountain, plunged into it and was drowned. But that same image, we ourselves see in all rivers and oceans. It is the image of the ungraspable phantom of life, and this is the key to it all" (3). The same idea is developed much more explicitly, however, in the wonderful chapter on the doubloon. The gold coin which is nailed to the mast to reward the man who first sights the white whale is, as the Negro Pip calls it, "the ship's navel." One morning, late in the cruise, all the leading characters of the book contemplate this navel, so to speak—and discover themselves. As Ahab recognized, "this round gold is but the image of the rounder globe, which, like a magician's glass, to each and every man in turn but mirrors back his own mysterious self" (428). Here is the Narcissus idea again. And after Ahab, Starbuck, Stubb, Flask, and the others have all read themselves in reading the coin, the little Negro, whose "insanity is heaven's sense" (413), thrice repeats his cryptic comment: "I look, you look, he looks; we

look, ye look, they look" (432). As William Ellery Sedgwick has pointed out in *Herman Melville: The Tragedy of Mind*, what Pip is saying, in effect, is that although the object (the coin) remains the same, and the process or verb ("look") remains the same, yet the one change in the subject of the verb makes the whole meaning different.

So the meaning of the coin—and the meaning of the white whale—depends on the subject, on the one who does the looking. There are therefore innumerable meanings for the white whale, just as there are innumerable readings of other examples of "Nature's cunning alphabet." This fact does not, of course, make every meaning equal in value to every other: that kind of philosophical relativism was foreign to Melville's thought. But all that needs saying here on this large topic is that, for Melville, the more nearly omniscient the observer, the more true and valuable his interpretation.

II

Very early in the book Melville says that not all whalemen even "knew of [the white whale's] existence; only a few of them, comparatively, had knowingly seen him; while the number who as yet had actually and knowingly given battle to him, was small indeed" (177). Most whalemen—the common people—had at best heard rumours and shared some general beliefs about this unseen and unknown whale: that he was immense, ferocious, malignant, and not without apparent intelligence. Such ordinary men, like their fellows aboard the *Pequod*, looked upon the white whale as dangerous and intelligent, and therefore perhaps "evil" in the sense of harmful—just as they would no doubt regard a vicious dog as a malignant creature. But such an attitude did not make them take up any quarrel with the creator or with the universe. They thought of the white whale as a particular danger, not as the deity or an agent of the deity, not

2 *Pierre, or The Ambiguities*, ed. Henry A. Murray (New York, 1949), 402.

as the devil or an agent of the devil, and not as a symbol of the inherent evil or unintelligibility of the universe. A few of the "superstitiously inclined," as Ishmael calls them, go a little further and conceive of the white whale as immortal and ubiquitous—but even that advance leaves them far removed from the interpretations of either Ahab or Ishmael.

These ordinary men were, in their interpretations, far closer to Starbuck, whose orthodox piety was shocked at Ahab's seeking "vengeance on a dumb brute . . . that simply smote thee from blindest instinct!" (162) Before this voyage, Starbuck had only "heard" of the white whale, and to him that whale always remained a "dumb brute," a natural even if concentrated manifestation of normal life in the universe of whaling, part of the danger and death one risked in "the business we follow" (162). Such perils, which had been fatal to both his father and his brother, were no doubt "evil" in one sense, but at worst were only the tragic accompaniments to a hazardous profession. He killed whales for a living, not for adventure, let alone any "heaven-insulting purpose" (167). He is a "staid, steadfast man" (112) who is best pleased when "duty and profit" go "hand in hand" (219). His attitude towards the white whale is simply that the risk is too great for the profit that might accrue. He is unconcerned with any possible glory, for he is no "crusader after perils" (113). He is piously and sincerely content to trust in God to run the universe while he does his duty to the owners and hunts whales for his living. He dies performing his duty and praying to his God.

To Stubb, the casual, happy-go-lucky second mate, whaling is simply glorious fun. "Think not" is his "eleventh commandment" (125) and "a laugh's the wisest, easiest answer to all that's queer" (168). Like Starbuck, he leaves the running of the universe to other hands; but whereas Starbuck trusts in a personal God, Stubb is a fatalist: he finds "unfailing comfort"

in his belief that "it's all predestinated" (168). Ahab has a similar fatalism—but, gifted with high intellectual powers, Ahab finds no comfort in it. Stubb willingly follows his captain who, he says, acts on the right principle: "live in the game, and die in it!" (494) Nevertheless, Ahab has little respect for jolly Stubb, whereas he has some for Starbuck who is capable of understanding Ahab's purposes and motives, while disapproving them. "Down, dog, and kennel!" (124) Ahab once snarls at Stubb; and later, when Stubb laughs at the wreck of Ahab's boat and calls it "the thistle the ass refused," Ahab calls him "a soulless thing . . . Did I not know thee brave as fearless fire (and as mechanical) I could swear thou wert a poltroon" (544). By whale-oil light Stubb eats whale-steak as a delight to his palate, just as he hunts whales for the thrill, the joyous adventure. He impiously prays to the corpusants, damns the devil out of bravado, and blasphemously scoffs at God (326). In short, he is almost completely devoid of a sense of values,[3] completely indifferent to spiritual and intellectual affairs. Life to him is a jolly game, a high-spirited frolic. His attitude towards the white whale is clearly that it is to be merely the crowning adventure, a daring challenge—nothing more. Even death becomes but an occasion for witticisms.

In Starbuck and Stubb, therefore, we have representatives of two large groups of readers: those who prefer to regard the white whale as merely a dangerous specimen of sea life, without philosophical or symbolic connotations; and those who give no thought to the matter at all provided the adventure be exciting. As Ahab says,

---

[3] It is true, nevertheless, that the first time Pip jumped from the whaleboat Stubb cut loose from a whale to save him, and apparently his abandoning Pip the second time is not to be held too much against him. It was Stubb, also, who was the only one aboard the *Pequod* who voiced the desire to help the captain of the *Rachel* search for his lost son. Whether he displays impulse or principle in such acts is difficult to decide.

"Starbuck is Stubb reversed, and Stubb is Starbuck; and ye two are all mankind" (544).

In Flask we have a slightly different point of view or interpretation. He is described as pugnacious, destructive, indifferent or cruel (he stamps carelessly on Daggoo's shoulders while perching there for better lookout, and he probes the ulcerous growth on the sick whale). He is the complete materialist, "so utterly lost . . . to all sense of reverence for the many marvels . . . and mystic ways [of whales] . . . that in his poor opinion, the wondrous whale was but a species of magnified mouse, or at least water-rat, requiring only a little circumvention and some small application of time and trouble in order to kill and boil. . . . he followed these fish for the fun of it" (116). If Starbuck is the careful man in the whale fishery, and Stubb the adventurer, then Flask is the ignorant and destructive mediocrity. All he sees in the gold doubloon is a certain number of cigars, and the white whale himself presumably is only worth so many more. In the face of death from Moby Dick his last thought is of money.

Apart from Ahab, the three harpooneers are the only persons aboard the *Pequod* who have previously encountered or seen the white whale. These three—the American Indian, the South Sea Islander, and the African Negro—have all experienced Moby Dick before, but their interpretations of him are as much a mystery as Queequeg's thoughts about the tattooing on his body. Perhaps uncomprehendingly, but certainly uncomplainingly, they do what they have to do skilfully and courageously. They are almost the only crewmen Ahab trusts to serve him faithfully in his pursuit of the whale (528), yet they do not seem to see in the white whale any of Ahab's meanings or any of the three mates'. Like Starbuck, they do their duty, but unlike him they feel no responsibility to the owners or to commercial interests. Unlike Ahab, they feel no hatred as they

chase the white whale, and unlike the "civilized part of the crew" they remain unmoved by such mysterious events as the "plaintively wild and unearthly" cry in the night (514) which others variously interpret as the cries of mermaids, the "voices of newly drowned men," a foreshadowing of future evils, and the wailing of seals. They remain "almost wholly unimpressed" by Ahab's creation of his own compass (509), and by his defiance of the corpusants. As the *Pequod* sinks, the three harpooneers remain at the mast-heads, "fixed by infatuation, or fidelity, or fate, to their once lofty perches," still maintaining "their sinking lookouts on the sea" (565). Tashtego during the thunder and lightning on the night of the corpusants, while lashing the main top-sail yard, had cried: "Stop that thunder! Plenty too much thunder up here. . . . We don't want thunder; we want rum. . . . Um, um, um!" (504) He is again at the main masthead when he dies, while dutifully nailing Ahab's flag to the mast, and taking down in his death-grasp "the bird of heaven" or skyhawk (565).

Fedallah's point of view or interpretation is also enigmatic. He has, of course, a mysterious affinity, sometimes a kind of identity, with Ahab, though they rarely speak to each other, and though Ahab "shunned Fedallah" (528) when he was choosing a man to hoist him aloft to a lookout point. Fedallah compares the wrinkles on the right whale's head to the lines in his hand (327), in a not dissimilar gesture to Queequeg's comparing his tattooing to the signs on the doubloon. Fedallah merely "makes a sign" to the doubloon and "bows himself" in a way which makes Stubb label him a "fire worshipper" (431). On the night of the corpusants, Fedallah kneels "beneath the doubloon and the flame" and is used as a footstool by Ahab in his harangue to the "clear spirit of the fire" (499). Fedallah is a fatalist, who foresees his own doom and that of Ahab, yet chooses to let Ahab misinterpret his prophetic messages (491–2). To Fedallah, the white whale means death and a horrible "hearse" —an instrument of a foreseen fate, just as Fedallah himself is an instrument of Ahab's all-consuming purpose. But the problem of which is the agent and which the principal here (as elsewhere) becomes involved, for to make Fedallah's fate come to pass Ahab and his quest are as "instrumental" as Moby Dick himself. For Fedallah, the meanings of the white whale and of Ahab coincide.

Ahab's complex conception of the white whale has received by far the most attention. It is not therefore necessary to discuss it here at any length. To Ahab, Moby Dick was a composite entity—physical power, wilful intelligence, and malignant divinity—a trinity of body, mind, and spirit in opposition to Ahab. Which of the three a reader chooses to emphasize as *the* meaning for Ahab is, as Melville clearly implies, a reflection of the reader's own personal character.

From his first encounter with Moby Dick, Ahab has hated him, and "at last came to identify with him, not only all his bodily woes, but all his intellectual and spiritual exasperations. . . . All that most maddens and torments; all that stirs up the lees of things; all truth with malice in it; all that cracks the sinews and cakes the brain; all the subtle demonisms of life and thought; all evil, to crazy Ahab, were visibly personified, and made practically assailable in Moby Dick. He piled upon the whale's white hump the sum of all the general rage and hate felt by his whole race from Adam down . . ." (183). Ahab is not sure whether the white whale is "agent" or "principal"; it is enough for him that the whale should be assailable. The whale may be only a "pasteboard mask," like "all visible objects," but in him Ahab sees "outrageous strength, with an inscrutable malice sinewing it," and he hates that "inscrutable thing" (162). As he says on the third day of the chase, "all the things that most exasperate and out-

rage mortal man, all these things are bodiless, but only bodiless as objects, not as agents. There's a most special, a most cunning, oh, a most malicious difference!" (555) Ahab's "great natural intellect" had itself become an agent, the "living instrument" of his monomania (184), which made him intent, not on profitable cruises or dutiful responsibility to his crew, not even on glory and adventure, but "on an audacious, immitigable, and supernatural revenge" (186), impious defiance, and despotic self-gratification.

III

Whereas Ahab's interpretations of the white whale have received much attention, Ishmael's have been almost equally neglected. But before Ahab reveals his problem and his purpose of hunting the white whale, Ishmael has already told us that "the problem of the universe" was revolving in him (156). When Ahab binds the crew with an oath to hunt Moby Dick to his death, the occasion produced in Ishmael "a wild, mystical, sympathetical feeling"; as he says, "Ahab's quenchless feud seemed mine" (176). He gave himself "up to the abandonment of the time and the place; but while yet all a-rush to encounter the whale, could see naught in that brute but the deadliest ill" (186).

Ishmael, however, is a thoughtful man— a Melville. And the problem of the universe and/or the whale went on revolving in him. He devotes an entire chapter to the attempt to say "what the white whale . . . at times . . . was to me." He begins with these words: "Aside from those more obvious considerations touching Moby Dick, which could not but occasionally awaken in any man's soul some alarm, there was another thought, or rather vague, nameless horror concerning him, which at times by its intensity completely overpowered all the rest; and yet so mystical and well nigh ineffable was it, that I almost despair of putting it in a comprehensible form. It was the whiteness of the whale that above all things appalled me. But how can I hope to explain myself here; and yet, in some dim, random way, *explain myself I must, else all these chapters might be naught*" (187, my italics). The rest of this famous chapter on the whiteness of the whale discusses *this* meaning—and it is surely significant that *no one else, not even Ahab,* appears to be troubled by this aspect of Moby Dick.[4] To Ahab and the others the whiteness is merely a useful but fortuitous aid in identifying a particular whale; only to Ishmael has the whiteness any further meaning at all.

Ishmael recognizes that there are innumerable "sweet, and honourable, and sublime" associations with whiteness (188), that, indeed, "whiteness . . . is at once the most meaning symbol of spiritual things, nay, the very veil of the Christian's Deity; and yet . . . it is the intensifying agent in things the most appalling to mankind" (194). The root of the horror inspired in him by whiteness,[5] Ishmael concludes, seems to be that whiteness symbolizes the "indefiniteness," the "heartless voids and immensities," the "dumb blankness" of the universe (194–5). Later, on reading about the "most wondrous phe-

[4] Pip is possibly the exception. At the end of the midnight scene on the forecastle during which the crewmen reveal the effects on them of the oath and the rum, Pip cries: "Lord help such jollies. . . . White squalls? white whale, shirr! shirr! Here have I heard all their chat just now, and the white whale—shirr! shirr!—but spoken of once! . . . Oh, thou big white God . . . have mercy on this small black boy . . ." (176).

[5] Whiteness is associated with most of the portentous events of the book. Not only is the white squid regarded as an unfavourable omen, but the white "spirit spout," first described by Fedallah in the Atlantic and frequently perceived thereafter on moonlit nights, is associated with the white whale, though never explained. The flame of the corpusants, defiantly addressed by Ahab, was white. Among other occurrences which might be mentioned the two most obvious are Ahab's white whalebone leg and, more significantly, the "lividly whitish" scar or brand which possibly streaked his body from crown to sole and for which numerous interpretations and explanations were offered by various members of the crew.

nomenon which the secret seas have hitherto revealed to mankind," the great squid, which appeared as a silent "great white mass . . . like a snow slide . . . no perceptible face or front . . . no conceivable token of either sensation or instinct; but . . . an unearthly, formless, chance-like apparition of life" (277), we are reminded of these phrases in Ishmael's conclusion. But in the chapter on "The Whiteness of the Whale" Ishmael goes on to interpret the whiteness as a symbol that the universe is a formless, indefinite blank, and that beauty and meaning are "but subtile deceits, not actually inherent in substances, but only laid on from without" by the observer (195). Here we quite obviously have again the idea of "I look, you look, he looks. . . ." The universe, this "rounder globe" is like the doubloon, and both are like the white whale—a blank existence upon which form or meaning is projected by the observer. Ishmael goes farther, to consider that light itself "remains white or colourless in itself" and requires a "medium" (presumably the "eyes" of some observer) if any colour is to be seen by the light (195). Even Ahab himself, when his "tormented spirit" was for a time dissociated from his monomaniac purpose, becomes a meaningless being. Melville employs the same metaphor of light to express this point, in the chapter entitled "The Chart," which explains how sometimes there would be a spontaneous rebellion of Ahab's "living principle or soul" against "the characterizing mind, which at other times employed it for its outer vehicle or agent. . . . Therefore, the tormented spirit that glared out of bodily eyes, when *what seemed Ahab* rushed from his room, was for a time but a vacated thing, a formless somnambulistic being, a ray of living light, to be sure, but without an object to colour, and therefore a blankness in itself" (201, my italics).

The meaning Ishmael finds in the white whale is obviously very different from any of Ahab's—and the difference is perhaps most briefly suggested by saying that to Ahab the white whale was a personification, a "pasteboard mask," or perhaps an effigy, of something otherwise unknown and unassailable; whereas to Ishmael the whale is merely a symbol. If afflicted with a monomania such as Ahab's, one can feel like assaulting and destroying a personification or effigy; but the only thing to do with a symbol is to understand it. Ishmael, therefore, saw the white whale as a symbol of what might be called a metaphysical hypothesis, and throughout the rest of the book he shows himself endeavouring to study the evidence for and against that hypothesis. He seeks not to destroy the whale for vengeance, profit, or pleasure, but simply to understand it, to comprehend it, to reduce the unknown to intelligibility. And this, he insists, is not a project to be pursued in a quiet study, ruminating over the partial and unreliable reports of other men (as provided in fragmentary books or faulty paintings of whales). As he puts it: "Only in the heart of quickest perils; only when within the eddyings of his angry flukes; only on the profound unbounded sea, can the fully invested whale be truly and livingly found out" (451).

The fact has been strangely overlooked that Ishmael, as well as Ahab, deliberately embarked in quest of the white whale. The others aboard the *Pequod* were pursuing other ends when they were irresistibly drawn into Ahab's wake. But Ishmael tells us in the first chapter that "chief among these motives" which induced him into going a-whaling "was the overwhelming idea of the great whale himself. Such a portentous and mysterious monster roused all my curiosity. . . . the great floodgates of the wonder-world swung open, and in the wild conceits that swayed me to my purpose, two and two there floated into my inmost soul, endless processions of the whale, and, mid most of them all, one grand hooded phantom, like a snow hill in the air" (6).

This curiosity, or passion to comprehend, explains why it is Ishmael (not Ahab, Starbuck, or anyone else) who is shown as being interested in every detail about whales, both species and individuals—the whales that appear in books, pictures, and doorknockers; that contribute food, oil, and corset stays; that are detected in mountain ridges and stars; that have been fossilized, worshipped, hunted, and scientifically studied; that have been dissected, analysed, and described to exhibit every possible characteristic. Understandably enough, he often feels that complete comprehension is impossible—"there is no earthly way of finding out precisely what the whale really looks like" (267); "the mystic-marked whale remains undecipherable" (306) and "dissect him how I may . . . I know him not, and never will" (377). Nevertheless, he must continue to make the attempt "to approve myself omnisciently exhaustive in the enterprise" (451), to pursue his "thoughts of this Leviathan" wherever they lead, through "the whole circle of the sciences, and all the generations of whales, and men, and mastodons, past, present, and to come, with all the revolving panoramas of empire on earth, and throughout the whole universe" (452).

This necessity to learn and include everything in order to comprehend the essential principle is the true artistic justification of Ishmael's compiling the mass of whaling details given in *Moby Dick*. He is attempting to see the whale not partially, as a personified malignancy, a natural peril, a challenge, or a monetary value, but omnisciently, as a possibly intelligible microcosm in a possibly intelligible cosmos. The meaning of the white whale, for Ishmael, seems to be either the totality or essential of all meanings—in a word, attainable only by omniscience.

Although Ishmael's details and measurements tell us much about the species to which the white whale belongs, knowledge of Moby Dick himself is provided before the final encounter by the several ships hailed by the *Pequod*. What information might have been given by the long-seasoned veteran whalers aboard the spectral and forlorn *Goney* was lost when her captain dropped his speaking trumpet in the very act of answering. Two of the others—the *Jungfrau* and the *Rosebud*—had never even heard of the white whale. The rolling *Bachelor* has heard of him but in its rollicking prosperity chooses not to believe in him. The *Town-Ho* regarded the white whale as an instrument of God's judgment and justice, and the *Jeroboam* went so far as to consider him "the Shaker God incarnated" (315). The *Samuel Enderby* had once encountered him, and her captain now wore a white whalebone arm as the price of his present wisdom; though he has seen him twice since, and recognizes that there would be both profit and glory in killing him, "he's best let alone" (439). The *Rachel* has lost a whole boat's crew, including the captain's twelve-year-old son. The *Delight* is burying the only body recovered of "five stout men" lost the previous day. For each ship Moby Dick has acquired a different meaning.

It is worth remembering that none of these ships sought the white whale; they came upon him (those that did) only by chance while they were hunting other whales, and each time (as in Ahab's own first encounter) Moby Dick was acting as the protector of those hunted whales. Only the *Pequod* deliberately sought out the white whale himself, and whereas on the other encounters he was shepherding other whales, he was a solitary when the *Pequod* came upon him. Moreover, only Ahab is able to "raise" the white whale on each of the three days of the chase. As he boasts: "I only; none of ye could have raised the White Whale first" (537). He is quite right: it is Ahab's whale they have been persuaded into chasing, and it is Ahab's whale they have found.

Indeed, it is not until the *third* day of the chase that the qualities perceived by Ahab in the whale become really apparent to the others aboard the *Pequod*. Ishmael gives us a careful description of Moby Dick when he is overtaken on the first day:

A gentle joyousness—a mighty mildness of repose in swiftness, invested the gliding whale. Not the white bull Jupiter swimming away with ravished Europa . . . not Jove, not that great majesty Supreme! did surpass the glorified White Whale as he so divinely swam. . . .

. . . No wonder there had been some among the hunters who namelessly transported and allured by all this serenity, had ventured to assail it; but had fatally found that quietude but the vesture of tornadoes. Yet calm, enticing calm, oh, whale! thou glidest on, to all who for the first time eye thee. . . .

And thus, through the serene tranquilities of the tropical sea, among waves whose hand-clappings were suspended by exceeding rapture, Moby Dick moved on, still withholding from sight the full terrors of his submerged trunk, entirely hiding the wrenched hideousness of his jaw. But soon the fore part of him slowly rose from the water; for an instant . . . and warningly waving his bannered flukes in the air, the grand god revealed himself . . . (538-9).

That first day the white whale treated all his pursuers as gently, if as warningly, as a patient mother might her wilfully erring children. And the second day he took away simultaneously both Ahab's "evil shadow," Fedallah, and Ahab's ivory leg—not even his remaining human one. No wonder Starbuck believed that "all good angels" were mobbing Ahab with warnings. "Oh, oh,—Impiety and blasphemy to hunt him more!" (552)

The third day ended the drama—except for the epilogue about Ishmael. Now it is certain that Ishmael is saved not for the technical reason that a narrator must be left alive to tell the story—for when throughout the book has Melville ever allowed himself to be cramped by the exigencies of technique? No. Ishmael was saved because he alone had learned anything from all their experiences, because he had, in effect, solved *his* problem, had triumphed over the symbolic white whale and the universe. He had, I think, proved his hypothesis—to his own satisfaction at least—and the *very means of his salvation* symbolizes the truth, for him, of *his* meaning of the white whale.

That marvellous concluding paragraph of the book contains words which can almost be taken as a summary description of Ishmael's role throughout the entire story:

So, floating on the margin of the ensuing scene, and in full sight of it, when the half-spent suction of the sunk ship reached me, I was then, but slowly, drawn towards the closing vortex. When I reached it, it had subsided to a creamy pool. Round and round, then, and ever contracting towards the button-like black bubble at the axis of that slowly wheeling circle, like another Ixion I did revolve. Till, gaining that vital centre, the black bubble upward burst; and now, liberated by reason of its cunning spring, and, owing to its great buoyancy, rising with great force, the coffin lifebuoy shot lengthwise from the sea, fell over, and floated by my side. Buoyed up by that coffin, for almost one whole day and night, I floated on a soft and dirge-like main. The unharming sharks, they glided by as if with padlocks on their mouths; the savage sea-hawks sailed with sheathed beaks. On the second day, a sail drew near, nearer, and picked me up at last. It was the devious-cruising Rachel, that in her retracing search after her missing children, only found another orphan.

IV

But let us look again at that coffin, which was, after all, not a coffin. This long wooden box, like everything else in the universe, shifts its meanings according to the point of view of the beholder.

First, consider its creator. Like his handiwork, the carpenter and coffin-maker is more things than one. Ahab addresses him once as "manmaker" (466) and later calls him "as unprincipled as the gods, and as much of a jack-of-all-trades" (518). He is not only carpenter and coffin-maker but painter, apothecary, surgeon, dentist, and leg-maker to Ahab. His attitude towards the society and universe in which he lives is one of negatives: indifference, "uncom-

promisedness," and unintelligence. As a creator, "he did not seem to work so much by reason or by instinct" or by training, "but merely by a kind of deaf and dumb, spontaneous literal process. He was a pure manipulater . . ." (464). His most remarkable characteristic was "a certain impersonal stolidity as it were . . . it seemed one with the general stolidity discernible in the whole visible world; which while pauselessly active in uncounted modes, still eternally holds its peace, and ignores you, though you dig foundations for cathedrals. . . . He was a stript abstract; an unfractioned integral; uncompromised as a newborn babe; living without premeditated reference to this world or the next. . . . He was like one of those unreasoning but still highly useful . . . contrivances [such as a pocket-knife with an assortment of tools attached]. . . . So, if his superiors wanted to use the carpenter for a screw-driver, all they had to do was to open that part of him . . . or if for tweezers, take him up by the legs, and there they were" (463-4). Thus the carpenter, like the doubloon and the white whale, had a multiplicity of uses and meanings.

Queequeg in his sickness had asked for a "canoe" like those "all whalemen who died in Nantucket were laid in" (473). And he had admired this Nantucket custom because it was agreeable to his own race's making canoes in which to send forth their dead warriors. But to the eyes of the carpenter and the crew the object requested was a coffin, not a canoe. And out of "some heathenish, coffin-coloured old lumber aboard, which, upon a long previous voyage, had been cut from the aboriginal groves of the Lackaday islands" (474) the carpenter made the coffin to fit one individual man by exact measurement.

But when Queequeg recalled some undone duties ashore he changed his mind about dying and changed the canoe-coffin into a sea-chest. Not only that. He spent many hours carving the lid, copying the tattooing on his body, with which he had earlier found resemblances upon the gold doubloon. "This tattooing," we are told, "had been the work of a departed prophet . . . who by those hieroglyphic marks had written out . . . a complete theory of the heavens and the earth, and a mystical treatise on the art of attaining truth" (477).

It was this composite creation which saved Ishmael—for when the *Pequod*'s original lifebuoy sank with the man it had been dropped to save, Queequeg was the one who suggested that the canoe-coffin-seachest-theory-of-the-universe-and-treatise-on-the-art-of-attaining-truth should be transformed into a lifebuoy. No means of salvation could be more fitting for Ishmael, the man whose constant art and endeavour had been to discover a truth by which he might live.[6]

What might be termed the coffin theme pervades the book from beginning to end. In the opening paragraph Ishmael tells us that he recognizes the time for him to get to sea by certain symptoms: "whenever it is a damp, drizzly November in my soul . . . whenever I find myself involuntarily pausing before coffin-ware-

houses, and bringing up the rear of every funeral I meet" (1). He first hears of Queequeg when a certain innkeeper named Peter Coffin assigns him the same bed. Tashtego almost found himself "coffined, hearsed, and tombed" (343) in the sinking whale's head until "delivered" by Queequeg's "obstetrics." To Fedallah, Moby Dick was the first hearse, the *Pequod* itself the second hearse in that it carried the coffin-lifebuoy. And the *Pequod*, moreover, is not only hearse but general coffin and tomb for the little world of men aboard. Ahab, who more than once dreamed of hearses, had been forewarned by Fedallah: "neither hearse nor coffin can be thine" (491). Ishmael survives by means of a "canoe" chosen by Queequeg for *his* special purposes (to be buried in at sea) ; but Queequeg succumbs aboard a "hearse" selected at the Nantucket wharf by Ishmael. Meanings fluctuate and change here too.

So, in its own way, the coffin-lifebuoy-treatise becomes one with the doubloon and the ship and the white whale—and they all symbolize the universe, incorporating Nature's "cunning alphabet whereby selecting and combining as he pleases, each man reads his own peculiar lesson according to his own peculiar mind and mood." Herman Melville's *Moby Dick*, like Nature, has its alphabet, and we are each left to read it for ourselves with whatever "outreaching comprehensiveness of sweep" (452) we are able to encompass.

---

[6] When the sociable little Pip, who lacked Ishmael's boldness and hard-won comprehension, was abandoned in the sea for a few hours, he went insane because of "the awful lonesomeness . . . the intense concentration of self in the middle of such a heartless immensity" (412). "The sea had jeeringly kept his [Pip's] finite body up, but drowned the infinite of his soul" (413). Pip had had no lifebuoy of any kind to sustain him.

Sherman Paul

Melville's "The *Town-Ho*'s Story"

OF THE nine encounters with whaling ships in *Moby-Dick*, "The *Town-Ho*'s Story" is the first on-the-sea report of the white whale. Unlike the other reports this story can stand alone artistically and was actually printed separately in *Harper's* in 1851. R. S. Forsythe says that "since this sailor's yarn is not closely woven into the fabric of the novel, there is no awkwardness in its publication as an independent work; it is complete in itself." [1] This, however, does not mean that the story is not integrally necessary to the deepest understanding of Moby-Dick, for "The *Town-Ho*'s Story" offers an alternative and variant meaning of the significance of the white whale. It is a tragic but not an unwarrantably pessimistic tale that inspires an awe of, but not an aversion to, the whale; it marks the beginning of that feeling of attraction for the whale which Melville nurses carefully in the seven remaining stories and without which the dramatic focus on Ahab's monomania would be diminished. Furthermore, the themes and characters of the story, and its symbolic techniques, make it Melville's "Ethan Brand," the kind of short story the significance of which, as in the case of Hawthorne and similarly of Melville, penetrates the main body of an author's work.

The story itself, stripped of long digressions for its recital, is told with yarnlike ease at the Golden Inn in Lima, Peru. Its portentous meaning, which, Melville wrote, "seemed obscurely to involve with the whale a certain wondrous, inverted visitation of one of those so-called judgments of God," [2] arises seemingly from the simple fabric of a sailor's recollection. The audience of entertainment-expecting Dons of "This dull, warm, most lazy and hereditary land" are driven to outbursts of incredulity much as the reader who at this point in *Moby-Dick* first encounters the whale and who must readjust his faculties and shift his expectations for even more "wondrous visitations" to come. The scene of the telling of the story in "corrupt" Lima, to men conditioned by Catholic mysteries and yet unbelieving, forms a contrast to the heightened all-pervading religious content of the tale and reaffirms Ishmael's devotion to the mysterious fatalities of life. The humor of their skepticism—for the faith of the landlocked, comfortable, aristocratic wine drinkers who never put to sea is another "tale" in the Holy Evangelists—moves Ishmael to ask for "the largest sized Evangelists," even to swear on the Testament. [3]

"The *Town-Ho*'s Story" contains Melville's germ of tragedy and his portrayal of the retributive justice of the whale. In this there is a glimmer of relief from the overwhelming sense of evil that engulfs Ahab. For here the whale carries out a cosmic decree that more nearly accords with our ideas of Christian justice. And there is more: an affirmation of the sanctity of personality and of the kind of democracy that recognizes kings in commoners. As Charles Olson has indicated, "Democracy, to Melville, merely gave man his chance to be just—in politics, society *and* intimate

---

[1] "Herman Melville's 'The *Town-Ho*'s Story,'" *Notes and Queries*, CLXVIII, 314 (May 4, 1935).

[2] *Moby-Dick* (London, 1922), I, 306.

[3] Ibid., p. 330.

Reprinted by permission from *American Literature*, XXI (1949), 212–222.

human relations." [4] The idea of the inviolability of man's personality was the key to what Melville called, in his "Hawthorne and His Mosses," "that unshackled, democratic spirit of Christianity in all things." [5] Christian democracy was that democracy in which the laws were more in accord with divine law and the natural dignity of all men. Melville thought that after eighteen hundred years it was democracy that should realize this fundamental Christianity, this unique value of the human being which, when recognized, was manifested by men in bonds of love, sympathy, and charity. Startled by the apathy of mankind toward humanity caught up in poverty and death in the streets of Liverpool, as described in *Redburn*, he went further to protest against the inhumanity of law in *White-Jacket*. Here, he cited Blackstone on the Law of Nature as a moral justification for mutiny [6] and dramatized man's instinctive sense of his own dignity as justification for defiance of authority. When White Jacket was arraigned at the mast to be flogged for no offense by a wilful captain who "would not forgive God Almighty," he decided to rush against the captain and pitch him into the sea. In describing White Jacket's justification for this defiance of authority, Melville wrote:

But the thing that swayed me to my purpose was not altogether the thought that Captain Claret was about to degrade me, and that I had taken an oath with my soul that he should not. No, I felt my man's manhood so bottomless within me, that no word, no blow, no scourge of Captain Claret could cut me deep enough for that. I but swung to an instinct in me—the instinct diffused through all animated nature, the same that prompts even a worm to turn under heel. Locking souls with him, I meant to drag Captain Claret from this earthly tribunal of his to that of Jehovah, and let Him decide between us. [7]

[4] "Lear and Moby Dick," *Twice a Year*, I, 188 (Fall-Winter, 1938).

[5] *Billy Budd and Other Prose Pieces* (London, 1924), p. 136.

[6] *White-Jacket* (London, 1922), p. 181.

[7] Ibid., pp. 352–353.

The sense of tragedy comes when this essential dignity is abused, whether through the self-willed arbitrary law of a captain or through Ahab's misuse of his own personality. In both it was the God-idea in man—as Starbuck recognized it—which should be used in better ways than revenge on man or animal.

Out of this conflict between the different orders of law and the warrant for the higher law which Melville dramatizes in terms of the dignity of man grows the problem of good and evil. *White-Jacket*, *Billy Budd*, and "The *Town-Ho*'s Story" have this as their basic situation: the instance of Ushant's beard as a symbol of his dignity brings him before the mast in *White-Jacket*; the essential innocence of Billy Budd is at the mercy of human law as executed by the all-knowing, godlike Captain Vere; Radney, the mate of the *Town-Ho*, goes beyond the law of the ship and the divine law and brings down upon himself the force of divine justice.

In Melville's development of this problem, "The *Town-Ho*'s Story" stands midway between *White-Jacket* and *Billy Budd*. For White Jacket's intention of letting God decide is fulfilled by the whale in the action between Steelkilt and Radney. Their story is a simple one. [8] When the whaler *Town-Ho* sprang a leak in the Pacific, it became necessary to man the pumps almost continuously. Steelkilt, "a Lakeman and desperado from Buffalo," exhausted by his turn at the pumps, was ordered to sweep down and remove some excrement from the deck. In so ordering, the mate Radney had overlooked the rules applying to such duties and had issued a command to Steelkilt only to "sting and insult" him. Radney was moved to do this because he was "ugly" and resented Steelkilt's physical nobility. It was only conventional, Melville points out, "that when a person placed in command over his fellow men finds one of them to be very significantly his superior in general pride of manhood . . . he will pull

[8] "The *Town-Ho*'s Story," *Moby-Dick*, I, 306–330.

down and pulverize that subaltern's tower, and make a little heap of dust of it." Steel-kilt "instinctively saw all this" but, like a "really valiant" man, refused to give way to passion and so arouse further anger; he merely refused on the grounds that it was not his duty. Again Radney ordered, cursing him, and threatened Steelkilt with a hammer. And when Radney, in defiance of Steelkilt's warnings, grazed him with the hammer, the latter smashed the mate's jaw.

Mutiny followed. Steelkilt and his fellow seamen entrenched themselves and refused to man the pumps until the captain swore not to flog them. In the face of the captain's indecision Steelkilt twice shouted, ". . . treat us decently, and we're your men; but we won't be flogged." When neither party would give in, Steelkilt followed the Captain's orders and allowed himself to be confined with his nine followers in the fore-castle. But "The fetid closeness of the air, and a famishing diet . . . constrained" all but three to surrender. Then Steelkilt, "maddened by his long entombment in a place as black as the bowels of despair"— a Melvillean hell—proposed to the two other seamen to break out and take the ship. The other two, however, betrayed him, and all three were bound and hoisted into the rigging for the remainder of the night. On the following morning the captain flogged the two betrayers into lifelessness, but Steelkilt forewarned the captain with a "hiss." (One is reminded here of old Ushant's saying after he was flogged that " 'tis no dishonour when he who would dishonour you, only dishonours himself. . . . My beard is my own.") [9] The captain, apparently recognizing in this defiance Steelkilt's inviolability, ordered him to be cut down, but Radney refused to take heed and personally laid on the punishment.

When the normal life of the ship was resumed, the seamen agreed to Steelkilt's plan of giving up the chase by no longer singing out for whales, and returning to port to desert ship. Meanwhile Steelkilt

planned his revenge—to crush Radney's skull and drop him into the sea. But at the moment of execution, "by a mysterious fatality, Heaven itself seemed to step in to take out of his hands into its own the damning thing he would have done." "Just between daybreak and sunrise," the top-watch spied out Moby-Dick and involuntarily cried, " 'Jesu, what a whale,' " calling out Christ's name instinctively at the critical moment when the whale had come to take from Steelkilt his revenge. In the hunt for Moby-Dick that followed, Radney was tossed into the sea and destroyed when his boat struck the whale. After the crew reached port, they deserted ship and, detaining the captain by the sheer force of Steelkilt's will, "forever got the start on their Captain." In the end, Steelkilt triumphed; God had decided, by means of Moby-Dick, between Steelkilt and Radney.

Melville's handling of the story sharpens this central idea. In the character of Steel-kilt he creates another handsome sailor, who, although an inlander, is, like Jack Chase, "wild-ocean born" and "wild-ocean nurtured." [10] He is of the pattern of Billy Budd and Chase in his personal strength and beauty, his seamanship, his qualities of leadership and geniality, and his "off-hand unaffectedness of natural regality." [11] The type of person Melville portrayed in Steel-kilt he describes in *Billy Budd* as "an amusing character all but extinct now, but occasionally to be encountered, and in a form yet more amusing than the original, at the tiller of the boats on the tempestuous Erie Canal or, more likely, vapouring in the groggeries along the towpath." [12] And like Jack Chase, who was "a stickler for the rights of man," [13] the canaller "was the champion (ashore) ; afloat the spokesman; on every suitable occasion always foremost." [14] Steelkilt became the embodiment

[9] *White-Jacket*, p. 461.

[10] *Moby-Dick*, I, 309.
[11] *Billy Budd and Other Prose Pieces*, p. 5.
[12] Ibid., p. 6.
[13] *White-Jacket*, p. 19.
[14] *Billy Budd and Other Prose Pieces*, p. 6.

of the American savage, the natural man, a being free from civilized hypocrisy. Melville describes him fondly as the fulfilment of his idea of the democratic hero, sharing that "democratic dignity which, on all hands, radiates without end from God . . . our divine equality!" [15] "Steelkilt was a tall and noble animal with a head like a Roman, and a flowing golden beard like the tasseled housings of your last viceroy's snorting charger; and a brain, and a heart, and a soul in him, gentlemen, which had made Steelkilt Charlemagne, had he been born son to Charlemagne's father." [16] He would have fitted Melville's description of the canaller as "the young Alexander curbing the fiery Bucephalus." [17]

One can hardly fail to see the physical mold of Steelkilt. What goes unemphasized in this characterization, only to rise foremost in that of Billy Budd, is Melville's corollary that "The moral nature was seldom out of keeping with the physical make." [18] Steelkilt, like Melville's cherished friend Jack Chase and "peacemaker" Billy Budd, whom all his fellows "love," maintains throughout the story a certain passiveness, intensified and dramatized by the exceptional strength and violence of the man. Except when threatened with flogging and abused by Radney, he follows orders. He has a sense of duty which Melville points up by having Steelkilt save the crew by cutting the line holding their boat fast to the whale (which in this instance, though fulfilling justice in the destruction of Radney, is still the symbol of universal physical force that gives the whale an almost Old Testament significance as the bearer of both wrath and justice). It is Steelkilt, also, who meets his captain with Christ's words, "I come in peace," [19] and who seeks revenge only when "maddened" by the hell of confinement and stung by flogging to "the ven-

15 *Moby-Dick*, I, 144.

16 Ibid., p. 311.

17 *Billy Budd and Other Prose Pieces*, p. 6.

18 Ibid., p. 6.

19 *Moby-Dick*, I, 329.

tricles of his heart." [20] Again, the heart as symbol of feeling and of man's innate dignity contrasts with the cold intellectuality of a Radney, Claggart, Bland, or Jackson. Each of them partakes of that depravity which "towards the accomplishment of an aim which in wantonness of malignity would seem to partake of the insane, he will direct a cool judgment sagacious and sound." [21] Against this background, Ahab's tragedy comes to mean the same thing as Radney's: Ahab's violation of his own personality or heart by his will makes him proudly assert that other men are his hands and feet, thereby violating them and the natural law; and this is reflected in his consequent inability to feel, to sympathize, and to look into man's eyes. His tragedy is a self-wrought loneliness arising from the separation of men from men by the separation of mind and heart. For Radney destruction came about through his own rash ignorance; for Ahab, through his acceptance of fate as a rationalization for his wilfulness.

Against this formula for monomania, Melville indirectly builds up Steelkilt's moral nature by creating in him a Christ-indwelling figure. Radney's offense had insulted Steelkilt "as though Radney had spat in his face." [22] And this action, symbolic of striking the godhead in man, is reminiscent of a similar incident of the individual versus authority in Matthew 27:30, where the soldiers spit on Christ. And there are other more marked symbolic Christian referents in Steelkilt's passivity, his betrayal "at midnight," his coming from the depths of the forecastle, and the stringing of the three seamen in the rigging. Probably the three mutineers are intended to remind one of Christ's crucifixion, for after the beating of the two betrayers Melville compares their lifelessness to "the two crucified thieves." [23] This is enough to sug-

20 Ibid., p. 324.

21 *Billy Budd and Other Prose Pieces*, p. 46.

22 *Moby-Dick*, I, 313.

23 Ibid., p. 322.

gest the Christian insight that Melville wished to provide in his characterization of Steelkilt. For Melville, befriended by Jack Chase, the humanity of helping "a poor stranger in a strait" was a Christlike thing, and even for a man of violence, a redeeming quality.[24]

Melville merely sketches the figure of Radney as a symbol of evil. He describes him as "brutal," "overbearing," "fearless," "ugly," "hardy," and "malicious." He provoked Steelkilt by failing to show him "that common decency of human recognition which is the meanest slave's right."[25] Where Ahab has strength of purpose and a tragic perception of his willingness to fulfil fate, Radney has only maliciousness. But Radney, too, had his saving part—like Jackson and Claggart, to whom he is more nearly akin, and whom Melville pities as men of sorrows. He is said to have "some good-hearted traits," just as Ahab had his "humanities." What these were in Radney's case the story never reveals, unless in his widow's grief we recognize the one bond of love that tied him to humanity. Coming at the very end of the tale, it bears the weight of final verity, the one redeeming feeling and value of this cosmic struggle.

But there seems to be more to Radney's tragedy than this. A forecast of doom can be sensed in the symbolic details of the story: the leak that compels the action that follows is never found because it is too far below the ship's water line; submerged in evil, in mystery, it is beyond man's probing. The leak widens mysteriously, and only Radney feels apprehensive over making port. The self-contained ship is somehow rent, and the sea-evil enters, and from this moment Radney "was doomed and made mad."[26] Melville says that Radney was moved by a "cozening fiend," was "predestined," was "branded for the slaughter by the gods."[27] In fact, "a strange fatality

pervades the whole career of these events, as if verily mapped out before the world itself was charted."[28] This can be seen in the symbolic merger of the white-bandaged Radney and the white whale, where the whale again takes on an evil significance, and evil blends with evil, at the same time that this judgment of God gives Steelkilt his salvation.[29] That the smallest event should be so ordered was the sign of fatality; the ways of necessity, as Babbalanja observed in *Mardi*, left more to man—the choice of evil and a self-imposed and self-willed fate.

There are two modes by which Melville further illumines what he means by Christian democracy: the moral contrast of the tale with the scene of its recital, and explanations in the story of references to America. The Peruvian backdrop of decadent Christianity and the ship-symbol serve to bring into focus the struggle for faith in America. The land of the Dons has no more autos-da-fé, but Don Pedro thought "that at your temperate North the generations were as cold and holy as the hills."[30] In explaining this Melville recreates the savage-civilized life of the American interior by imaginatively developing its parallels to the antipodal societies he himself has found in the world—the primitive life of *Typee* and the regimentation of a frigate. The interior is a world in itself; its great lakes are oceans with romantic Polynesian isles like the great oceans and bordered by a variety of life as ancient and barbaric, as new and civilized as any provided by history. It has its "paved capitals of Buffalo and Cleveland," its "ancient and unentered forests." The link between this "Christian cornfield" and the "barbaric seas" is the Erie Canal, whose "one continual stream of Venetianly corrupt and often lawless life" flows "by rows of snow white chapels, whose spires stand almost like milestones." To the cornfield of churches the waterborne evil of the canal brings the old and

[24] Ibid., p. 317.
[25] Ibid., pp. 309–310.
[26] Ibid., p. 310.
[27] Ibid., pp. 312, 314, 315.
[28] Ibid., p. 327.
[29] Ibid., p. 327.
[30] Ibid., p. 317.

new corruptions, the wicked "Mark Antony" of a canaller, and the challenge of its commerce and vulgarity. But it is not the canaller whom Melville despises; rather, it is the American pagan "under the long-flung shadow, and snug patronizing lee of churches" which serve as mileposts along the way. This disunity and cross-purpose, represented by the canal which separates as well as connects, is Melville's picture of the outrunning of the religious support of democracy and of the ever-grasping, ever-extending rapaciousness of American life.[31]

This apparent failure in the basis of American democracy has its counterpart in the mutiny that takes place on the *Town-Ho*. The ship-as-society or world-in-itself is a recurrent symbol in Melville's work and in "The *Town-Ho*'s Story" becomes a stage on which is acted one possible failure in human institutions. The captain, "believing that rare good luck awaited him in those latitudes," little heeds the sea-evil, relies wholly on his pumps and stout men. But the evil reaches deeper and brings on a mutiny by enlarging the sense of separation that had taken place between Steelkilt and Radney, or, symbolically between those who rule and those who obey. Melville suggests that all would have been well if Rad-

[31] Ibid., pp. 308–309, 315–317.

ney had only recognized that portion of the right of manhood in Steelkilt which was due even a slave—but Radney "did not love Steelkilt." Law, to have religious sanction, must be tempered with love, Christian love and compassion, and for this fundamental right, like the French in 1848, the "sea-Parisians"[32] patrolled their barricades. More was at stake than the ship *Town-Ho*; it was a matter of the humane basis of society, of Christian democracy.

The vindication of mutiny in the name of personality and the retributive role of the whale are the secret parts of the story that Ahab never hears. Ahab, as one who himself felt oppressed, might have responded to Steelkilt's rebellion on the grounds of personality. For in his soliloquy on fire Ahab proclaims his inviolate part, "the queenly personality" that "lives in me, and feels her royal rights."[33] But as oppressor, intent on shaping the world to his monomaniac vision of it, he had seen the cosmic evil, but could not hearken to his humanities and give love its redemptive place. The central meaning of "The *Town-Ho*'s Story" is the reaffirmation of the heart with which Melville arms his readers for the greater tragedy to come.

[32] Ibid., p. 318.

[33] *Moby-Dick*, II, 282.

Don Geiger

Melville's Black God: Contrary Evidence in "The *Town-Ho*'s Story"

THAT Herman Melville in *Moby-Dick* rejected important features of the Calvinistic version of God has been frequently maintained, if not universally accepted. The episode of "The *Town-Ho*'s Story," Chapter LIV, in the context of the whole book [1] presents impressive evidence for this interpretation. Yet the story has proved difficult for critics to explain in their infrequent comments on the episode.

Once the story is considered in terms of its thematic implications, the temptation is apparently to think of it as a condensed illustration of the meaning of the book as a whole. This is the opinion, I think, even of Mr. Sherman Paul, who suggests that in this episode "there is a glimmer of relief from the overwhelming sense of evil that engulfs Ahab. For here the whale carries out a cosmic decree that more nearly accords with our ideas of Christian justice." [2] Mr. Paul (whose entire article should be read for a study of the episode's democratic theme), though he here provides a valuable hint for tracing out a distinction between the meanings of the episode and the book as a whole, seems personally to think of the difference as one of degree: "Against this background, Ahab's tragedy comes to mean the same thing as Radney's. . . ." [3]

Mr. Lawrance Thompson, because he has perhaps a securer sense of the book's argu-

ment against God, does not make this mistake. Instead, however, he plainly takes the episode for an "epitome" of the total book's portrait of a wicked God. [4] Now there is nothing in this episode which contradicts the meanings which Mr. Thompson attributes to the whole book. But in insisting that the chapter is an epitome of the whole, he is forced to disregard what is so clear to Mr. Paul and, I think, to any disinterested reader of the chapter. That is, simply, this chapter records the divine punishment of injustice and, correlatively, the divine enforcement of justice.

Mr. Thompson's difficulty is caused, I think, simply because Melville is interested in this chapter in giving the God His due. Mr. Thompson suggests that Melville had been led into "a quaintly childish oversimplification: if the Calvinistic God did not inspire love, that God must inspire hate. If He was not white, He was black." [5] But Melville's is not a mere propaganda art in which he paints God in the unrelieved colors of villainy: and "The *Town-Ho*'s Story" is a vivid example of Melville's consideration of the evidence which might justify the God whom he ultimately rejects.

The meaning of the episode does not admit of a simple translation into paraphrase, of course, but we might roughly phrase the attitude or opinion revealed in this way: "O I grant you, Calvinist, that you have seen some of the features of God, and that the God you see may even at times be a

[1] Herman Melville, *Moby-Dick*, ed. Luther S. Mansfield and Howard P. Vincent (New York, 1952), pp. 240–261.

[2] Sherman Paul, "Melville's 'The *Town-Ho*'s Story,'" *American Literature*, XXI, 213 (May, 1949).

[3] *Ibid.*, p. 217.

[4] Lawrance Thompson, *Melville's Quarrel with God* (Princeton, 1952), p. 207.

[5] *Ibid.*, p. 422.

Reprinted by permission from *American Literature*, XXV (1954), 464–471.

just God. But notice, even in His acts of justice He reveals a barbarous character whose justice may well become as irregular and inhumane as His laws are liable to become capricious." This irregular justice and inhumane law are shown, then, in the fate of Ahab and the crew of the *Pequod*.

But let us turn to the episode itself for a clearer understanding of its meaning. It is presented by a flashback, in which Ishmael tells the story to a group of high-born Spanish gentlemen (thus describing to these orthodox Catholic landsmen an even more marvelous divinity than the miraculous one to which they pay their skeptical and gentlemanly respects). As Ishmael prepares to tell the story, he summarizes by saying that it "seemed obscurely to involve with the whale a certain wondrous, inverted visitation of one of those so-called judgments of God which at times are said to overtake some men." [6] It is an "inverted" visitation because it upsets the secular arrangement of human power; it is a judgment of "God" because it punishes, not the man guilty of a secular offense (Steelkilt), but the man guilty of an offense against natural, or divine right (Radney).

The *Town-Ho* represents roughly the state (particularly, of course, the American, democratic, puritan state). Steelkilt (we may notice a double-pun: Steel-kills and Steel-dressed, or armored-in-steel) is a common citizen (ordinary seaman) aboard this boat. But though this is his social status, he is one of nature's noblemen: "Steelkilt was a tall and noble animal with a head like a Roman, and a flowing golden beard like the tasseled housings of your last viceroy's snorting charger; and a brain, and a heart, and a soul in him, gentlemen, which had made Steelkilt Charlemagne, had he been born son to Charlemagne's father." [7] Steelkilt too is a "Lakeman, in the land-locked heart of our America, had yet been nurtured by all those agrarian free-booting impressions popularly connected

[6] *Moby-Dick*, p. 241.

[7] Ibid., p. 245.

with the open ocean. For in their interflowing aggregate, those grand fresh-water seas of ours—Erie, and Ontario, and Huron, and Superior, and Michigan,—possess an ocean-like expansiveness, with many of the ocean's noblest traits. . . ." [8]

Radney is Steelkilt's social superior, chief mate of the *Town-Ho*, an agent of the state's authority. But in the eyes of nature, he is Steelkilt's inferior, as "ugly as a mule. . . ." [9] He is, too, though he has spent his life on the sea, a spiritual landsman, for Radney, "though in his infancy he may have laid him down on the lone Nantucket beach, to nurse at his maternal sea; though in after life he had long followed our austere Atlantic and your contemplative Pacific; yet was he quite as vengeful and full of social quarrel as the backwoods seaman, fresh from the latitudes of buck-horn handled Bowie-knives." [10] Thus, Steelkilt (to the world's eye, a landsman) and Radney (to the world's eye, a seaman) in reality bear, in important characteristics, just the reverse relationship to one another.

Though Steelkilt is a wild "mariner," naturally superior to his social superior, he can be expected not to disrupt society, if he is justly treated. He "might yet by inflexible firmness, only tempered by that common decency of human recognition which is the meanest slave's right; thus treated, this Steelkilt had long been retained harmless and docile." [11] But Radney becomes envious of Steelkilt's natural superiority. "Now, as you well know, it is not seldom the case in this conventional world of ours—watery or otherwise; that when a person placed in command over his fellow-men finds one of them to be very significantly his superior in general pride of manhood, straightway against that man he conceives an unconquerable dislike and bitterness; and if he have a chance he will

[8] Ibid., pp. 242–243.

[9] Ibid., p. 245.

[10] Ibid., p. 243.

[11] Ibid., pp. 243–244.

pull down and pulverize that subaltern's tower, and make a little heap of dust of it." Thus, Radney "did not love Steelkilt, and Steelkilt knew it." [12]

One evening Radney comes on several sailors, Steelkilt among them, working at the pumps to bail out water that has issued into the *Town-Ho* through a mysterious leak. They have been joking that Radney is solicitous of the fate of the ship only because "of his being part owner in her." Though he knows Radney is approaching, Steelkilt, foreshadowing his social unmanageability, keeps up the "bantering." In revenge, Radney orders the men to work to the limit of their endurance, after which he orders Steelkilt to clean the deck of "some offensive matters consequent upon allowing a pig to run at large." Steelkilt is already worn out, and, in any event, this is an insulting order because "this broom business is the prescriptive province of the boys" aboard the ship.[13]

Steelkilt is reluctant to quarrel, though the order is manifestly unjust: ". . . that strange forbearance and unwillingness to stir up the deeper passionateness in any already ireful being—a repugnance most felt, when felt at all, by really valiant men even when aggrieved—this nameless phantom feeling, gentlemen, stole over Steelkilt." He replies reasonably, then, that the work should not be his, but "Radney replied with an oath, in a most domineering and outrageous manner unconditionally reiterating his command" and threateningly picks up a hammer. After other threats by Radney, at last Steelkilt warns him to keep the hammer away, but Radney insultingly touches the hammer to Steelkilt's cheek. Steelkilt immediately breaks the mate's jaw.[14]

This begins Steelkilt's rebellion against the established authority of the *Town-Ho*, in which he is joined by several others. Ordered to work by the captain, they refuse

[12] Ibid., p. 245.

[13] Ibid., pp. 247–248.

[14] Ibid., pp. 247–248.

to do so, but, since Steelkilt is unwilling to act violently against the captain, they voluntarily enter the forecastle, where they are locked in. From this imprisonment, where they are slowly starved by the captain's orders, all but two of the men have deserted the forecastle by the fifth day (in Steelkilt's dark retreat and his desertion by friends, there are overtones—in terms of what follows—of Jesus's having hidden from those who did not believe in Him, five days before the Passover).[15]

At this point, Steelkilt is maddened into planning a desperate attack on the entire ship the following morning. The two men remaining with him agree to the plan, but in fact betray Steelkilt (reminding us somewhat, in the context of the episode, of the betrayals of Judas and Peter).

Despite this, they are sentenced with Steelkilt to a flogging, and the captain beats the two men with a rope "till they yelled no more, but lifelessly hung their heads sideways, as the two crucified thieves are drawn." [16] Thus, clearly, does the scene become an emblem of the crucifixion and Steelkilt becomes an angry Christ. A gag taken from his mouth, Steelkilt hisses: "What I say is this—and mind it well—if you flog me, I murder you!" The captain, unfrightened, takes up the rope but Steelkilt warns him again, and yet a third time: "Steelkilt here hissed out something, inaudible to all but the Captain; who, to the amazement of all hands, started back, paced the deck rapidly two or three times, and then suddenly throwing down his rope, said, 'I won't do it—let him go—cut him down: dy'e hear?' " [17]

Mr. Thompson sees this as the freeman's rebellion against God, referring to the "God-like Captain." [18] This interpretation is accurate in part: to the extent that Steel-

[15] "The Gospel According to John," *The Revised Standard Edition of the New Testament* (New York, 1946), chap. xii, p. 217.

[16] *Moby-Dick*, p. 254.

[17] Ibid.

[18] Thompson, op. cit., p. 208.

kilt has merged with the character of Christ, his "captain" becomes related to the godhead. But we may best understand the figure of the captain, in this connection, as representing the false but frequent Puritan (Calvinist) identity of the will of the church authority or even the secular authority with the will of God. The true will of God remains to be revealed, in the monstrous might of Moby Dick.

Thus the captain is in this scene essentially emblematic not of a divine but of a secular authority; and in this scene of crucifixion, like the governor Pilate, he washes his hands of the affair. We are reminded of the Pilate of Mark's gospel, who thought Jesus innocent: "Why, what evil has he done?" but nevertheless, under the urgings of the chief priests, "delivered him to be crucified." [19] For despite the captain's refusal to execute the punishment in his own authority, the punishment is administered: the chief mate Radney snatches up the rope and, though made to pause by Steelkilt's "hiss," at last whips the pinioned Steelkilt.[20]

To avenge this unjust punishment, Steelkilt plans to murder Radney. But before he can accomplish his vengeance, "Heaven itself seemed to step in to take out of his hands into its own the damning thing he would have done." [21] The agent is Moby Dick, who, sighted and followed by the *Town-Ho*'s crew, deliberately and savagely kills Radney. Thus the whale becomes an emblem of divine justice, able to avenge social injustice against all the arrayed forces of secular society.

Later Steelkilt, who has deserted the ship at the first opportunity, comes across the captain at sea. "The captain presented a pistol." But Steelkilt "laughed him to scorn; assuring him that if the pistol so much as clicked in the lock, he would bury

him in bubbles and foam." The captain realizes that the forces of the divinity are aligned against him, apparently, for he yields to the threat and cries, "What do you want of me?" Steelkilt asks for sufficient time to make good his escape and makes the captain swear to the proper conditions, forcing him to conclude his oath with, "If I do not, may lightnings strike me!" [22] Thus, the divinity has not only punished crime; He has also enforced justice.

But this is not, as has been thought, a parable of just any *Christian* justice, but of a species of Christian justice. In the crucifixion scene, for example, it is a special Christ who threatens murder in a continuous devilish and viperish hissing; and the God who strikes through Moby Dick is closer to the God of Vengeance than He is to the God of Love. The God of the *Town-Ho* episode is, in fact, a barely distorted caricature of the orthodox Calvinist God. Though His methods of punishment are beyond human understanding and only dimly reflected in the natural means (the power of Moby Dick) by which He enforces His laws, His evaluation of human events (the injustice of Radney) presents a clear moral lesson for the edification of human understanding. We are shown then only a special, Calvinist version of Christian justice, more marked by wrath and punishment than by love.

The God revealed in the *Town-Ho* episode has some of the same characteristics of the God who reveals Himself to Ahab and the crew of the *Pequod*, but Ahab's tragedy is not the "same thing" as Radney's, and the differences between their fates are more important than their similarities.

It is true that there is a sense in which Ahab is justly executed for a Radney-like crime. For example, Ahab does "proudly assert that other men are his hands and feet, thereby violating them and the natural law." [23] But Ahab is no Radney, naturally

[19] "The Gospel According to Mark," *The Revised Standard Edition of the New Testament* (New York, 1946), chap. xv, p. 108.

[20] *Moby-Dick*, p. 370.

[21] Ibid., p. 257.

[22] Ibid., p. 259.

[23] Paul, op. cit., p. 217.

inferior to his social subordinates, and his execution brings with it the destruction of the crew which he has, in the power of his natural authority, victimized. Consequently, we feel much greater sympathy with the criminality of mighty Ahab at the same time that we can hardly discern the operations of divine justice as it affects the rest of the *Pequod*'s crew.

But the most important difference between the episode and the book as a whole involves us in a comparison not between Ahab and Radney but between Ahab and Steelkilt. Both have been maliciously treated. But the inhumane treatment of Steelkilt is of human origin whereas Ahab has been cruelly wounded by a playfully malicious universe. Consequently, the God of the *Town-Ho* episode, however barbarous in His methods, punishes a human crime and so is, in human eyes, a just God (a Calvinist God, indeed), however harsh.

In the case of Ahab, however, he is only attempting to right a wrong perpetrated not by man but by the nature of the universe. But for the monstrous God revealed by the book as a whole, even this assertion of human right is a crime. While God will punish a human crime, He defends His own malicious actions. This is certainly, as Mr. Thompson suggests, a tyrannous God; a ruler who refuses redress to His subjects for the evil consequences of the bad laws He has Himself legislated.

This is Melville's ultimate image of the Calvinist God of the Puritan. However just He may occasionally be, He is without love or mercy, or even common fairness. It is no wonder that the book's epilogue shows the sole survivor of the disaster, Ishmael, floating on a coffin lifebuoy like an "orphan": the features of the God are not the features of a human Father ("He" has become "It"), and lonely Ishmael floats like a man already dead in an inhumane universe.

James Dean Young

The Nine Gams of the *Pequod*

IN THE fifty-second chapter of *Moby-Dick* Melville presents the first of a series of meetings at sea. These social meetings, or gams, have been considered usually as essential varying interludes,[1] as individual dramatic scenes,[2] or as separate significant episodes.[3] They have never been considered as an integrated series. By taking the gams as a frame of reference, one may gain new insights into the structure and significance of the narrative, for no other group of chapters contributes such coherence to the developing action. Since the significance of several meetings appears only after other gams take place, the following examination of contexts and interrelations of the nine gams will be fairly detailed.

The suggestions of Melville's conception of the ship as society, as world-in-itself, or as microcosm are rather numerous and explicit. The *Pequod*, of course, is a special kind of world, dominated by Ahab, and takes many of its qualities from the man who makes its laws and commands. The ship, like Ahab, is self-sufficient; it is governed by attitudes and actions which are independent of other societies and other worlds, yet the *Pequod* has some relations with these other worlds. And here is the ambiguity: however independent our separate lives may be, we cannot escape entirely from relation and communication with others. This is so because our individuality itself may require some relation in order to exert and maintain its essential independence. The individual, like the ship, is still a microcosm related to a macrocosm and a cosmos. The gams are, then, relations to the world, inevitable relations which must be accepted. If possible, these relations should be made valuable even though they can be used only as relative guides. Other individuals are what we are not; they may provide what we lack, or add to what we already have. In any of their complex relations with us, they may voice warnings which we find inapplicable; they may exhibit attitudes which we find impossible; or they may act and persuade us to act in manners and directions which we know to be inadequate. But whatever our profit in these relations, the other worlds are alternatives to ours; the nine gams of the *Pequod* are meetings with other possible worlds.

The first problem in any relation to the world is one of communication; it is the problem of having a gam at all. A gam is a social meeting, "when, after exchanging hails," the whaleships "exchange visits by boats' crews: the two captains remaining, for the time, on board of one ship, and the two chief mates on the other." It is with this problem of exchange that Melville begins in the fifty-second chapter, entitled "The Albatross."

Just as we know that white is the color of purity and goodness, we also know that the albatross is a bird of good omen; but as Melville changes the connotations of

[1] F. O. Matthiessen, *American Renaissance* (New York, 1941), pp. 418–421.

[2] Newton Arvin, *Herman Melville* (New York, 1950), pp. 155–158.

[3] Herman Melville, *Moby-Dick*, ed. L. S. Mansfield and H. P. Vincent (New York, 1952), p. 762; W. H. Auden, *The Enchafèd Flood* (New York, 1950), pp. 63–66; Howard P. Vincent, *The Trying Out of Moby Dick* (Boston, 1949), pp. 243, 341–342; Nathalia Wright, *Melville's Use of the Bible* (Durham, N.C., 1949), pp. 78–93.

Reprinted by permission from *American Literature*, XXV (1954), 449–463.

whiteness, so he changes the meanings of the albatross: "in the wondrous bodily whiteness of the bird chiefly lurks the secret of the spell." The *Albatross* now becomes the omen of evil: "As if the waves had been fullers, this craft was bleached like the skeleton of a stranded walrus. All down her sides, this spectral appearance was traced with long channels of reddened rust, while all her spars and her rigging were like the thick branches of trees furred over with hoar-frost." [4]

But it is an omen of evil which is accepted and passed by. Relations to the world are necessary and are to be accepted for what they are. Any relation is essentially evil in so far as it attempts to modify or encroach upon the autonomy of the individual's world. But this evil is necessary, so necessary that all difficulties must be overcome; anything more than physical proximity is difficult, especially when physical proximity itself might be a matter of chance. The greatest difficulty is one of communication, for in the first gam, a silent and ominous meeting, there are no "exchanging hails"; the *Albatross* is a specter-ship whose fishermen, "mildly eyeing us as they passed, said not one word to our own look-outs." What is dramatized in the first gam occurs to some degree in each one, since all communications are hazardous, tentative, and unsatisfactory: "But as the strange captain, leaning over the pallid bulwarks, was in the act of putting his trumpet to his mouth, it somehow fell from his hand into the sea; and the wind now rising amain, he in vain strove to make himself heard without it. Meanwhile his ship was still increasing the distance between." [5]

The falling trumpet is, of course, symbolic of the problem of communication. As an exchange the first gam is futile, but not without meaning even to the seamen of the *Pequod*. When words fail, appear-

ances will serve; it was not the communication but the appearance of the phantom ship which prophesied the evil to befall the *Pequod*. "In various silent ways the seamen of the Pequod were evincing their observance of this ominous incident at the first mere mention of the White Whale's name to another ship." At the moment the two wakes cross, the prophecy of doom becomes real, especially to a madman, for even the "shoals of small harmless fish . . . darted away with what seemed shuddering fins, and ranged themselves fore and aft with the stranger's flanks . . . yet, to any monomaniac man, the veriest trifles capriciously carry meanings. . . . But in pursuit of those far mysteries we dream of, or in tormented chase of that demon phantom that, some time or other, swims before all human hearts; while chasing such over this round globe, they either lead us on in barren mazes or midway leave us whelmed." [6] The first gam, then, is an indication of the future as well as a description of the present. A world commanded by a monomaniac is certain to be whelmed, because the aid of other worlds is impossible when communication is attended with insurmountable difficulties.

The single chapter separating the first and second meetings is an exposition on "The Gam." Since this chapter does not become especially significant until the gam with the *Enderby,* the sixth of the series, discussion of it will be necessarily delayed.

The gam with the *Town-Ho* is the second meeting at sea and occurs in the third chapter of the initial group of three chapters concerned with the gams. Most of the chapter is devoted to a retelling of "The *Town-Ho*'s Story," as told at the Golden Inn at Lima. Although the total version of the story was related to Tashtego during the gam, and subsequently to the rest of the crew on the *Pequod*, Ahab never learns of the "secret part of the tragedy," the circumstance of the *Town-Ho*'s story, "which seemed obscurely to involve with the whale

[4] Herman Melville, *Moby-Dick,* ed. Willard Thorp (New York, 1947), p. 222; chap. lii.

[5] Ibid., p. 223; chap. lii.

[6] Ibid., pp. 223–224; chap lii.

a certain wondrous, inverted visitation of one of those so called judgments of God which at times are said to overtake some men." This second gam contains both a warning and a prophecy, neither of which Ahab ever receives. The seamen on the *Pequod* "who came to full knowledge of it . . . kept the secret among themselves." For the reader and the crew the second gam is a prefiguration of the *Pequod*'s tragedy; for Ahab it is a warning which cannot be applied because the sign of danger is held secret. Communication is still difficult, and yet even if it were not, we cannot doubt that Ahab would find either no prefiguration in the gam or reason to be incensed by the prophecy, and thereby precipitate himself to a more rapid destruction in a gesture of defiance. The "strange delicacy" which governed the crew in their silence is certainly a part of their realization that if the warning were communicated to Ahab, it would be ignored or misapplied. We have, then, in this second gam an illustration of Ahab's lack of cognizance due to the lack of communication. This could be, of course, mere lack of cognizance; since the knowledge or warning has no personal application, it is not useful, and therefore it is not necessarily true.

The nature of the warning in the *Town-Ho*'s story is also important: Steelkilt, the "handsome sailor," mutinies against the inhumanity of the "malicious" Radney. Radney himself administers the punishment for mutiny in a scene which underscores the Christlike qualities of the "handsome sailor." Before Steelkilt is able to avenge himself, "heaven itself seemed to step in to take out of his hands into its own the damning thing he would have done." Moby Dick is encountered "between daybreak and sunrise of the morning of the second day," and through him the retributive "judgment of God" is enacted: Radney is destroyed. Whether the White Whale be agent or principal, divine justice is fulfilled; the very naming of God at the Whale's appearance, almost an incantation of the Christian deity,

reflects Ishmael's comprehension of the secret portion of the story: "Jesu, what a whale! It was Moby Dick." [7] The warning of the second gam, then, is one against the monadic intellectuality and inhumanity of a Radney, a Claggart, or an Ahab; it is a warning which would not be applied even if it were heard.

The third gam, with the *Jeroboam*, provides a companion story to that of the *Town-Ho*; this story, too, is a warning and a prophecy, but it is also the first of four evenly spaced gams in the middle portion of the book. This gam is related closely to the previous gam and prepares for meetings with the ships that are ruled by captains whose attitudes are impossible for Ahab. The background for the meeting with the *Jeroboam* is provided by the "Town-Ho's company." This time Ahab hears the prophecy, but ignores it, just as Mayhew and Macey, the captain and the mate of the *Jeroboam*, had done. Gabriel, "in his gibbering insanity, pronouncing the White Whale to be no less a being than the Shaker God incarnated," hurls forth prophecies "of speedy doom to the sacrilegious assailants of his divinity." The White Whale is again divine, not now a just God, but a wrathful and jealous God. Gabriel's plea to "think of the blasphemer—dead, and down there!—beware of the blasphemer's end!" has already been answered; when to be enraged with a dumb thing seemed blasphemous to Starbuck, Ahab cried: "Talk not to me of blasphemy, man; I'd strike the sun if it insulted me." The third gam, then, is another warning which cannot be applied; God destroys those who assail his divinity as well as those who assail their fellowmen.

Throughout the third gam there is a constant underscoring of the difficulties of communication: although the epidemic on board the *Jeroboam* "did by no means pre-

[7] This is not the instinctive call of the topwatch as stated by Sherman Paul in "Melville's 'The *Town-Ho*'s Story,'" *American Literature*, XXI, 212–221 (May, 1949).

vent all communication," the gam is attended by constant interruptions, both from the sea and from Gabriel. The letter for Macey arrives after his death; "most letters never reach their mark; and many are only received after attaining an age of two or three years or more." If communication is accomplished, it may be too late; most communications, like the message of the *Albatross* and the prophecy of the *Town-Ho*, are never received.

Aside from being ineffective, the prophetic gams of the *Town-Ho* and the *Jeroboam* have something in common: God is equated with the White Whale, but this equation is either secret or made known through insanity. In either case the prophecy is one only in retrospect; only the stupid, superstitious crew see any significance in the events at the time; only after Ahab's world is destroyed does Ishmael see the prefigurations of events. Prophecies, even when they are understood, are not really substantial ground enough on which to base an attitude or an action. The signs and warnings of the world or the sea cannot be known clearly; they can be interpreted only with difficulty. This is the essential problem of any relation to the world, and it is the underlying theme for the first three gams. The problem becomes less important, although always present to some degree, in the remaining gams which present the alternatives of attitude and action. That each ship suffers the consequences of its own attitude and action only reinforces the consistency and inevitability of the *Pequod* tragedy.

The gams immediately following that of the *Jeroboam* are more or less evenly spaced, somewhat mechanically spread through the middle section of the book. Although Melville speaks of men-of-war and pirates "when they chance to meet at sea," he never speaks of the chance meeting of whalers. Indeed, the opening of the fourth gam removes the possibility of chance from the *Pequod*'s meetings: "The predestinated day arrived, and we duly met the ship

Jungfrau." Both the sequence and the meetings themselves suggest that the gams were planned as a series and are important as events in the life at sea.

Contrary to what one might expect from this predestination, the gams are not isolated from the context of the narrative; they are ganglia which focus and connect the linear narrative. Immediately preceding the gam with the *Jeroboam* and in preparing for it, Melville considers the head of the whale as "The Sphynx." This conceit enables Ahab to soliloquize on the problem of prophecy:

"Speak, thou vast and venerable head . . . tell us the secret thing that is in thee. Of all divers, thou hast dived the deepest . . . thou hast seen enough to split the planets and make an infidel of Abraham, and not one syllable is thine!"

"Sail ho!" cried a triumphant voice from the main-masthead.[8]

Ahab's musings are interrupted by the gam with the *Jeroboam:* the prophecy of madness, a warning which cannot be heeded even though it is understood.

Preceding the next gam is the sequel to "The Sphynx," another chapter of preparation entitled, "The Nut," which begins: "If the Sperm Whale be physiognomically a Sphynx, to the phrenologist his brain seems that geometrical circle which it is impossible to square."[9] The chapter continues as a discussion of the problem of knowledge and its appearances. This discussion is dramatized in the gams which follow it, just as the previous discussion was dramatized in the gam with the *Jeroboam*.

In both "The Sphynx" and "The Nut" the central subject is the head of the whale. In the former it is large and mysterious, capable of superhuman feats of intellect, especially the power of prophecy. In the latter it is large and unconstrainable:

It is plain, then, that phrenologically the head of this Leviathan, in the creature's living intact state, is an entire delusion. As for his true brain,

[8] *Moby-Dick*, p. 293; chap. lxx.
[9] Ibid., p. 327; chap. lxxx.

you can then see no indications of it, nor feel any. The whale, like all things that are mighty, wears a false brow to the common world. . . . I should call this high hump the organ of firmness or indomitableness in the Sperm Whale. And that the great monster is indomitable, you will yet have reason to know.[10]

The whale's indomitableness is almost in proportion to its size; its intelligence is like man's, but greater. A whale's skull, "scaled down to the human magnitude" and placed "among a plate of men's skulls," would be involuntarily confounded with them. Ironically enough, it would not be confounded with the skull of Derick, master of the *Jungfrau*, who presents to Ahab the first of the three impossible attitudes.

The first of these attitudes is innocence. As Derick DeDeer (or "die Deern," in low German appropriate to Breman, for "girl") boarded the *Pequod* to borrow oil for his lamp, "Ahab abruptly accosted him . . . but in his broken lingo, the German soon evinced his complete ignorance of the White Whale." Communication is difficult, though not impossible; Derick's ignorance is primarily that of innocence, so that in the subsequent chase the "Yarman" loses the whale to the Nantucketers. After the action of the chapter has shifted to a detailed account of the skill and proficiency of the *Pequod*'s crew, in order to emphasize both the rejection and the impossibility of innocence,

a cry was heard . . . announcing that the Jungfrau was again lowering her boats; though the only spout in sight was that of a Fin-Back, belonging to the species of uncapturable whales, because of its incredible power of swimming. Nevertheless, the Fin-Back's spout is so similar to the Sperm Whale's that by unskilful fishermen it is often mistaken for it. And consequently Derick and all his host were now in valiant chase of this unnearable brute . . . and thus they all disappeared far to leeward, still in bold, hopeful chase.[11]

[10] Ibid., pp. 327–329; chap. lxxx.
[11] Ibid., p. 339; chap. lxxxi.

"Oh! many are the Fin-Backs," as Moby Dick proves to be since he is "unnearable"; "and many are the Dericks," as those who have no knowledge of Moby Dick prove to be since they are in some degree innocent.

The second impossible attitude is inexperience. The barriers to communication with the *Rose-Bud* are still those of language, somewhat reduced by the English-speaking Guernsey-man, and distance, somewhat reduced by "a sleepy, vapory, midday sea." Yet the communication with the French captain is a parody of communication; and "in order to hold direct communication . . ." Stubb had to "come close to the blasted whale; and so talk over it." Stubb's first question concerns language, his second the White Whale; in answer to the latter he is asked:

"*What* whale?"
"The *White* Whale—a Sperm Whale—Moby Dick, have ye seen him?"
"Never heard of such a whale. Cachalot Blanche! White Whale—no." [12]

The answer of the Guernsey-man is important, for he does not evince "his complete ignorance of the White Whale," but merely states that in his experience he has "never heard of such a whale." Both his question of "*What* whale?" and his final answer suggest that he knew something of whales, that he has had some experience in whaling, even though it was limited; he is not ignorant nor innocent, but merely inexperienced. The *Bouton-de-Rose* may not "shun blasted whales," but it would not chase fin-backs with the *Jungfrau*. Handicapped by the lack of experience and communication, the French captain allows Stubb to tow the second whale away, and thereby trick him out of the ambergris that the "problematical" whale contained; "no knowing fisherman will ever turn up his nose at such a whale as this."

But again, since knowledge of Moby Dick is not available, and since the attitude of inexperience is impossibly dissatisfying

[12] Ibid., pp. 379–380; chap. xci.

to the man of experience, there is little to be gained by Ahab in this fifth gam. Only by the "happy-go-lucky" Stubb could more "have been secured were it not for impatient Ahab's loud command to Stubb to desist, and come on board, else the ship would bid them good-bye."

Like the previous gams, the fifth gam is a focal point, prepared for by chapters which precede it and reverberating in chapters which follow it. The discussions of "Fast-Fish and Loose-Fish" and "Heads or Tails" are necessary for any appreciation of the trickery, guile, and experience of Stubb. The gam itself necessitates the additional remarks on "Ambergris"; only after the technical strategy of the gam is clear, however, can it be seen that "Fast-Fish" is also the preparation for "The Castaway," interrupted and made specific by the gam. "All men's minds and opinions," "the principle of religious belief," "the ostentatious smuggling verbalists," and even Pip are Loose-Fish.

The third impossible attitude is indifference. As the language and distance barriers are removed, communication is improved; but even with the improvement, the difficulties are real and perhaps more subtle than mere physical obstacles. The gam with the *Samuel Enderby* begins with Ahab's question: "Hast seen the White Whale?" The answer is significantly an evasion of an answer. The stranger captain holds up "a white arm of sperm whale bone, terminating in a wooden head like a mallet" and asks, "See you this?" Although the answer is ambiguous, it leads Ahab to suppose not only that the captain has seen the Whale, but that he can supply information which will aid in locating him. This hope is indeed Ahab's motivation as he himself boards the stranger ship; this is the only gam in which Ahab is so moved, for he is intent on information. Ahab realizes that he has something organically in common with Captain Boomer; this is dramatically presented by the crossing of an ivory leg with an ivory arm. During the gam, Ahab

listens impatiently to the "bye-play between the two Englishmen"; when he is certain that he will receive neither information nor aid, his departure is violent and immediate. The action of the gam shows that the attitude of the English captain is impossible, and strongly underscores the fact that Ahab is isolated, solitary, and monadic in his monomania. Even though real information, like real communication, is impossible, the attitude of indifference is impossible also.

The stranger captain does not share Ahab's monomania even though he too has been injured by the Whale; nor does Ahab share the captain's neutrality toward the discoveries about whales which have made the house of Enderby and Sons famous. Both the captain's character and nationality suggest why he, even with an ivory arm, escapes the tragedy of Ahab. Captain Boomer (whose name echoes the hollow sounds of his facetiousness) was at first "ignorant of the White Whale"; after the encounter which bore him "down to Hell's flames," he is capable, partially through his reasonableness and humanity and partially through the rationality of his English character, of profiting from the knowledge it gave him. Only to Ahab would this reasonableness seem triviality and this rationality indifference; both are impossible attitudes for a monomaniac. With all common sense Captain Boomer says: ". . . ain't one limb enough? What should I do without this other arm?" His knowledge of Moby Dick provides basis for the perception that "Moby Dick doesn't bite so much as he swallows." Ahab is swallowed, together with the *Pequod;* Captain Boomer is satisfied with one lowering, even though he realizes that "there would be great glory in killing him." He knows that Moby Dick is "best left alone." Ishmael, saved from the *Pequod* by his humanity, perceives in another gam with the *Enderby* what Ahab could not see. The ship was "a noble craft every way. . . . It was a fine gam we had, and they were all trumps —every soul on board. . . . And that fine gam I had—long, very long after old Ahab touched her planks with his ivory heel—it reminds me of the noble, solid, Saxon hospitality of that ship; and may my parson forget me, and the devil remember me, if I ever lose sight of it." [13]

While Ahab has lost sight of humanity and common sense, he still recognizes that Moby Dick is best let alone; although Ahab is capable of reason, he is not a reasonable man: "What is best let alone, that accursed thing is not always what least allures. He's all magnet!" Understanding does not lessen Ahab's monomania; it makes it tragic. At Ahab's abrupt departure Captain Boomer again perceives accurately. "Is your Captain crazy?" he whispers to Fedallah, who of all the *Pequod's* crew lacks the power of such judgment. The rapid action and the very violence of Ahab's departure have been long ago prepared for in "The Gam." When Ahab leaves "with back to the stranger ship, and face set like flint to his own," he is still in complete control of himself and his own world. This act is the climactic rejection of other possible attitudes; although Ahab could realize the extent of his predicament and the inevitability of its outcome, such realization would be only momentary, because his madness never allows his sanity to surface itself again. The departure from the *Enderby* is the beginning of his final descent to destruction. Ahab has rejected the attitudes of innocence, inexperience, and indifference, because he was not, nor could he be, innocent, inexperienced, or indifferent. Moby Dick was "all magnet."

The remaining three gams each present a basis for action, the action itself, and the consequences of such action. As it has been with the three alternative attitudes, each is more or less inadequate for Ahab.

Between the gams with the *Enderby* and the *Bachelor*, many preparations have been made for the encounter with Moby Dick; most important of these are Ahab's new leg and the newly forged harpoon. In the chapter entitled "The Gilder," immediately preceding the seventh gam, there is a short but important discussion of the land-sea antithesis which concludes with two short monologues, one by Starbuck and the other by Stubb. The essentials of these monologues are enacted in the following two gams.

The alternative of action presented by the *Bachelor* is the same alternative which Stubb finds most adequate: "And Stubb, fishlike, with sparkling scales, leaped up in that same golden light: 'I am Stubb, and Stubb has his history; but here Stubb takes oaths that he has always been jolly!' " [14] Stubb is an intelligent animal, who, if he were captain, would be captain of a *Bachelor*. This Nantucket ship "had just wedged in her last cask of oil, and bolted down her bursting hatches, . . . had met with the most surprising success." Now the ship "was joyously, though somewhat vain-gloriously, sailing round among the widely-separated ships on the ground, previous to pointing her prow for home." The captain of the *Bachelor*, just as Stubb might do, thrusts his hands into his pockets "in self-complacent testimony of his entire satisfaction." But when the inevitable question is asked by Ahab, the stranger captain can only reply:

"No; only heard of him; but don't believe in him at all," said the other good-humoredly. "Come aboard!" [15]

The basis for action is no belief at all; it is the animal's basis for action. Since the action is entered into for its own sake, it is successful; but the success is without intellectual conflict just as the action is without real understanding. The alternative is inadequate for Ahab: action for itself is "too damned jolly"; both the lack of belief and the success it brings are rejected:

[13] Ibid., p. 416; chap. ci.

[14] Ibid., p. 459; chap. cxiv.

[15] Ibid., p. 461; chap. cxv.

"How wondrous familiar is a fool!" muttered Ahab; then aloud, "Thou art a full ship and homeward bound, thou sayst; well, then, call me an empty ship, and outward-bound. So go thy ways, and I will mine. Forward there! Set all sail, and keep her to the wind!"[16]

Immediately after this profession of faith and strength, Ahab is momentarily reminded of the precariousness of his actions and of the security of the land: "And as Ahab, leaning over the taffrail, eyed the homeward-bound craft, he took from his pocket a small vial of sand, and then looking from the ship to the vial, seemed thereby bringing two remote associations together, for that vial was filled with Nantucket soundings."[17]

The second alternative of action, presented by the *Rachel*, is essentially that alternative which Starbuck finds most adequate in his monologue near the end of "The Gilder": "Loveliness unfathomable. . . . Let faith oust fact; let fancy oust memory; I look deep down and do believe."[18] Long before the gam with the *Rachel*, the antagonism between Ahab and Starbuck had been developed and resolved in "The Musket" and "The Needle." Just as Stubb might have been the captain of the *Bachelor*, Starbuck might have been the captain of the *Rachel*; neither is a captain because each has surrendered to Ahab's commands.

Before any exchange has been made between the *Pequod* and the *Rachel*, the old Manxman mutters, "Bad news; she brings bad news." This bad news is, of course, the answer to Ahab's "Hast seen the White Whale?": "Aye, yesterday." This is the first affirmative answer; the *Rachel* believes in the Whale, has seen the Whale, and has lost a boat in the encounter with the Whale. But with this loss, the interest of the *Rachel*'s captain has shifted from the White Whale to the lost men. After admitting knowledge of the Whale, the stranger captain asks, "Have ye seen a whale-boat adrift?" The actions of the *Rachel* are now made with partial understanding, even though the conflict brought no success. Partial defeat is illuminated by the partial understanding, for the actions of the *Rachel* are based no longer on the belief in Moby Dick, but on the belief in man. This humanity saves Ishmael, since he is eventually rescued by the *Rachel*; this same humanity would have saved Starbuck and most of the *Pequod*'s crew, if they had not been subdued by the superior intellect and will of Ahab. It is not Starbuck, but Stubb, who reacts with complete animal spontaneity to the situation, yet not without recognizing his subservient understanding: "What says Ahab? We must have that boy."

But just as Ahab's plea for aid on board the *Enderby* had been ignored, so Ahab ignores the plea of the *Rachel*'s captain; the alternative of believing in man more than the Whale, and of acting on that belief, is inadequate: ". . . now the stranger was still beseeching his poor boon of Ahab; and Ahab stood like an anvil, receiving every shock, but without the least quivering of his own."[19] Again, immediately after the rejection, Ahab is reminded of the necessity and virtue of humanity, but he is reminded at the same time of its impossibility for him: "Captain Gardiner, I will not do it. Even now I lose time. Good bye, Good bye. God bless ye, man, and may I forgive myself, but I must go."[20]

The final alternative of action is presented by the *Delight*; this last gam is both an alternative and a warning, this time unambiguous, which recalls the gam with the *Albatross*. On the "most miserably misnamed" *Delight* were beheld "the shattered, white ribs, and some few splintered planks, of what had once been a whale-boat; but you now saw through this wreck, as plainly as you see through the peeled, half-unhinged, and bleaching skeleton of

16 Ibid., p. 461; chap. cxv.

17 Ibid., p. 461; chap. cxv.

18 Ibid., p. 459; chap. cxiv.

19 Ibid., p. 492; chap. cxxvii.

20 Ibid., p. 492; chap. cxxviii.

a horse." [21] Again, as with the *Enderby*, the answer to Ahab's question is ambiguous; the "hollow-cheeked" captain replies, " 'Look!' . . . and with his trumpet he pointed to the wreck." As before, the evasion of an answer is sufficient for Ahab. The *Delight* has believed in the White Whale, but through the conflict which brought partial destruction, this belief has been modified. The stranger captain now says that "the harpoon is not yet forged that will ever" kill Moby Dick. The belief of former action has been modified; the *Delight* is now governed by understanding, gained through conflict, which prevents all action. All the *Delight* can do now is bury its dead. Aided by this understanding, the *Delight* can see the impending doom of the "intense *Pequod*," and can forebode that pursuit of the White Whale is "in vain . . . ye fly our sad burial; ye but turn us your taffrail to show us your coffin!"

As with the other alternatives, Ahab perceives its necessity in the very act of rejection: "But the suddenly started Pequod was not quick enough to escape the sound of the splash that the corpse soon made as it struck the sea; not so quick, indeed, but that some of the flying bubbles might have sprinkled her hull with their ghostly baptism." [22] The alternatives of

action for the *Pequod* were, then, these: (1) disbelief in the Whale and action on that disbelief; (2) belief in man and action on that belief; or (3) belief in the Whale and inaction on that belief. The *Pequod* itself presents the other possibility: belief in the Whale and action on that belief; the belief is complete, the action is one of total understanding, and the conflict brings total destruction.

All nine gams of the *Pequod* are important relations to the world. Each gam deals to some degree with the problem of communication and the problem of alternative; each is a focal point in the action and part of the matrix for the narrative. The first group of three gams means very little as a warning, but it clearly prefigures the tragedy, and ends in the climactic meeting with the *Jeroboam*. The second group of three gams defines the alternative attitudes and is climaxed in the gam with the *Enderby*. The final group of three gams presents the alternative actions, which are also warnings, and is climaxed in the gam with the *Delight*. The series of gams is a stable reference for understanding the structure and action of the narrative; no other group of chapters forms such an integrated series. Through these meetings at sea, the *Pequod* experiences difficult relations to the world: communication is uncertain, and alternatives are inadequate.

[21] Ibid., p. 499; chap. cxxxi.

[22] Ibid., p. 500; chap. cxxxi.

R. E. Watters

Melville's "Isolatoes"

THE unhappy fate of the man whom choice or chance has alienated from the human community greatly interested Hawthorne, as is well known. The theme held a similar fascination for Melville—even before he became acquainted with many of Hawthorne's tales.[1] The probable discussions subsequently with his friend and neighbor, however, may well have strengthened his interest in the Ishmael *motif*. As might be expected, Melville explored the moral and philosophical implications of the theme, and out of them he evolved a doctrine of racial and social community as an ideal to set opposite the isolated individual. This positive doctrine[2] need concern us here,

however, only in so far as it is implicit in his delineation of individuals who, because of birth or achievement or action or character—a white jacket of some kind, in short—were set apart from normal human relationships. These persons may appropriately be called "Isolatoes," a term coined by Melville himself in describing the crew of the Pequod: "They were nearly all Islanders. . . . 'Isolatoes' too, I call such, not acknowledging the common continent of men, but each Isolato living on a separate continent of his own."[3] In each of his books one character at least is just such an exile, either by accident or volition.

II

Many of the Isolatoes are presented as involuntary outcasts from the human community. In *Typee* the narrator is estranged because he had moved in a different sphere of life from the "dastardly and mean-spirited wretches" who mainly composed the crew.[4] And later, in the valley with the natives, he was again a person set apart from the common life of his neighbors. In *Omoo* the narrator is also isolated as "a man of education."[5] Taji's similar exclusion in *Mardi* is explained in a passage which is probably also autobiographical:

. . . Aboard of all ships in which I have sailed, I have invariably been known by a sort of drawing-room title. . . . It was because of something in me that could not be hidden; stealing out in an occasional polysyllable; an otherwise incompre-

[1] The date of Melville's first reading of Hawthorne is uncertain. He discusses "Hawthorne and His Mosses" in *The Literary World* for August, 1850, asserting that he had just come upon the book during July. In this review there is a reference to *The Scarlet Letter* (published a few months earlier) and to *Twice-Told Tales* (1837), but although the reference is eulogistic, it seems not to have been founded on much close knowledge. For instance, in February, 1851, Melville wrote to Duyckinck: "I have recently read . . . 'Twice Told Tales' (I had not read but a few of them before). I think they far exceed the 'Mosses' . . . ." [see Willard Thorp, *Herman Melville: Representative Selections* . . . (New York, 1938), pp. 327 ff. and 385.] The assertion made by several critics that Melville reviewed *The Scarlet Letter* for *The Literary World* in March, 1850, has been thoroughly refuted by Willard Thorp, "Did Melville Review *The Scarlet Letter?*" *American Literature*, XIV, 302–305 (November, 1942). Melville's enthusiasm for *The Mosses* in the summer of 1850 was so unbounded that one is forced to conclude that Hawthorne had made little or no impact upon him previously. Yet the five novels Melville wrote before this time all employ in some degree the theme of isolation.

[2] For a discussion, see the present writer's "Melville's 'Sociality,'" *American Literature*, XVII, 33–49 (March, 1945).

[3] *Moby Dick*, I, 149. All references to Melville's writings are to the Standard Edition (London, Constable & Co., 1922–24).

[4] *Typee*, p. 25.

[5] *Omoo*, p. 131.

Reprinted by permission from *PMLA*, LX (1945), 1138–1148, with a few alterations by the author.

hensible deliberation in dining; remote, unguarded allusions to Belles-Lettres affairs; and other trifles. . . .[6]

Taji found no one among the crew "with whom to mingle sympathies"[7] except Jarl, who himself was experiencing "that heart-loneliness which overtakes most seamen as they grow aged."[8] In *White Jacket*, the notorious garment symbolized, among other things, the wearer's conspicuous difference and detachment from all but a few members of the crew. Redburn's naivete, landlubberliness, and odd clothes made him "a sort of Ishmael in the ship."[9] The narrator in *Moby Dick* begins by calling himself Ishmael, having been made one, he says, by circumstances. But from the moment when he felt that Queequeg, himself a wanderer in an alien land, was "a human being just as I am,"[10] his initial isolation began to thaw. The thorough Ishmael in this novel, as we shall see, is Captain Ahab.

Isabel, in *Pierre*, is another involuntary Isolato. As a child she had to discover for herself that she even belonged to the general community of humanity,[11] so harshly had she been treated by the people among whom she lived. She wrote to Pierre eventually because she could no longer "endure to be an outcast in the world."[12] Israel Potter, through no fault of his own, became another Ishmael, wandering from youth to age in the wilderness of estrangement from his native land.[13]

[6] *Mardi*, I, 16.

[7] *Ibid.*, I, 3.

[8] *Ibid.*, I, 15.

[9] *Redburn*, p. 79.

[10] *Moby Dick*, I, 30.

[11] *Pierre*, p. 172.

[12] *Ibid.*, p. 88. Another female Isolato was the Chola widow, Hunilla, whom Melville called a "lone, shipwrecked soul" (*The Piazza Tales*, p. 227).

[13] The explicit *motif* of *Israel Potter* is, of course, Israel's forty years in the wilderness. This was obviously suggested by Potter's name, but Melville's use of the suggestion illustrates again his interest in the general theme.

Melville's poetry presents others in the same role. As Weaver says, "the most recurring note" of *Clarel* is a "Parched desire for companionship,"[14] a yearning for spiritual brotherhood. *John Marr and Other Sailors*, published only three years before Melville's death, contains the last of his involuntary Isolatoes. The old seaman, John Marr, cannot establish "sympathetic communion" with the prairie settlers among whom he had gone to live. He lacked the "common inheritance" upon which such familiarity rests—the shared experiences of a common past.[15] When he once reminisced of his life at sea he was silenced with "Friend, we know nothing of that here."[16]

All these individuals, through the accidents of birth or upbringing or circumstances or temperament, found themselves lacking the requirements for familiar social intercourse with their fellows. Some of them escape at last into a social environment congenial to themselves. Some of them succumb as involuntary victims. But none of them succeed in adjusting themselves to the social group which disowned them.

III

Perhaps because of the greater possibilities for tragedy, Melville was more profoundly interested in those whose isolation was voluntarily chosen or preferred. No doubt every man, on occasion, must imitate Father Mapple's "act of spiritual isolation" in pulling up the rope ladder to the pulpit to signify "his spiritual withdrawal for the time from all outward worldly ties and connexions."[17] But in Melville's opinion prolonged isolation either chills the heart or corrupts the mind—or both.

Melville's two greatest voluntary Isolatoes, Ahab and Pierre, have hypnotized some readers into a mistaken conception of

[14] R. M. Weaver, *Herman Melville, Mariner and Mystic* (New York, 1921), p. 361.

[15] *Poems*, p. 198.

[16] *Ibid.*, p. 199.

[17] *Moby Dick*, I, 48.

his general attitude towards individualism. According to F. L. Pattee, Melville "was a Nietzschean when Nietzsche was but a schoolboy. Be hard, smite down, trample, be a superman, or else be yourself trampled —that was the law of Nature,—of God if there be a God." [18] R. H. Gabriel views Melville as "the supreme individualist of the nineteenth century," and Ahab as "the personification of Melville's individualism." [19]

Although occasionally Ahab could regret the cold isolation his monomania produced,[20] most of the time he deliberately preferred his solitude, deliberately spurned as far as possible the assistance of other agents, human and non-human. Proudly he boasted: "Ahab stands alone among all the millions of the peopled earth, nor gods nor men his neighbors!" [21] He challenges the immortal gods to "swerve" him from his chosen course.[22] He also curses "that mortal interdebtedness which will not do away with ledgers. I would be free as air; and I'm down in the whole world's books. . . ." [23] In his pride he resents his debts to the carpenter "for a bone to stand on" and to his ancestors and parents "for the flesh in the tongue I brag with." [24] He tramples on human science as symbolized in the quadrant, and later makes his own compass. He is even glad his mates do not share his fierce hatred of the whale, lest his own hate might be lessened

thereby.[25] His vanity makes him crave to be first in sighting Moby Dick, and when he succeeds he boasts: "I only; none of ye could have raised the White Whale first." [26] He will acknowledge no ties of neighborliness to his fellow Nantucketer, the captain of the Rachel, who cites the Golden rule in vainly begging Ahab to help search for the lost boy. Indeed, Ahab's first thought on hearing of the Rachel's encounter with Moby Dick is a fear that some other person might have killed the whale. He craved not the mere destruction of what he considers to be evil but the egocentric delight in his own destroying it. When he thinks of his fellow men, they are as projections of himself, subordinated to his selfish purpose: "Ye are not other men, but my arms and legs; and so obey me." [27] In his last speech he reveals nothing but self-centered egotism: my ship, my crew, "my topmost greatness," "my topmost grief," "I grapple with thee," and so on.[28] Not a word of remorse, not a word of sympathy for the men he had brought to death.

The fate Melville assigned to this "Nietzschean" individualist was not even partial victory, but total defeat. Professor Gabriel misinterprets the outcome when he writes: "In the end Ahab saved his soul, maintained inviolate his personal integrity, by going down in unconquered defeat while Moby Dick swam on for other Ahabs to pursue." [29] The man left to continue the chase, had he so desired, was Ishmael, who had found values in this "wolfish world" which Ahab was blind to; and Ishmael was saved by the captain of the Rachel, whose searchings were prompted by love. Ahab did not save even his soul —in his own opinion, at least—since as he darts the last harpoon he cries: "From hell's heart I stab at thee; for hate's sake

[18] "Herman Melville," *American Mercury*, X, 39 (January, 1927).

[19] *The Course of American Democratic Thought* (New York, 1940), pp. 73, 74.

[20] Most notably in two remarks to Starbuck. First, when Ahab cried "Close! stand close to me, Starbuck; let me look into a human eye; it is better . . . than to gaze upon God." Secondly, after his whalebone leg had been snapped off: "Ay, ay, Starbuck, 'tis sweet to lean sometimes . . . and would old Ahab had leaned oftener than he has" (*Moby Dick*, II, 329, 350).

[21] *Moby Dick*, II, 341.

[22] *Ibid.*, I, 210.

[23] *Ibid.*, II, 240.

[24] *Ibid.*, II, 239–240.

[25] *Ibid.*, I, 207.

[26] *Ibid.*, II, 333.

[27] *Ibid.*, II, 361.

[28] *Ibid.*, II, 366.

[29] Gabriel, *op. cit.*, p. 74.

I spit my last breath at thee." [30] The Pequod itself, "like Satan, would not sink to hell till she had dragged a living part of heaven [the skyhawk] along with her." [31] The delight Father Mapple had promised to the man "who against the proud gods and commodores *of this earth,* ever stands forth his own inexorable self" [32] never descended upon Ahab, for he not only opposed the powers of earth but defied those of heaven.

Not Pattee nor Gabriel but Professor Matthiessen gives the true interpretation:

Melville created in Ahab's tragedy a fearful symbol of the self-inclosed individualism that, carried to its furthest extreme, brings disaster both upon itself and the group of which it is a part. He provided also an ominous glimpse of what was the result when the Emersonian will to virtue became in less innocent natures the will to conquest. [33]

Pierre was like Ahab in two ways: he was determined to eradicate something he believed to be evil, and he was proudly self-reliant. He was ready to sacrifice his whole social group (mother, fiancee, relatives, friends, dependents—everybody) to achieve something which he, like Ahab, considered necessary and good. Pierre's desire to bestow upon Isabel the spiritual, emotional, and material benefits of her patrimony was undoubtedly admirable; so was Ahab's desire to annihilate evil in the universe as epitomized for him in Moby Dick. The issue can be stated simply: Is a man justified in severing most of his human relationships to pursue a personal ideal— particularly when that ideal may involve ambiguity or error?

When Isabel's letter frightened away "the before undistrusted moral beauty of the world" Pierre cried:

Myself am left, at least. . . . With myself I front thee! Unhand me all fears. . . . Henceforth I will know nothing but Truth. . . . Fate, I have a choice quarrel with thee. . . . I will lift my hand in fury, for am I not struck? . . . Thou Black Knight, that with visor down, thus confrontest me, and mockest at me; lo! I strike through thy helm, and will see thy face, be it Gorgon! . . . I will be impious, for piety hath juggled me. . . . From all idols, I tear all veils. . . . [34]

Such assertive self-dedication echoes not only Ahab's egotism but the very imagery in his "pasteboard masks" speech. In the process of rectifying the wrong, moreover, Pierre again followed Ahab. Not till the last possible moment did Ahab confide in anyone his purpose in the Pequod's voyage. Pierre concealed his purpose from the world also, even from his beloved Lucy. He even hid from Isabel, who shared his major secret, the identity of Lucy and the full desperateness of their plight. Because he considered himself "driven out an infant into the desert," [35] he had little faith in either his companions or humanity at large. After his first interview with Isabel, for instance, he felt a desire to shun every human habitation, human activity, or even "remembrances and imaginings that had to do with common and general humanity." [36] His repudiation was complete.

Unlike Ahab, however, Pierre found his action at least partly justified by his subsequent experiences. His mother's family pride, the Reverend Falsgrave's worldliness, and his Cousin Glen's materialism— all thrust him away from his social group. But Pierre's own pride, like Ahab's, made him loath to lean on anyone:

Pierre was proud. . . . A proud man likes to feel himself in himself, and not by reflection in others. He likes to be not only his own Alpha and Omega, but to be distinctly all the intermediate gradations. [37]

[30] *Moby Dick*, II, 366.

[31] *Ibid.,* II, 367.

[32] *Ibid,* I, 59. My italics.

[33] F. O. Matthiessen, *American Renaissance: Art and Expression in the Age of Emerson and Whitman* (New York, 1941), p. 459.

[34] *Pierre*, pp. 89, 90–91.

[35] *Ibid.,* p. 125.

[36] *Ibid.,* p. 192.

[37] *Ibid.,* p. 363.

Finally, Pierre resembles Ahab in not believing that his defiance and renunciation would save even his individual soul from the total defeat:

Had I been heartless, now, disowned, and spurningly portioned off the girl at Saddle Meadows, then had I been happy through a long life on earth, and perchance through a long eternity in Heaven! Now, 'tis merely hell in both worlds. Well, be it hell.[38]

In truth, the Melville hero who does save his soul is not Ahab or Pierre or Taji but Billy Budd, who lived and died, not in isolation, not in hate or self-assertion, but in community and love and sacrifice.

Many minor self-determined Isolatoes are scattered through Melville's works. In *Clarel*, Mortmain and Vine are two examples; Ungar is another, a man specifically described as "a wandering Ishmael from the West." [39] The John Paul Jones of *Israel Potter* is as ruggedly individualistic as Ahab. He calls himself "an untrammeled citizen and sailor of the universe," and agrees to serve his native country only under "unlimited orders: a separate, supreme command; no leader and no counsellor but himself." He even prefers to sleep in a chair alone than to share a bed.[40] In *The Confidence Man*, Frank Goodman calls the Missourian "an Ishmael" [41] and explains his "philosophy of disesteem for man" as springing from "a certain lowness, if not sourness, of spirits inseparable from sequestration." [42] Melville devotes a short story to the life of a Jimmy Rose, who sequestered himself from friends as well as creditors after his financial collapse, until, "in his loneliness, [he] had been driven half mad." [43] The Dansker in *Billy Budd* contributed to the tragedy of Billy's fate because he preferred the isolation of his aloof and guarded cynicism to the frankness of friendship.

The most complete and moving portrait among the minor Isolatoes, however, is that of Bartleby the Scrivener. He simply and sweetly "preferred not to" when asked to participate in the normal life and duties of his new employer's office. Bartleby was a man who was "by nature and misfortune prone to a pallid hopelessness." [44] After years as a clerk in the Dead Letter office, where he had sorted for the flames the unsuccessful attempts of men to communicate with one another—where he had, in short, witnessed the breakdown of social fellowship—he would not or could not adapt himself to the necessary usages of society. Melville ends the sketch with the cry: "Ah Bartleby! Ah humanity!" Both the man and mankind lose by such Ishmaelism— an opinion antithetical to Emerson's panegyric: "the great man is he who in the midst of the crowd keeps with perfect sweetness the independence of solitude." [45]

IV

In fact, none of Melville's Isolatoes find much comfort in Emersonian self-reliance. The involuntary ones, at least, are not self-sufficient individualists who lean only on the impalpable Over-Soul, but rather lonely men in search of a human shoulder. In *Moby Dick* Ishmael succeeded in such a quest. Queequeg's fellowship "redeemed" his heart: "I felt a melting in me. No more my splintered heart and maddened hand were turned against the wolfish world." [46] Queequeg's race and color might have made him an Ishmael, but he is revealed as the direct opposite of Ahab. To save a

---

[38] *Ibid.*, p. 502.

[39] *Clarel*, II, 199.

[40] *Israel Potter*, pp. 73, 74, 79–80.

[41] *The Confidence Man*, p. 185.

[42] *Ibid.*, p. 178.

[43] *Billy Budd*, etc., p. 263.

[44] *The Piazza Tales*, p. 65.

[45] *Complete Works* (Boston, 1903–04), II, 54. Since the present article was written, Egbert S. Oliver, in "A Second Look at 'Bartleby,'" *College English*, VI, 431–439 (May, 1945), has suggested that in writing his tale Melville intended "a reductio ad absurdum of the convictions Thoreau expressed" in his wish to dissociate himself from the community.

[46] *Moby Dick*, I, 62.

stranger who had mocked at him he risks his life; Ahab would not pause to help a Nantucket neighbor. Queequeg insisted that Ishmael decide the future of both by choosing a ship, but Ahab silenced all interference in his risking the ship and his crew. Finally, Queequeg invited Ishmael to share equally in his religious worship, but Ahab harangued the corposants with his foot upon Fedallah.

Not only Queequeg but the other harpooneers, the mates, and the crew found values hidden to Ahab, because they shared common duties, common dangers, and common feelings. They subordinated their egos to assist their fellow man, Ahab: "all the individualities of the crew," their virtues and vices, "were welded into oneness." [47] "I, Ishmael, was one of that crew; my shouts had gone up with the rest. . . . A wild, mystical, sympathetical feeling was in me; Ahab's quenchless feud seemed mine." [48] The harpooneers protected one another with whale-spades from snapping sharks. Daggoo and Queequeg willingly risked their lives to save Tashtego when he was engulfed in the sinking whale's head. Human interdependence was further impressed upon the crew in such operations as the one employing the "monkey-rope," in which the man on board ship staked his very life on protecting the man who worked on the slippery whale alongside from falling into the shark-filled sea. Ahab took no such risks for his fellows, felt no such responsibilities for their safety. The crew found other values in such ordinary duties as the squeezing by hand of spermaceti globules. This act produced in Ishmael "a strange sort of insanity," wherein he found himself squeezing his co-workers' hands.

I forgot all about our horrible oath; in that inexpressible sperm, I washed my hands and my heart of it. . . . Such an abounding, affectionate, friendly loving feeling did this avocation beget . . . [that I longed to say]—Oh! my dear fellowbeings,

why should we longer cherish any social acerbities . . . let us squeeze hands all round; nay, let us squeeze ourselves into each other; let us squeeze ourselves universally into the very milk and sperm of kindness.[49]

The same "strange sort of insanity" characterized the negro Pip, who, as even Ahab recognized was "full of the sweet things of love and gratitude." [50] Pip begged Ahab to use him to replace the leg lost to Moby Dick, and promised never to desert Ahab as Stubb did Pip. But Ahab remained unswerved by Pip's abounding affection, which he called something "too curing for my malady." [51] Ahab persisted in his demoniac isolation of spirit, while he bent other men to his will; yet he found neither happiness nor success. Although all the crew except Ishmael died, they did not die like Ahab, alone in hate and selfish concentration of purpose, but rather with brave fidelity and conscious of their humanity. Even the materialistic Flask thought of his mother!

Not admiration for their self-reliance but the deepest pity for their loneliness dominated Melville's attitude towards his Isolatoes. As Bartleby's employer put it: "What miserable friendlessness and loneliness are here revealed! His poverty is great; but his solitude, how horrible!" [52] The horror of loneliness is expressed again and again by Melville. In his first novel, *Typee*, he cites as a social crime far worse than wars, hangings, or even cannibalism, "the horrors we inflict, upon these wretches, whom we mason up in the cells of our prisons, and condemn to perpetual solitude in the very heart of our population." [53]

[49] *Ibid.*, II, 172.

[50] *Ibid.*, II, 302.

[51] *Ibid.*, II, 316.

[52] *The Piazza Tales*, p. 39.

[53] *Typee*, p. 167. In a volume of Schopenhauer, which Melville read in 1890 or 1891 (about forty-five years after he wrote the above protest), he marked the following passage: ". . . when possible, the apparent severity of the punishment should exceed the actual: but solitary confinement achieves the reverse. Its great severity has no

[47] *Ibid.*, II, 345.

[48] *Ibid.*, I, 222.

Pip, who was deserted for many hours after his jump from the whaleboat, went insane less from fear than from his discovery, as a "lonely castaway" in the "shoreless ocean," that "the awful lonesomeness is intolerable. The intense concentration of self in the middle of such a heartless immensity, my God! who can tell it?" [54] Even Ahab, when in "The Symphony" chapter his "intense concentration of self" is momentarily diffused by a trace of human sympathy—even Ahab acknowledges the human horror of loneliness:

When I think of this life I have led; the desolation of solitude it has been; the masoned, walled-town of a captain's exclusiveness, which admits but small entrance to any sympathy from the green country without—oh, weariness! heaviness! Guinea-coast slavery of solitary command! [55]

Denied even the privilege common to "the meanest shipwrecked captains" of going down with his ship, he dies with only one emotion other than his consuming hatred: "Oh, lonely death on lonely life!" [56]

Melville's abounding pity for all his Isolatoes, the voluntary no less than the involuntary, no doubt issued from his own love of companionship, often thwarted as that may have been. He was himself no lover of solitude, though he probably experienced something of the involuntary Isolato's plight on shipboard because of his different upbringing. But no man who repudiated fellowship in a preference for privacy would have chosen to spend many months in the confinement of a whaler,

especially after already experiencing crews' quarters on Atlantic crossings. John Marr's reminiscences about the jovial companionship he once knew on ships suggest a similar indulgence by Melville himself. The letters Melville wrote to Duyckinck and especially to Hawthorne give overt evidence of what conversation, sympathy, appreciation, fraternity, meant to him. Even before meeting Hawthorne he had responded to the "depth of tenderness . . . boundless sympathy . . . omnipresent love" which he had detected in *The Mosses*.[57] And when he received Hawthorne's "joy-giving" letter about *Moby Dick* he felt a oneness of himself and his neighbor—"ineffable socialities . . . infinite fraternity of feeling." [58]

Frank Goodman's remark in *The Confidence Man* suggests what Melville considered to be the prime cause of voluntary Ishmaelism:

. . . . Misanthropy, springing from the same root with disbelief in religion, is twin with that . . .; for, set aside materialism, and what is an atheist, but one who does not, or will not, see in the universe a ruling principle of love; and what a misanthrope, but one who does not, or will not, see in man a ruling principle of kindness? . . .[59]

Except momentarily, Ahab expunges kindness from his heart, yet demands of God: "Come in thy lowest form of love, and I will kneel and kiss thee; but . . . come as mere supernal power [and I remain indifferent]." [60] Yet he would not recognize that "lowest form of love" when it was displayed through humanity (Pip and Starbuck), through the serenity of the ocean, and even through the gentleness of Moby Dick himself on the first day of the chase—when the whale merely splintered Ahab's leg but spared every man who took to boats after him, except Ahab's "evil shadow" Fedallah. Ahab would not

witnesses, and is by no means anticipated by any one who has not experienced it; thus it does not deter." *The World as Will and Idea*, translated by R. B. Haldane and J. Kemp, Vol. III, 413 (London, 1890). This volume is not in the Melville Collection in Harvard's Houghton Library.—Permission to use this material was granted by Kenneth B. Murdock as Chairman of the Committee on Higher Degrees in the History of American Civilization at Harvard University.

[54] *Moby Dick*, II, 168–169.

[55] *Ibid.*, II, 328.

[56] *Ibid.*, II, 366.

[57] Thorp, *op. cit.*, p. 331.

[58] *Ibid.*, pp. 394–395.

[59] *The Confidence Man*, p. 210.

[60] *Moby Dick*, II, 282.

recognize what was so plain to Starbuck: "All good angels mobbing thee with warnings:—what more wouldst thou have?" [61]

Whether or not Melville himself could "see in the universe a ruling principle of love," he at least believed such a principle was essential to humanity and to religion. As Braswell says, "Christ's doctrine of love and his promise of immortality were among the lasting influences in Melville's life." [62] Melville called the Sermon on the Mount "that greatest real miracle of all religions . . . an inexhaustible soul-melting stream of tenderness and loving-kindness." [63] In *Mardi* he presented Serenia as an ideal land which practiced the teachings of that sermon. In this Land of Love all men, rich and poor, masters and servants, were called brothers. They all united in a "fond, filial, reverential feeling" for Alma [Christ],

whose "great command is Love." [64] Love is the greatest human virtue, as Melville suggests in *Billy Budd*—not rationality or self-reliance; and although men can think alone they must love together.

Throughout his works, then, Melville displayed his belief that happiness is not obtainable by the individual in isolation, but may be found in shared experiences—in a community of thought and action and purpose. The man whose solitude is thrust upon him is to be deeply pitied. The man whose isolation is self-imposed through repudiation of his social ties creates sorrow for himself and pain for others. In his criticism of the voluntary Isolato—the man who would forsake the common continent of humanity to maroon himself on his own island—Melville may conceivably have had in mind John Donne's memorable metaphor: "No man is an *Iland*, intire of it selfe; every man is a peece of the *Continent*, a part of the *maine*."

[61] *Ibid.*, II, 351.

[62] William Braswell, *Melville's Religious Thought* (Durham, N.C., 1943), p. 122.

[63] *Pierre*, p. 289.

[64] *Mardi*, II, 368, 370.

Milton R. Stern

Some Techniques of Melville's Perception

IN THE 1930's after Melville vessels had begun to display their ample accommodations, R. P. Blackmur wrote in somewhat hostile fashion that Melville "made only the loosest efforts to tie his sermons into his novels: he was quite content to see that his novels illustrated his sermons and was reasonably content if they did not." In the 1950's after the ship plans were better understood (albeit some specialized new quarters—particularly nurseries, bathrooms, and bedrooms complete with one-way glass—had been added from the outside), R. W. B. Lewis opined that "Melville understood the nature of plot, plot in general, better than any one else in his generation." [1]

Despite the voluminous evidence in *Mardi* and, often, in *Pierre*, the tricks by which a Melville novel proceeds are not so divorced from the editorial statements of Melville's typically nineteenth-century narrators as Blackmur assumed they are. Conversely, despite the clean machinery of *Typee* or the profuse complexities of *Moby-Dick*, one cannot agree with Lewis' implication that Melville understood the poetic relationship between the detail and the over-all narrative better than, say, a writer like Thoreau. In the history of the Melville studies that lie between these two poles lingers the general uncertainty about the nature of the sermons and the purpose of the plots—an uncertainty no longer about the fact of Melville's artistry, but about the thematic direction of his particular brand of magic. In "placing" Mel-

ville, one still is forced to begin with discovery of the philosophical significance of his techniques.

Generally, Melville adjusts the thematic progress of his details by means of four basic techniques which, in themselves, are by no means peculiar to him; he uses common instruments whose thematic functions, rather than originality, define his position in American literature. [2] Perhaps it is because he forged neither new method nor new genre (despite *Moby-Dick*) that he has had so little effect upon practicing writers. His essential methodological contribution was rhetorical, but (again, except for *Moby-Dick*) in the sense of a diction that was dying out: stylistically, after all, he did write some atrocious books. Moreover, transcendentalism already had prepared for the symbolic imagination and artistry that marked him in spite of the conservative Knickerbocker influences on his early career. [3] Still further, quest, innocence, self and society, guilt, freedom, fate, and isolation were common, conscious preoccupations of his literary age. Nor did he contribute a new setting for theme, for with the exception of *Mardi* he elevated to new

[2] While from the final point of view it is true that technique (instrument) cannot be divorced from theme (function), yet heretically I suggest that in practical criticism they always are divorced. They have to be, for the critic arbitrarily must decide upon his own starting point among all the possible starting points offered by a work in order to make an entering break in the circle. For the purpose of this article I do not handle technique for a discussion of aesthetic success or structural analysis, but am quite willing to use technique and theme as ancillary to one another.

[3] See Perry Miller, *The Raven and the Whale* (New York, 1956), esp. pp. 23–25, et passim.

[1] "The Craft of Herman Melville," *VQR*, XIV (1938), 281; *The American Adam* (Chicago, 1955), p. 133.

Reprinted by permission from *PMLA*, LXXIII (June, 1958), 251–259.

dimensions realistic materials that were old. Once high romanticism had done its liberating work, it was not to be until James and Twain that new channels and cadences for the old, old questions were matured. Rather, Melville combined a style which lay within the expectations of his age with a cosmic view that did not lie within those expectations. It was this combination that puzzled the critics who thought that "the author of 'Typee,' 'Piddledee' &c" had gone mad. If he did not offer a new fad to talk about, nor even a new way to talk, his greatness lay in his offering of new ideas: like the romantics who made him possible, he offered a new way to see. In brief, the functions of Melville's techniques indicate that Melville used everything the romantics had to offer to come at a perception of the universe that is essentially closer to naturalism than to romantic, cosmic idealism. Therefore, in enumerating the following general categories my purpose is not to isolate techniques peculiar to Melville, but to set off the distinguishing direction of the thought with which he utilized devices common to all artists. If technique determines theme, theme also determines technique, for there is as much a "politic" as an "aesthetic" shoring up the fullness of literature that speaks to the human condition.

I. REINFORCEMENT

The simplest instrument Melville uses, this is almost a Dreiseresque repetition of similar details which, by quantitative intensification, becomes a vehicle for the expression of a controlling idea. Often overused, as in the presentation of the follies of the world in *Mardi*, it spoils many of Melville's books because it pushes the narrative along by means of a reiterative, recapitulating statement that is at the root of Blackmur's objections. *Mardi* and *Pierre*, particularly, are made overlong and talky.

In its rarest form, reinforcement appears on the level of the single word. For example, Mrs. Glendinning muses thus about Pierre:

A noble boy, and docile . . . he has all the frolicsomeness of youth, with little of its giddiness. And he does not grow vain-glorious in sophomorean wisdom. I thank heaven I sent him not to college. A noble boy, and docile. A fine, proud, loving, docile, vigorous boy. Pray God he never becomes otherwise to me. His little wife that is to be, will not estrange him from me; for she too is docile,—beautiful and reverential, and most docile. Seldom yet have I known such blue eyes as hers, that were not docile, and would not follow a bold black one, as two meek, blue-ribboned ewes follow their martial leader. How glad I am that Pierre loves her so, and not some dark-eyed haughtiness with whom I could never live in peace; but who would ever be setting her young married state before my elderly widowed one, and claiming all the homage of my dear boy—the fine, proud, loving, docile, vigorous boy!—the lofty-minded, well-born, noble boy; and with such sweet docilities! See his hair! He does in truth illustrate that fine saying of his father's, that as the noblest colts, in three points—abundant hair, swelling chest, and sweet docility—should resemble a fine woman, so should a noble youth.

Most immediately apparent here is the use of reinforcement as a comic technique. Mrs. Glendinning's reiterations disclose her own imperialism in human relations. In her moment of proud, seeming invincibility, her blindness exposes her and foretells that she will be unable to cope with the rebellion that is to come in precisely the form she fears most. But the passage holds a greater significance than comic foreshadowing. For at the moment of Mrs. Glendinning's musings, Pierre *is* the Typee-like, docile animal she pictures. Mrs. Glendinning stands in the same relationship to Pierre that he stands to his own noble colts, who "well knew that they were but an inferior and subordinate branch of the Glendinnings, bound in perpetual feudal fealty to its headmost representative. Therefore these young cousins never permitted themselves to run from Pierre; they were impatient in their paces, but very patient in the halt."

Indeed, all the rebelling fathers in the history of the house of Glendinning had been patient in the halt. Each in turn had settled down as a colony under imperial rule, a docile "worshipper of the household gods" that represent smug blindness to the cosmic and social truths Pierre is to discover. Pierre is the Typee animal because he believes that his mindless existence is a human realization of an idealized cosmos. He *is* vainglorious in sophomorean wisdom, but Mrs. Glendinning can find only self-justification in the "wisdom" of the early Pierre. She fears knowledge of the actual. For she too assumes, but on a social level of political and economic prerogative, that the quality of life in Saddle Meadows is the actualized ideal. The reinforcement emphasizes ideal appearances only to indicate their falseness. Melville reverses the idealistic assumption of reality: the ideal is appearance and the actual is real. One is more likely to mistake the ideal than the actual, and Melville repeats an identical warning in all his books. "Judge not things by their names," he insists in *Mardi*; do not evaluate the world or the human condition by the sunlit blue day or the musings of the lean-browed young Platonist on the masthead. With almost no exception the forewarning reinforcement constantly indicates that in its "frozen but teeming North," an empty white blankness, existence always prepares new, external, historical surprises as well as moral anomalies—new whales to be caught—with which to deny the assumption of a China Wall, or absolute condition for existence.

On the level of setting, one might single out reinforcement in the repetition with which Typee's seeming perfection is related to mindless isolation and an inability to communicate. The aspiration-denying horror at the heart of the primitive ideal is the darkness that Tommo, a contemporary man, must discover, and that is what gives philosophical tension to the plot of *Typee* and meaning to the cannibalism.

On the level of mood, or atmosphere, one might return to *Pierre* for the incremental intensification of Pierre's despondency, fever, and physical weakness. And here again, the reinforcement serves to supply the descriptive details which validate the irony whereby Pierre destructively consumes the very humanity he would redeem by means of absolute behavior.

On the total level of theme, the isles of *Mardi,* the gams of *Moby-Dick,* and the avatars of the confidence man undercut idealistic practice by disclosing that an historical definition of behavior, not an absolute assumption, is the only operational guide by which man maintains existence, identity, and effectiveness. In short, Melville's comic use of reinforcement as revelation is basically an instrument of irony. It consistently implies what is sometimes stated, as in "The Mast-Head" of *Moby-Dick:* a true sense of life is obtained only from a view based upon natural identity. The primacy of history shows one that the "ideal"—the absolute moral pattern, the ultimate condition of being—is a man-made projection rather than a true definition of cosmic reality. Melville insists ironically that following the absolute assumption only leads to the denial of that assumption. Obversely, this basic ironic view demands a misanthropic shudder at the nature of the actual to which man must turn.[4] For how man butchers the

---

[4] Alfred Kazin, one of the few critics to emphasize Melville's basic naturalism, mistakenly concentrates upon the misanthropic shudder. But contrary to Kazin's contention that Melville adopted nature's rather than man's point of view, one must recognize Melville's emphasis upon brotherhood, not isolation, as a prescription for man thrown back upon himself—*because* of a view of nature. This is the sense of life in the midst of horror which allows Ishmael to rejoin humanity and lack of which makes Ahab villainous as well as noble. The inexplicable joy which Kazin appears to find in the loneliness of "man losing his humanity and being exclusively responsive . . . to the trackless fathomless nothing that has been from the beginning . . ." seems to inhibit his ability to see

possibilities offered by the actual! Herein lies the major "ambiguity" in Melville's evaluation of man. The finality of the grave, the fact of mortal limitation, makes all men equal and interdependent: even that isolato, Ahab, recognizes at moments that " 'tis sweet to lean." Man becomes a cosmic orphan, deposed as the spiritual center of the universe. An orphan and an Ishmael, he wanders the frozen infinity of a whitely indifferent cosmos that teems with "joyous, heartless, ever-juvenile eternities" of coequal life forms, and that portends the backstab of annihilation in its morally atheistic colorlessness.

So man is thrown back upon himself for sustenance, values, and morality. Consequently Melville rejects the transcendental basis for the joy of the romantic Whitmanesque Messiah, and at the same time reaffirms an ecological, cosmic democracy. Even socially, the positive companion of the misanthropic shudder is a heightened, naturalistic emphasis upon the brotherhood of all men, and here Melville is in the center of his philosophical tradition. The irony strongly accounts for the "ambiguity" whereby Melville views with classical horror and disdain the uncontrolled mess made by uncontrolled man, and at the same time insists upon demo-

cratic brotherhood and interdependence. As he summed it up in a statement to Hawthorne, "It seems an inconsistency to assert unconditional democracy in all things, and yet confess a dislike to all mankind—in the mass. But not so."

For man always swindles himself with the absolute by which he "squares his life," and kills himself with the realities he ignores. Thus Ahab, who has had the experience which smashes surfaces, is initiated into the "wisdom that is woe" only so far as a view of cosmic benevolence is concerned. But rather than abandon an assumed absolute by which to guide his human behavior, he inverts it from the comfortable, hypocritical, and unexamined optimism of the land to the metaphysical opposite represented by Fedallah. Because he refuses to recognize the reinforcing and mounting suggestions that eternity is in his own eye, he develops the monomania which is the "woe that is madness." Sincere determination, courage, and a transcendental, cosmic directness make Ahab noble and inspiring in relation to the people whose lives are all on the surface—Aunt Charity and the lee shore's Captain Bildad. But a false view of reality and identity makes old Ahab the villain in relation to the total Anacharsis Clootz expedition of universal human life. Or, coming at it from the opposite direction, Melville's idealistic *young* men are woeless and unmarked by experience: like Pierre they are victimized by the very truth imparted by the historically experienced oldster, whom the youths, in reinforcing repetition, misunderstand or deride. When the transcendentalist, speaking out of the supposedly Edenic American youth, says that cosmic moral reality exists in the eye of the free, untrammeled, and self-reliant perceiver, Melville's wizened, seaborn reinforcement replies that aye, that's just the point.[5]

Ahab's villainy or to see that what Ishmael has learned is what allows him to be saved. (Kazin suggests that the only real reason for Ishmael's salvation is the necessity for a narrator.) Missing Ishmael's true stake in the game, he confuses Ahab's heroic stature with the role of the hero: Melville's sense of life disappears in a concentration upon Melville's sense of loss. In his generally perceptive discussion of Melville's naturalism, Kazin does not discover the lesson Melville learned from idealistic thought, or that Melville found a transcending dignity for humanity on naturalistic grounds. In Melville's statement about "the endlessness, yea, the intolerableness of all earthly effort," Kazin does not see that the endlessness and intolerableness also become nobility. See Kazin's Introduction to *Moby-Dick* (Boston, 1956), pp. v–xiv [revised version, pp. 52–59 above].

[5] Lewis (*The American Adam*) poses this problem centrally in his brilliant contribution to American studies.

II. CONTRAST

Melville employs this technique so frequently that it is practically impossible to sum its characteristics in one brief statement. Heuristic, like reinforcement, it does not have the promissory qualities of reinforcement. Instead of necessarily preparing for a summary action in the future, it is a summary action in the present. For instance, in *Mardi*, Pani's repeated self-revelations form a proleptic statement about the final reaction of religion to the "transcendental boy" who visits Maramma to seek God. But the actual slaying of the boy, in immediate juxtaposition to the words of the priests, creates the sudden static exposure of the difference between the supposed and actual functions of religion. If reinforcement generally prepares one for a moral shock, contrast generally *is* that shock of recognition. Usually the device is given a religious, social, or political, rather than a directly ontological, weighting. Wilson in *Omoo*, Captain Riga, the city of Liverpool, and the prosy old guide book in *Redburn*, Captain Claret in *White-Jacket*, Bildad in *Moby-Dick*, and Falsgrave in *Pierre* are cases in point.

One of the best samples is offered by *Mardi*, that germinal book. Arriving in Odo, Taji is distressed to see King Media establish his own person in the place of the temple's idol. A fake deity himself, Taji explains Media's "superhuman" status, which, supposedly, frees Media from the necessities and limitations of natural existence. But at once Media is shown taking his sacred place in the fane in order to *dine*. After the refreshments have been consumed with typical Rabelaisian zest, Media "celestially" lays his hand on his divine belly to signify the social delight and animal gusto with which he relishes a good meal.

Although one really cannot divorce such instances from their anticipatory functions, the contrast between the status and actions of Media is complete in itself as a revelation (now) of the realities Media is to admit during his long and garrulous voyage (in the future). The Media episode is valuable because it is typical and because it indicates the general thematic energy of the technique—an emphasis upon empirical evaluation. Although contrast is used for many purposes (subtleties of characterization, suspense, psychological insight), Melville steadily uses it to suggest that experience must be tested in the conditionings of historical necessity. Not the absolute assumptions which transcend the history and nature from which they are projected, but rather the limitations of natural existence become reality: history becomes primary rather than ancillary, as *Billy Budd* alone makes plain.

The unconditional democracy of all things is Melville's empirical translation of romantic, nineteenth-century concepts of plenitude. The teeming universe embraces all life forms in egalitarian indifference. The forms are related by the processes of life, but as coequals they all have their own reality external to each other. Men may believe in any kind of unific spiritual essence, but they always have to act empirically, according to the material differences taught by historical experience. If one goes to the Emersonian woods and finds there that "the name of the nearest friend sounds then foreign and accidental: to be brothers, to be acquaintances, master or servant, is then a trifle and a disturbance," it is precisely then that, like the hollow-eyed lad on the masthead, one slips his hold on reality. His subjective measure of the supernatural may be a reality to Melville's idealist, but always the actuality within which the idealist works his "reality" is measured by the infinite number of possible relationships between the independent externals of the natural universe. The nub of the matter is quite simple: total possibility that may affect man is external to and independent of his subjective ability to shape the universe to his ideal. If there is an "unconditional," then that absolute of "democracy" is relativity. The conditions of life demand that the actual be defined by relations rather than by equations, and thus Melville's naturalism finds expression in symbolism rather than allegory or the lists of facts typical of the narrowly naturalistic novel. In *Pierre*, indeed, Melville consciously uses democratic America as a truer symbol of actuality than the hierarchical ideal traditions of aristocratic Europe. On a cosmic level, ecology in a sense replaces the supernaturalism, or ethical monism, of theology. On a social level, the brotherhood of mortality becomes the humanitarian replacement of preconceived systems of human inequality.

Always the absolute assumptions shown up by contrast demonstrate that idealism inverts men from the ways of understanding, as "The Try-Works" of *Moby-Dick* suggests. The idealistic assumptions turn men's eyes away from the proper government of their affairs, away from an honest realization of their common mortality and their transiency as individual entities. Such realization is necessary for the brotherhood that can channel private quest unselfishly into the less impermanent entity, the Anacharsis Clootz expedition itself. There must be an empirical grasping of fact, a seizure of the tiller when it gives its first hitching hints, in order that the government of human affairs may direct the expedition to a true haven ahead in the one and only world rather than rush with fiery, blinding idealism from all havens astern. In the largest example, the contrast between the private assumption and the common actuality is translated into the difference between the pained, commandeering vainglory of Captain Ahab and the painful, administrative selflessness of Captain Vere.

III. THE MULTIPLE VIEW

"I look, you look, he looks; we look, ye look, they look," says that "unearthly idiot," Pip. The lost slave-bastard-orphan has discovered that the doubloon, like any midmost, equatorial reality, is an external actuality that offers a moral blank with an infinite number of possible faces. "And some certain significance lurks in all things, else all things are little worth, and the round world itself but an empty cipher, except to sell by the cartload, as they do hills about Boston, to fill up some morass in the Milky Way." The looking and the looker create certain significances, segments of potential thematic energy. Melville reserves for the reader the total kinetic energy of the meaning lurking "in the middle of the world," and the lurking meaning is the shocking recognition of a naturalistic universe. No one character sees the whole golden circle, for no one can see infinite possibility: Pip sees the relationship of the coin to the viewer—he sees that the coin is the mystery of all existence. Though he can see the nature of existence for the reader, he cannot see all its possible facts, and it is this limitation imposed by the nature of the human condition itself that is at the core of Melville's heavily modified attitude toward science. (But one must be careful to distinguish Melville's attitude from Ahab's.) Each character reveals himself at the moment he reveals the external portion which, in mistaken subjective fashion, he blindly mistakes for an ethical or physical whole. As crazy Pip says, punning, "And I, you, and he; and we, ye, and they, are all bats." Stubb caps it all by muttering a truth whose profundity he cannot allow himself to recognize. After hearing the Manxman's interpretation of the Ecuadorian coin, he says, "There's another rendering now; but still one text. All sorts of men in one kind of world, you see."

As the term implies, the multiple view is the filtering of a constant through diverse intelligences. The constant, in sections, and each separate intelligence, in toto, are thereby reciprocally defined. "The Doubloon" is the most apparent and conscious example of the technique, but Melville wrings from this instrument a steady relativism in many books and on many levels. Thouars and Paulet of *Typee* both view the problems of colonial administration. *Mardi* gives us Donjalolo's ambassadors to the outside world and shows us Babbalanja explaining the footprint to the foolish disputants on the Isle of Fossils. *Pierre*'s Memnon, or Terror, Stone is reflected by many perceptions. The important point is that the relativism of the multiple view shares a common thematic basis with the anti-absolutism of reinforcement and the empiricism of contrast, and that all are motivated by a unifying perception of experience. When Melville says that "some certain significance lurks in all things, else all things are little worth," he is making a "spiritual" statement that could have come from Emerson or Thoreau or Whitman. Yet Melville's relativism gives this statement community with transcendental idealism only in the implication that meaning is not realized until the object is touched by the human mind. It is significant that this is the point of contact between Melvillean and transcendental thought, for it is precisely at this point that idealism can break down into naturalism (which is, I believe, the importance of Emerson's humanism as well as Thoreau's scientism) and that naturalism can break up into romantic idealism.[6]

Even more to the point is Melville's insistence that significance lurks in the thing as well as the viewer. Thereby Melville insists upon the external independence of the matter of experience, contradicting the causal relationships implicit in Emerson's statement that it makes no "difference . . . whether Orion is up there in the heaven, or some god paints the image in the firmament of the soul." The multiple view makes it clear that no one perceiver can bring out the totality of the thing. The internal significance finds itself as symbol in the external thing, but it finds that only. Thus at the same moment that Melville suggests an Emersonian epistemology, he also suggests that a subjective evaluation of total experience, of the cosmos, can be monomania and insanity. It no longer makes any difference that the subjective evaluation may proceed by means of a disciplined and objective return to nature as in the case of Emerson and Thoreau, who, like Melville, insisted that experience must be the necessary foundation that has to be put under the air castle of the vital vision. For once the equation between total possibility and a single, absolute, cosmic spirituality is made, then one begins to slip his hold on reality and must distort the meanings of experience. Like the eighteenth-century materialist of the Jeffersonian Circle, who insisted that malarial swamps must have a good purpose in the great chain of being, only man hasn't discovered it yet, the cosmic idealist is seen by Melville as a man who limits his own insistence that man assigns moral signficance to things. For with fact and the assessment of fact subordinated to theoretical assumption, man must see experience all one way. Either all creation is promissory of ethical benevolence, as it is for the historical transcendentalist, or it is promissory of ethical evil, as it is for the idealistic Ahab. The contradictions of all-color and all-colorlessness cannot coexist, and the living need of man to assign shifting moral values according to relative facts disappears and is forbidden in his attempt to fit the cosmos into the envelope of a par-

---

[6] Two articles in an issue of *AL*, xxviii (1956), offer a discussion about the relation of perception to surface and to submerged meaning. For the stylistic implications of appearance and reality in the later 19th century generally, see Leo Marx, "The Pilot and the Passenger: Landscape Conventions in the Style of *Huckleberry Finn*," pp. 129–146. Marx discusses the levels of reality that the century found beneath the surface. For a discussion of the nature of these levels as viewed by Melville, see J. A. Ward, "The Function of the Cetological Chapters in *Moby-Dick*," pp. 164–183. Ward skirts close to, but never states, what I take to be the over-all demonstration of his article: Melville used fact to provide a basis for a naturalistic perception that he expresses romantically, poetically, and symbolically.

ticular perception. Neither man nor fact is so limitless, says Melville, and the problem of identity is to be reckoned in the visible truth of the natural condition.

Consequently, the human personality and identity of all of Melville's questers—who begin or end as experienced men—increasingly disintegrate in the course of the quest as those men try to prove that they have limitless identities. The burning away of the hot heart's humanity comes from a transcendental view of reality as an externalization of the mind, which in turn is symbolized by the inversion that comes, O man! from looking too long in the face of the fire of idealism. Total reality, eternal infinitude, remains an independent actuality with which man can cope, internally or externally, only by recognizing that he does not live in a transcendentalist's universe. The symbol-making magic of the human mind allows man to internalize the independent cosmos from necessarily limited experience, and in this manner the ennobling poetic perception, or metaphoric truth, is made compatible with—indeed comes from—the empirical basis in necessarily limited fact.

In sum, Melville's poetically antimaterialistic statements are not antimaterialistic *in se* as much as they are a suggestion that man must accept the independent, amoral, and ultimate reality of the material world as the stuff from which he can fashion for himself an identity which is nobler than the merely physical. Finally, the thing and the meaning become one, but only so long as the thing, or surface, discloses no new facts arising from the depths of possibility. It is as important to see that Melville and the Transcendentalists were trying to find an organic metaphor for the human condition as it is to see that Melville's transcendentalism was not Transcendental. The formal problem of point of view in Melville is really a problem of philosophical theme: by never indicating whose view in the multiplicity is *the* one (the fractured

point of view in *Moby-Dick*, for instance), Melville uses the belief of the transcendentalists to display its shortcoming.

The white whale himself offers good evidence for the argument that the "naturalistic" perception need not yield the palm to the idealistic in the search for human grandeur and the organic metaphor. The control, or constant, is provided by Ishmael's discussion of whiteness.

Is it that by its indefiniteness it shadows forth the heartless voids and immensities of the universe, and thus stabs us from behind with the thought of annihilation, when beholding the white depths of the Milky Way? Or is it, that as an essence whiteness is not so much a color as the visible absence of color, and at the same time the concrete of all colors; is it for these reasons that there is such a dumb blankness, full of meaning, in a wide landscape of snows—a colorless, all-color of atheism from which we shrink?

Melville makes a mistake when he has Ishmael say, "*Or* is it, that as an essence . . ." For Melville is not offering an alternative. Rather he is emphasizing a nontranscendental view of experience as he intensifies the implications of naturalistic perception by linking it with man's shaken craving for the assumptions of cosmic idealism.

When one adds to the whiteness of the whale what Pip sees in the ocean, then the total, constant meaning of the white whale becomes clear. Pip sees an amoral, infinite, eternal universe so crammed with blithe, heartless life forms that man can no longer consider himself the center of the universe.[7] For such a universe offers man no home and father which transcend the facts Pip sees. The reading of the universe in the image of man as the spiritual center, in the face of Pip's facts, would be a wrenching of history to fit theory, and is, for Mel-

[7] To weave this thread into its proper place, it might be suggested that it is this that differentiates Melville's from Ahab's view of science, for Ahab replaces the cosmos with himself and thus replaces facts with his own demonized idealism.

ville, the basic error by which idealism loses truth. Man is orphaned into but another creature in the totality of existence, experience of which offers neither individual immortality nor any pattern of human morality. As individual animals, men must recognize that they are one with the plenitudinous universe; but as a social creature man must gain his uniqueness and transcend his animal mortality not by emulating or merging with nature, but by struggling with it. Man must internalize the meaning of the facts of infinite, physical eternity by socially and historically turning to the home and father that only he can create for himself out of the naturalistic realizations that lead to brotherhood rather than to Vandover's Brute. Note that until he comes to a naturalistic acceptance of plenitude ("heaven hath no roof"), Babbalanja seeks the absolute because he cannot accept the denial of ego which comes from seeing so many life forms crammed with vitality seemingly "only to perish." [8] Note that his serenity comes from the alternative of social love, even though the history provided by the Serenian Good Society is a "history" of vague utopianism for which there is no positive basis in all of *Mardi*'s facts. And note too that although the men who finally recognize the truth— Pip, Ishmael, Pierre—are all referred to as orphans, all of them (except Pierre for whom it is too late) insist that man must turn toward earth, social love, and brotherhood in the face of the overwhelming external reality. Thus by admitting that man creates "home" and "father" out of himself, whether or not those terms are idealized and religionized, and by denying the cosmic deification of those terms, Melville arrives at his organic metaphor. If the idealized identity of man is a cosmic blasphemy rather than religious devoutness, then the material facts of man's condition must become one of his identity. So Melville sees that growing out of what he considers to

[8] My debt to Matthiessen is obvious.

be man's actual condition is a godlike, creative nobility as well as a physical transiency and a psychic woe engendered of a view of the white whale.

The white whale becomes reality, total existence. It is God, or empty white time, that is itself the endless immensity which promises the annihilation that is the constant woe of Melville's demonized men. Yet, the colorlessness of all-color offers its own eternal emptiness as the medium in which all possibility exists, and individual death is transmuted into general life. It is not man, but "God," existence itself, that offers "the visible absence of color, and at the same time the concrete of all colors . . . a colorless, all-color of atheism." Moreover, the whale is also the plenitude that empty time makes out of itself. He is the total fact as well as the total meaning. Not only is he the symbol of the lurking significance in all external things, but he is the symbol of all the things themselves. *The* supreme monster of all the dark side of life, he is also always *one* of those monsters, diving deeper and faster than any, feeding even on the faceless, shapeless, all-shape of the blank, white squid—growing himself, as it were, out of the nature of reality. Yet if one may say that the whale is the symbol of the God that makes life, and is also the symbol of life, then it is important to recognize that the organic merger of God and life is made in the most fundamental terms of philosophical naturalism. Life isn't "Spirit" in Emerson's sense any more than the assumptions of ecology need be the assumptions of cosmic idealism. While Melville's aim is the same as the transcendentalist's, and while his merger of life and death may seem Whitmanesque, his perception of experience strips away the supernatural qualities from the promissory conclusions of transcendentalism. Except for the fourth technique, the relativism of the multiple view carries the deepest explanation of Melville's ability to conclude a work like *Clarel* with a statement that only seems to work against all the rest of the poem: "Death but routs life into victory."

IV. CIRCULAR REFLEXION

The subtlest of Melville's instruments, and one that is most productive of the "ambiguities," this technique is the most difficult to define because its structure is that of the symbol. Although it is a particularly embodied action or statement or image, the significance of its parts is enriched by relationships to elements outside the immediate cluster of associations. Yet those outward-reaching relationships are what give a circular perfection to the particular action or statement or image. Only on a logical level can the parts of the cluster be said to have a beginning or an end; on the level of metaphor, the associations create a self-expanding universe of meaning, or symbolic energy, wherein every part pulls forward every other part, and "beginning" and "end" must be abandoned for "relationship." The parts do not have that equation with a set meaning which is the method by which allegory proceeds from idea to particular. Rather the parts are given an operational definition which is relativistic, which proceeds from particular to idea, which makes symbolism a reflexive process of discovery rather than equation, and which offers symbolism fully as much "realism" as, say, the so-called photographic methods of naturalistic writing. In the fact that his symbolism is akin to the great bulk of symbolic literature, Melville discloses his reaction to transcendental equation. His circular reflexion is not organic in the transcendentalist's sense. It is structural symbolism, wherein the meaning comes out of the preparations which set up a shock of recognition, rather than from metaphysical position. If Melville can agree with Emerson that words are signs of natural facts, he parts company with transcendental idealism in insisting that the meanings of those facts are contextual, not absolute.

It is the definition of parts by use and by relation that displays the thematic unity of circular reflexion with the rest of Melville's devices. A dramatic instance is found in *Mardi*. When Taji finally consents to visit Hautia, he is guided by three maiden heralds who sail on before him. Behind him, in direct pursuit, are the three sons of Aleema. When day dawns, Flozella-a-Nina looms ahead; before Taji, in the water, are three radiant pilot fish, and in pursuit astern are three ravenous sharks.

On a logical level, this is simply a condensation of setting, much like the cutting and splicing by which a movie editor uses the camera to suggest continuity. But because of associations that lie beyond the particular images, the parts of this setting begin to swing about and line up as though drawn by several magnets, and they reach out to the general theme of the novel. Reaching back to "My Lord Shark and His Pages," this image unites Hautia and the sons of Aleema, who, until this moment, had always seemed to be opposed forces. Ahead of Taji is hauteur; behind is guilt and vengeance. Ahead of him is slavery to a mindless animality that takes pride in its own unregenerate denial of aspiration; behind him is the inhumanity of absolute, undeviating principle. The instruments of pride lead him toward death just as they lead toward him the pursuing results of his crimes. Combined within Taji himself, those forces kill the ideal, or Yillah, that is also within him as his own idealistic projection of experience. (Every voyager who pursues Yillah offers a different definition of her.) The image reaches ahead to Taji's realization that somehow Yillah and Hautia are one, just as Hautia and Aleema have suddenly been united into new meaning; for Taji's pursuit of the absolute was born of his pridefully assumed superiority to the too frequent "leaden hours" of historical identity. In the newly reflected light, Taji takes on the lineaments of the sons of Aleema, of Yillah, and of Hautia. It is he whose own pride, or cosmic idealism (which turns out to be blasphemy), bore and killed his own ideal and noblest aspiration. It is he who kills himself literally and symbolically. When he recognizes that Hautia has been with him from the beginning, he realizes that he has been pursuing his own projections. Then, Melville says, "two wild currents met" in Taji and "dashed" him "into foam." Like Ahab, unwilling to accept the reality of the human condition instead of his private vision, he renounces the conditions of existence, he renounces humanity, he renounces his own identity, and he abdicates as his own soul's emperor. With eternity in his own eye, he commits the "soul suicide" of the "last, last crime" which is a renunciation of life itself.

In keeping with all the conversational essays in *Mardi*, all phenomena are but separate faces of the faceless totality of time. Similarly, on subordinate levels, many things become one because they have the same effect. Hautia, Yillah, Taji, and the sons of Aleema ultimately are the same because of the results of their actions: they cause a denial of life. In this technique also, the conditional, not the absolute, becomes reality, and qualities are instrumentally defined.

The close approximation of techniques makes it clear that the richly "linked analogies" of Melville's own language will not really allow either a structural or thematic separation of one technique from another. The arbitrary divisions, however, do suggest the artist's devices, which allow one to isolate aspects of Melville's prose in order to use the how to approach the why. And when one sums up the implicit why that underlies these barely shadowed techniques, there is found a perception not generally associated with the mid-nineteenth century. Perhaps Melville's novels indicate the extent of the culture lag between the destruction of the optimistic American image and the rise of realism and naturalism. At any rate, Melville's guiding perception assumes anti-idealistic definition, empiricism, a kind of materialism, relativism,

and an instrumental evaluation of experience. Yet Melville remains mid-nineteenth century because he does not conform to what we have conditioned ourselves to expect from literary naturalism. He does not test the validity of the meaning of his books with lists of social, economic, biological, and political facts; rather he tests his materials by the poetic superlogic of his symbolism, using to his ends the poetic mode of the romantic mind.[9]

One can only conclude that if Melville is to be reckoned by romanticism or naturalism, he is of such gigantically protean proportion that he forces a redefinition of the criteria. Because Melville combined the literary methods of romanticism with a perception that was barometrically sensitive to the anti-idealistic themes that a widening American experience inevitably had to produce, his very relationship to American literature is symbolic. For all our Melville scholarship, it was not until recent books like *Symbolism and American Literature* and *The American Adam* that we have begun to explore entrances to that relationship. To what extent does transcendental monism imply a duality which can turn one to a recognition of natural fact? To what extent does a naturalistic duality imply, by denial of the supernatural, a singleness which can turn one to a recognition of organic metaphor? To what extent must naturalism in literature be re-examined and liberated from realistic techniques? How may it use the symbolic imagination? What are its assumptions as the ontology of the conditional? To what extent do the assumptions of romanticism make it the ontology of the absolute? How far must it use symbolic expression? In sum, to what extent can the two gigantic opponents share literary instruments and human aims: what are the total, cultural (not just the "interior") relationships between specific techniques and specific perceptions, or themes?

Perhaps what the definitive study of Mel-

[9] See Charles Feidelson, *Symbolism and American Literature* (Chicago, 1953), passim.

ville—if there can be such a thing—demands is a catholic reappraisal, not of Melville scholarship, but of the rich profusion of methods that the critical sophistication of our age has made available. At any rate, it is not until we begin to answer such questions that we can see the shape of a viable, persistent, thematic tradition, in which the "vision" of Herman Melville might be instructive.

Robert Penn Warren

Melville the Poet

F. O. MATTHIESSEN has undertaken to give in twenty-two pages a cross-section of the rather large body of the poetry of Herman Melville.[1] If he had intended to give merely a little gathering of his poet's best blossoms, his task would have been relatively easy. But he has also undertaken, as he says in his brief but instructive preface, to "take advantage of all the various interests attaching to any part of Melville's work." So some items appear because they present the basic symbols which are found in the prose or because they "serve to light up facets of Melville's mind as it developed in the years after his great creative period."

In one sense all one can do is to say that Mr. Matthiessen, with the space permitted by the series to which this book belongs ("The Poets of the Year"), has carried out his plan with the taste and discernment which could have been predicted by any reader of his discussion of Melville's poetry in the *American Renaissance*. But I shall take this occasion to offer a few remarks supplementary to the preface and to point out other poems and passages in Melville's work which I hope Mr. Matthiessen admires or finds interesting but which could have no place in his arbitrarily limited collection.

First, I wish to comment on Melville's style. It is ordinarily said that he did not master the craft of verse. Few of his poems are finished. Fine lines, exciting images, and bursts of eloquence often appear, but they appear side by side with limping lines, inexpressive images, and passages of bombast. In a way, he is a poet of shreds and patches. I do not wish to deny the statement that he did not master his craft, but I do feel that it needs some special interpretation.

If, for example, we examine the poems under the title "Fruit of Travel Long Ago," in the *Timoleon* volume of 1891, we see that the verse here is fluent and competent. In his belated poetic apprenticeship, he was capable of writing verse which is respectable by the conventional standards of the time. But the effects which he could achieve within this verse did not satisfy him. Let us look at the poem called "In a Bye-Canal." This first section gives us verse that is conventionally competent:

> A swoon of noon, a trance of tide,
> The hushed siesta brooding wide
>   Like calms far off Peru;
> No floating wayfarer in sight,
> Dumb noon, and haunted like the night
>   When Jael the wild one slew.
> A languid impulse from the car
> Plied by my indolent gondolier
> Tickles against a palace hoar,
>   And hark, response I hear!
> A lattice clicks; and lo, I see
> Between the slats, mute summoning me,
> What loveliest eyes of scintillation,
> What basilisk glance of conjuration!

But the next eight lines are very different. The metrical pattern is sorely tried and wrenched.

> Fronted I have, part taken the span
> Of portent in nature and peril in man.
> I have swum—I have been
> 'Twixt the whale's black fluke and the white
>   shark's fin;

[1] *Selected Poems of Herman Melville*. Edited by F. O. Matthiessen. New Directions. $1.00.

The enemy's desert have wandered in,
And there have turned, have turned and
    scanned,
Following me how noiselessly,
Envy and Slander, lepers hand in hand.

Then the poem returns to its normal movement and tone:

All this. But at the latticed eye—
"Hey, Gondolier, you sleep, my man;
Wake up!" And shooting by, we ran;
The while I mused, This surely now,
Confutes the Naturalists, allow!
Sirens, true sirens verily be,
Sirens, waylayers in the sea.
Well, wooed by these same deadly misses,
Is it shame to run?
No! Flee them did divine Ulysses,
Brave, wise, and Venus' son.

The poem breaks up. The central section
simply does not go with the rest. It is as
though we have here a statement of the
poet's conviction that the verse which belonged to the world of respectability could
not accommodate the rendering of the experience undergone " 'Twixt the whale's
black fluke and the white shark's fin." [2]
Perhaps the violences, the distortions, the
wrenchings in the versification of some of
the poems are to be interpreted not so much
as the result of mere ineptitude as the result of a conscious effort to develop a nervous, dramatic, masculine style. (In this connection, the effort at a familiar style in
John Marr and Other Sailors, especially in
"Jack Roy," is interesting.) That Melville
was conscious of the relation of the mechan-
ics of style to fundamental intentions is
ably argued by William Ellery Sedgwick
in *Herman Melville: The Tragedy of Mind*
in connection with the verse of *Clarel*. Mr.
Sedgwick argues that the choice of short,
four-beat lines, usually rhyming in coup-
lets, a form the very opposite to what would

have been expected, was dictated by a desire to conform himself in his new perspective. "The form of *Clarel* was prop or support to his new state of consciousness, in
which his spontaneous ego or self-con-
sciousness no longer played an all-com-
manding role." I would merely extend the
application of the principle beyond *Clarel*,
without arguing, as Mr. Sedgwick argues
in the case of *Clarel*, that Melville did develop a satisfactory solution for his problem.

If we return to "In a Bye-Canal," we may
observe that the poem is broken not only
by a shift in rhythm but also by a shift in
tone. The temper of the poem is very mixed.
For instance, the lines

Dumb noon, and haunted like the night
When Jael the wild one slew

introduce a peculiarly weighted, serious
reference into the casual first section which
concludes with the playful *scintillation-
conjuration* rhyme. Then we have the grand
section of the whale and the shark. Then
the realistic admonition to the gondolier.
Then the conclusion, with its classical allu-
sion, at the level of *vers de société*. Probably no one would argue that the disparate
elements in this poem have been assimi-
lated, as they have, for example, in Mar-
vell's "To His Coy Mistress." But I think
that one may be well entitled to argue that
the confusions of temper in this poem are
not merely the result of ineptitude but are
the result of an attempt to create a poetry
of some vibrancy, range of reference, and
richness of tone.

In another form we find the same effort
much more successfully realized in "Jack
Roy" in the difference between the two following stanzas:

Sang Larry o' the Cannakin, smuggler o' the
    wine,
At mess between guns, lad in jovial recline:
"In Limbo our Jack he would chirrup up a
    cheer,
The martinet there find a chaffing mutineer;
From a thousand fathoms down under hatches
    o' your Hades

[2] Can this be an echo of the "wolf's black jaw"
and the "dull ass' hoof" in Ben Jonson's "An
Ode to Himself" (*Underwoods*)? In both Jonson
and Melville, the content is the same: the affirmation of independence in the face of a bad and envious age.

He'd ascend in love-ditty, kissing fingers to
  your ladies!"

Never relishing the knave, though allowing for
  the menial,
Nor overmuch the king, Jack, nor prodigally
  genial.
Ashore on liberty, he flashed in escapade,
Vaulting over life in its levelness of grade,
Like the dolphin off Africa in rainbow
  a-sweeping—
Arch iridescent shot from seas languid sleeping.

Or we find the same fusion of disparate
elements in "The March into Virginia,"
one of Melville's best poems:

Did all the lets and bars appear
To every just or larger end,
Whence should come the trust and cheer?
Age finds place in the rear
All wars are boyish and are fought by boys,
The champions and enthusiasts of the state:
. . . . .
No berrying party, pleasure-wooed,
No picnic party in the May,
Ever went less loath than they
Into that leafy neighborhood.
In Bacchic glee they file toward Fate,
Moloch's uninitiate;
. . . . .
But some who this blithe mood present,
As on in lightsome files they fare,
Shall die experienced ere three days are spent—
Perish, enlightened by the volleyed glare; [3]
Or shame survive, and, like to adamant,
The throe of Second Manassas share.

On a smaller scale, Melville's effort to
get range and depth into his poetry is illustrated by the occasional boldness of his
comparisons. For example, in "The Portent," the beard of John Brown protruding
from the hangman's cap is like the trail of
a comet or meteor presaging doom.

Hidden in the cap
Is the anguish none can draw;
So your future veils its face,

[3] Melville's double use of the word *enlightened*
here is interesting and effective. The poem "Shiloh: a Requiem" echoes the metaphorical sense
of the word in the line, "What like a bullet can
undeceive?"

Shenandoah!
But the streaming beard is shown
(Weird John Brown),[4]
The meteor of the war.

Or in one of the early poems, "In a Church
of Padua," we find the confessional compared to a diving-bell:

Dread diving-bell! In thee inurned
What hollows the priest must sound,
Descending into consciences
Where more is hid than found.

It must be admitted that Melville did not
learn his craft. But the point is that the
craft he did not learn was not the same
craft which some of his more highly advertised contemporaries did learn with such
glibness of tongue and complacency of
spirit. Even behind some of Melville's fail-
ures we can catch the shadow of the poem
which might have been. And if his poetry
is, on the whole, a poetry of shreds and
patches, many of the patches are of a massy
and kingly fabric—no product of the local
cotton mills.

But to turn to another line of thought:
Both Mr. Matthiessen and Mr. Sedgwick
have been aware of the importance of the
short poems in relation to Melville's general development. Mr. Sedgwick does give
a fairly detailed analysis of the relation of
Battle-Pieces to *Clarel.* "Even in the *Battle-
Pieces*," he says "we feel the reservations
of this [religious] consciousness set against
the easy and partial affirmations of patri-
otism and partisan conflict." And he quotes,
as Mr. Matthiessen has quoted in the preface to the present collection and in the
American Renaissance, an extremely significant sentence from the prose essay
which Melville appended to the *Battle-
Pieces:* "Let us pray that the terrible historic tragedy of our time may not have
been enacted without instructing our whole
beloved country through pity and terror."
And Mr. Sedgwick refers to one of the para-
doxes of "The Conflict of Convictions," that

[4] The depth and precision of the word *weird* is
worthy of notice.

the result of the Civil War may betray the cause for which the North was fighting:

> Power unanointed may come—
> Dominion (unsought by the free)
> And the Iron Dome
> Stronger for stress and strain,
> Fling her huge shadow athwart the main;
> But the Founders' dream shall flee. . . .

But even in this poem there are other ideas which relate to Melville's concern with the fundamental ironical dualities of existence: will against necessity, action against idea, youth against age, the changelessness of man's heart against the concept of moral progress, the bad doer against the good deed, the bad result against the good act, ignorance against fate, etc. These ideas appear again and again in the poems. In the present poem the lines

> Senior wisdom suits not now
>   The light is on the youthful brow,

are matched in "Apathy and Enthusiasm,"

> And the young were all elation
> Hearing Sumter's cannon roar,
> And they thought how tame the Nation
> In the age that went before.
>
> . . . .
>
> But the elders with foreboding
> Mourned the days forever o'er
> And recalled the forest proverb,
> The Iroquois' old saw:
> *Grief to every graybeard*
> *When young Indians lead the war.*

Or in "The March into Virginia":

> Did all the lets and bars appear
> To every just or larger end,
> Whence should come the trust and cheer?
> Youth must the ignorant impulse lend—
> Age finds place in the rear.
> All wars are boyish and are fought by boys,
> The champions and enthusiasts of the state.

Or in "On the Slain Collegians":

> Youth is the time when hearts are large,
> And stirring wars
> Appeal to the spirit which appeals in turn
> To the blade it draws.
> If woman incite, and duty show

> (Though made the mask of Cain),
> Or whether it be Truth's sacred cause,
> Who can aloof remain
> That shares youth's ardour, uncooled by the
>   snow
> Of wisdom or sordid gain?

Youth, action, will, ignorance—all appear in heroic and dynamic form as manifestations of what Mr. Sedgwick has called Melville's "radical Protestantism," the spirit which had informed *Moby Dick*. But in these poems the commitment is nicely balanced, and even as we find the praise of the dynamic and heroic we find them cast against the backdrop of age, idea, necessity, wisdom, fate. Duty may be made the "mask of Cain" and "lavish hearts" are but, as the poem on the Collegians puts it, "swept by the winds of their place and time." All bear their "fated" parts. All move toward death or toward the moment of wisdom when they will stand, as "The March into Virginia" puts it, "enlightened by the volleyed glare."

Man may wish to act for Truth and Right, but the problem of definitions is a difficult one and solution may only be achieved in terms of his own exercise of will and his appetite for action. That is, his "truth" and the Truth may be very different things in the end. "On the Slain Collegians" sums the matter up:

> What could they else—North or South?
> Each went forth with blessings given
> By priests and mothers in the name of Heaven;
>   And honour in both was chief.
> Warred one for Right, and one for Wrong?
> So be it; but they both were young—
> Each grape to his cluster clung,
> All their elegies are sung.

Or there is "The College Colonel," the young officer who returns from the war, a crutch by his saddle, to receive the welcome of the crowd and especially, as "Boy," the salute of age. But to him comes "alloy."

> It is not that a leg is lost,
> It is not that an arm is maimed.
> It is not that the fever has racked—
> Self he has long disclaimed.

But all through the Seven Days' Fight,
And deep in the Wilderness grim,
And in the field-hospital tent,
And Petersburg crater, and dim
Lean brooding in Libby, there came—
Ah heaven!—what TRUTH to him.

The official truth and the official celebration are equally meaningless to him who has been "enlightened by the volleyed glare"—who has known pity and terror.

The event, the act, is never simple. Duty may be made the mask of Cain. In "The Conflict of Convictions," it is asked:

Dashed aims, at which Christ's martyrs pale,
Shall Mammon's slaves fulfill?

And in the same poem, in the passage which Mr. Sedgwick quotes, Melville conjectures that the Iron Dome, stronger for stress and strain, may fling its huge, imperial shadow across the main; but at the expense of the "Founders' dream." But other dire effects of the convulsion, even if it involves Right, may be possible. Hate on one side and Phariseeism on the other may breed a greater wrong than the one corrected by the conflict. The "gulfs" may bare "their slimed foundations," as it is phrased in the same poem in an image which is repeated in "America." The allegorical female figure, America, is shown sleeping.

But in that sleep contortion showed
The terror of the vision there—
A silent vision unavowed,
Revealing earth's foundations bare,
And Gorgon in her hiding place.
It was a thing of fear to see
So foul a dream upon so fair a face,
And the dreamer lying in that starry shroud.

More effectively, "The Apparition: a Retrospect" presents the danger of the hidden Evil which may be released even by the act undertaken for Good:

Convulsions came; and, where the field
Long slept in pastoral green
A goblin-mountain was upheaved
(Sure the scarred sense was all deceived),
Marl-glen and slag-ravine.

The unreserve of Ill was there,
The clinkers in her last retreat;
But, ere the eye could take it in,
Or mind could comprehension win,
It sunk!—and at our feet.

So, then, Solidity's a crust—
The core of fire below;
All may go well for many a year,
But who can think without a fear
Of horrors that happen so?

Even if the victory of Right and valor is attained, there is no cause for innocent rejoicing. As, in "The College Colonel," the hero looks beyond the cheering crowd to his "truth," so in "Commemorative of a Naval Victory," the hero must look beyond his "festal fame":

But seldom the laurel wreath is seen
Unmixed with pensive pansies dark;
There's a light and shadow on every man
Who at last attains his lifted mark—
Nursing through night the ethereal spark.
Elate he never can be;
He feels that spirits which glad had hailed his worth,
Sleep in oblivion.— The shark
Glides white through the phosphorous sea.

There is more involved here than the sadness over the loss of comrades. The shark comes as too violent and extravagant an image for that. The white shark belongs to the world of the "slimed foundations" which are exposed by the convulsion. It is between the whale's black fluke and the white shark's fin that wisdom is learned. He is the Maldive shark, which appears in the poem by the name, the "Gorgonian head" (the "Gorgon in her hiding place" appears too in the bared foundations of earth glimpsed in the dream of "America"), the "pale ravener of horrible meat," the Fate symbol.

We may ask what resolution of these dualities and dubieties may be found in Melville's work. For there is an effort at a resolution. The effort manifests itself in three different terms: nature, history, and religion.

In reference to the first term, we find the simple treatment of "Shiloh":

Foemen at morn, but friends at eve—
Fame or country least their care:
(What like a bullet can undeceive!)
But now they lie low,
While over them the swallows skim
And all is hushed at Shiloh.

Mortal passion and mortal definition dissolve in the natural process, as in "Malvern Hill":

We elms of Malvern Hill
Remember everything;
But sap the twig will fill:
Wag the world how it will,
Leaves must be green in Spring.

The focal image at the end of "A Requiem for Soldiers Lost in Ocean Transports" repeats the same effect:

Nor heed they now the lone bird's flight
Round the lone spar where mid-sea surges pour.

There is, however, a step beyond this elegiac calm of the great natural process which absorbs the human effort and agony. There is also the historical process. It is possible, as Melville puts it in "The Conflict of Convictions," that the "throes of ages" may rear the "final empire and the happier world." The negro woman in "Formerly a Slave" looks

Far down the depth of thousand years,
And marks the revel shine;
Her dusky face is lit with sober light
Sibylline, yet benign.

In "America," the last poem of *Battle-Pieces*, the contorted expression on the face of the sleeping woman as she dreams the foul dream of earth's bared foundations, is replaced, when she rises, by a "clear calm look."

. . . It spake of pain,
But such a purifier from stain—
Sharp pangs that never come again—
And triumph repressed by knowledge meet,
And youth matured for age's seat—
Law on her brow and empire in her eyes.

So she, with graver air and lifted flag;
While the shadow, chased by light,
Fled along the far-drawn height,
And left her on the crag.

"Secession, like Slavery, is against Destiny," Melville wrote in the prose Supplement to *Battle-Pieces*. For to him, if history was fate (the "foulest crime" was inherited and was fixed by geographical accident upon its perpetrators), it might also prove to be redemption. In *Mardi*, in a passage which Mr. Sedgwick quotes in reference to the slaves of Vivenza, Melville exclaims: "Time—all-healing Time—Time, great philanthropist! Time must befriend these thralls." Melville, like Hardy, whom he resembles in so many respects and with whose war poems his own war poems share so much in tone and attitude, proclaimed that he was neither an optimist nor a pessimist, and in some of his own work we find a kind of guarded "meliorism," like Hardy's, which manifests itself in the terms of destiny, fate, time, that is, in the historical process.

The historical process, however, does not appear always as this mechanism of meliorism. Sometimes the resolution it offers is of another sort, a sort similar to the elegiac calm of the natural process: the act is always poised on the verge of history, the passion, even at the moment of greatest intensity, is always about to become legend, the moral issue is always about to disappear into time and leave only the human figures, shadowy now, fixed in attitudes of the struggle. In "Battle of Stone River, Tennessee," we find the stanzas which best express this.

With Tewksbury and Barnet heath,
In days to come the field shall blend,
The story dim and date obscure;
In legend all shall end.
Even now, involved in forest shade
A Druid-dream the strife appears,
The fray of yesterday assumes
The haziness of years.
    In North and South still beats the vein
    Of Yorkist and Lancastrian.
            • • • • •

But Rosecrans in the cedarn glade
And, deep in denser cypress gloom,
Dark Breckinridge, shall fade away
Or thinly loom.
The pale throngs who in forest cowed
Before the spell of battle's pause,
Forefelt the stillness that shall dwell
On them and on their wars.
   North and South shall join the train
   Of Yorkist and Lancastrian.

In "The March into Virginia" the young men laughing and chatting on the road to Manassas are "Moloch's uninitiate" who "file toward Fate."

All they feel is this: 'tis glory,
A rapture sharp, though transitory,
Yet lasting in belaurelled story.

The glory of the act ends in legend, in the perspective of history, which is fate. Human action enters the realm where it is, to take a line from "The Coming Storm,"

Steeped in fable, steeped in fate.

Nature and history provide the chief terms of resolution in *Battle-Pieces*. Only rarely appears the third term, religion, and then in a conventional form. For instance, there is "The Swamp-Angel," which deals with the bombardment of Charleston:

Who weeps for the woeful City
Let him weep for our guilty kind;
Who joys at her wild despairing—
Christ, the Forgiver, convert his mind.

It is actually in the terms of nature and history that the attitude which characterizes *Clarel* first begins to make itself felt. Mr. Sedgwick has defined Melville's attitude as the result of a "religious conversion to life." In it he renounced the quest for the "uncreated good," the individualistic idealism of *Moby Dick*, the "radical Protestantism." Mr. Sedgwick continues: "Behind *Clarel* lies the recognition that for ripeness, there must be receptivity; that from the point of view of the total consciousness it is not more blessed to give than to receive. One receives in order to be received into life and fulfilled by life. . . . Melville's act was toward humanity, not away from it. He renounced all the prerogatives of individuality in order to enter into the destiny which binds all human beings in one great spiritual and emotional organism. He abdicated his independence so as to be incorporated into the mystical body of humanity." There is the affirmation at the end of *Clarel:*

But through such strange illusions have they passed
Who in life's pilgrimage have baffled striven—
Even death may prove unreal at the last,
And stoics be astounded into heaven.

Then keep thy heart, though yet but ill-resigned—
Clarel, thy heart, the issues there but mind;
That like the crocus budding through the snow—
That like a swimmer rising from the deep—
That like a burning secret which doth go
Even from the bosom that would hoard and keep;
Emerge thou mayst from the last whelming sea,
And prove that death but routs life into victory.

Or we find the same attitude expressed by the comforting spirit which appears at the end of "The Lake":

She ceased and nearer slid, and hung
In dewy guise; then softlier sung:
"Since light and shade are equal set,
And all revolves, nor more ye know;
Ah, why should tears the pale cheek fret
For aught that waneth here below.
Let go, let go!"

With that, her warm lips thrilled me through,
She kissed me while her chaplet cold
Its rootlets brushed against my brow
With all their humid clinging mould.
She vanished, leaving fragrant breath
And warmth and chill of wedded life and death.

And when, in the light of these poems we look back upon "The Maldive Shark" we see its deeper significance. As the pilot fish may find a haven in the serrated teeth of the shark, so man, if he learns the last wisdom, may find an "asylum in the jaws of the Fates."

This end product of Melville's experience has, in the passage which I have already quoted from Mr. Sedgwick, been amply defined. What I wish to emphasize is the fact that there is an astonishing continuity between the early poems, especially *Battle-Pieces*, and *Clarel*. Under the terms of nature and history, the religious attitude of *Clarel* and "The Lake" is already being defined.

Upon looking back over these remarks, I find that I have named or quoted from most of the poems of Melville which I find interesting and which do not appear in Mr. Matthiessen's collection. But by the way of conclusion I shall quote one more poem, which is notable, I think, for another facet of Melville's style and temper and for the poetic quality of the last stanza:

CROSSING THE TROPICS

While now the Pole Star sinks from sight,
The Southern Cross it climbs the sky;

But losing thee, my love, my light,
O bride but for one bridal night,
The loss no rising joys supply.

Love, love, the Trade Winds urge abaft,
And thee, from thee, they steadfast waft.

By day the blue and silver sea
And chime of waters blandly fanned—
Now these, nor Gama's stars to me
May yield delight, since still for thee
I long as Gama longed for land.

I yearn, I yearn reverting turn,
My heart it streams in wake astern.

When, cut by slanting sleet, we swoop
Where raves the world's inverted year,
If roses all your porch shall loop,
Not less your heart for me will droop
Doubling the world's last outpost drear.

O love, O love, these oceans vast:
Love, love, it is as death were past!